Solution-Focused

Solution-Focused Practice

Effective Communication to Facilitate Change

Guy Shennan

First published 2014 by
PALGRAVE MACMILLAN

Palgrave Macmillan in the UK is an imprint of Macmillan Publishers Limited, registered in England, company number 785998, of 4 Crinan Street, London N1 9XW.

Palgrave Macmillan in the US is a division of St Martin's Press LLC, 175 Fifth Avenue, New York, NY 10010.

Palgrave Macmillan is the global academic imprint of the above companies and has companies and representatives throughout the world.

Palgrave® and Macmillan® are registered trademarks in the United States, the United Kingdom, Europe and other countries

ISBN: 978–0–230–35912–3

This book is printed on paper suitable for recycling and made from fully managed and sustained forest sources. Logging, pulping and manufacturing processes are expected to conform to the environmental regulations of the country of origin.

A catalogue record for this book is available from the British Library.

Library of Congress Cataloging-in-Publication Data

Shennan, Guy, author.
    Solution-focused practice : effective communication to facilitate change / Guy Shennan.
        p. ; cm.
    Includes bibliographical references and index.
    Summary: "This book provides a comprehensive and accessible guide for anyone who wishes to incorporate solution-focused practice in to their helping conversations with people, whether these take place within structured sessions or in more unplanned and spontaneous ways" – Provided by publisher.
        ISBN 978–0–230–35912–3 (paperback)
        I. Title.
        [DNLM: 1. Counseling – methods. 2. Psychotherapy – methods. WM 55]
    RC480.5
    616.89′14—dc23   2014021337

Printed and bound by CPI Group (UK) Ltd, Croydon, CR0 4YY

*To my Mum, and in memory of my Dad and
my older brother, Andrew*

Contents

Preface   x

Acknowledgements   xv

1 **Introduction**   1

2 **The Solution-Focused Process**   11
   Introduction   11
   The transcript   12
   General overview   16
   The solution-focused process   18
   Constructing questions   24
   Conclusion   28

3 **Contracting**   29
   Introduction   29
   The solution-focused assumption   30
   Establishing outcome-based 'contracts'   30
   Contracting with children and young people   40
   Contracting with externally mandated clients   41
   Conclusion   47

4 **Description I: The Preferred Future**   49
   Introduction   49
   A little history of the preferred future   50
   Describing preferred futures   53
   Concrete interactional sequences   65
   Handling difficulties within preferred futures   69
   Using future-focused questions outside planned contexts   70

5 **Description II: Instances**   75
   Introduction   75
   A little history of the focus on what is working   76
   Eliciting instances   78
   Questions to follow up instances   80
   Asking about instances outside planned contexts   89

	Documenting change: The use of lists	90
	Focusing on change: Sparkling moments	91
6	**Bridging the Preferred Future and Its Instances: Scaling Questions**	**97**
	Introduction	97
	The development of scaling questions	98
	The general progress scale: An overview	99
	The general progress scale: The details	101
	Scale variations	112
	Scaling with children	115
7	**Acknowledgement and Possibility: Coping Questions and More**	**118**
	Introduction	118
	The scope of this chapter	119
	Listening (revisited)	119
	Acknowledgement...	120
	...and possibility	121
	Coping questions	122
	Stopping it from getting worse	126
	Working close to the problem: Exception-seeking	127
	Going into the past	129
	Going into the future	130
	Case example: The family who stayed together	131
	A both/and, 'enduring and enjoying' scale	138
8	**Putting It All Together**	**141**
	Introduction	141
	Session structure: Simple versions	141
	Typical first session structure: Detail	143
	Typical follow-up session structures: Detail	150
	Typical structure following a positive response	151
	Typical structure following an initially negative response	154
	Putting it all together: The example of Anna	156
9	**Applications and Adaptations**	**163**
	Introduction	163
	A widely-applicable approach	163
	Supervision and consultation	165
	Working with more than one person	169
	Working with children	180

10	**Becoming a Solution-Focused Practitioner**	**182**
	Introduction	182
	Getting started	183
	Practice tips	188
	Frequently-asked questions	191
	Keeping going	196
	The last word	198

Appendix 1: A List of Solution-Focused Questions 199

Appendix 2: Resources 202

Notes 205

References 208

Index 217

Preface

In September 1995, I spent one of the most significant weeks of my working life, driving each day from Derby to Birmingham, becoming increasingly excited as the solution-focused approach gradually unfolded in front of me. On a four-day introductory course, in the company of practitioners from the health, social care, education and organisational sectors, I was gaining a powerful sense of the potential usefulness and applicability of solution-focused practice and could hardly wait for the chance to put it into practice. I spent the weekend that followed counting down the hours until Monday morning came around and I could get back to work. At this time I was a social worker, working with families in some of the most difficult situations imaginable, and I usually welcomed weekends as times to recharge the batteries and replenish the soul. However, this weekend was only getting in the way.

What I was finding particularly exciting was the sense that I *could* use this therapeutic approach in my everyday work context. I had trained as a social worker between six and eight years earlier and had been fortunate to study on a course where practice models were taken seriously and where we had been encouraged and assisted in learning to use them as part of our social work practice. Unfortunately, having qualified it was apparent that there was a growing disconnect between the planned and reflective world of learning and the pressurised and politicised world of practice. It was difficult if not impossible to sustain a planned intervention over a period of time, especially one which paid attention to the client's agenda, as statutory and agency demands and crisis management came to dominate. Practice was reactive rather than proactive, and as a practitioner I felt like I was constantly spinning plates and unable to prevent some smashing on the ground. But something about solution-focused practice seemed different. It felt as if I would be able to use it, and it turned out that this feeling was well-founded, as the following three scenarios suggest.

Not long after the course, I was conducting a duty interview in the local social services office, where a mother and her teenage daughter were at each other's throats. In trying to explain their problems to me, their talk had inevitably descended into blaming. How would it not do? I took a deep breath and intervened the first moment that neither of them were speaking:

> Listen, can I ask a strange-sounding question? Just imagine that when you both go to sleep tonight, a miracle happens and the problems between you have gone, just like that. But you don't know it's happened, because you're asleep at the time. So when you wake up tomorrow morning, what's the first thing you'd notice that would tell you this miracle has happened?

I visited a family on a Monday morning after the father had called the Emergency Duty Team on the Friday night at his wits' end. When I arrived, he had just returned from taking his son to school. He was angry that no social worker had visited on Friday night or later over the weekend to offer support, after his wife had been admitted to a psychiatric unit and the police had returned his son who had run away from home. Having apologised that the emergency team had been too short-staffed to visit, I asked him:

> How did you get through the weekend, and how on earth did you not only get through it with your son, but in such a way that you were able to get him to go to school with you this morning?

I was in a meeting at a family centre with two parents and their daughter who was in foster care, and the parents were saying there was no way she could come home, though that was the local authority's plan. I set up 0–10 scales, where 10 represented the situation being right for the daughter to be at home again and 0 meant that a return would never be possible, from their various points of view. The parents and daughter were at 1, 2 and 1, respectively. I asked each of them in turn:

> How come you're at that point on the scale, and not at 0?

In the detailed case examples that appear throughout this book, you will see the sorts of responses that such questions can lead to. Suffice to say for now that in each of these scenarios, positive developments ensued and it was clear that the solution-focused questions I had asked had contributed to this.

Activity: Questions of interest?

I will be suggesting activities at intervals throughout the book, some inviting reflection, some to try out an exercise, and they have been designed to help you to get the most out of your reading. Here I would simply ask you to consider what you find interesting about what I asked on these three occasions. Is there anything that seems to connect the questions, any underlying principles or assumptions? I asked them as a social worker with children and families. How might similar questions translate into your work context?

At this time, solution-focused practice was still very much a new kid on the block, and its novelty and some radical differences with more traditional helping approaches were part of its attractiveness for many, myself included. Since then, it has bedded down and become an approach of choice for practitioners across all the helping sectors, in health, social care, education, coaching and so on. The widening of my own practice and training contexts reflects this. In the week that I am writing this preface, I have provided counselling and mentoring sessions for prolific adult offenders, trained a team of inner-city youth workers, taught first-year clinical psychology doctorate students, worked with a management consultant on a study about the origins of solution-focused brief therapy, and arranged a one-day workshop for occupational therapists and physiotherapists and a group coaching session for a team of educational psychologists, all in or using the solution-focused approach.

Two features of the approach that I believe account in particular for its widespread adoption are its proven *usefulness* and its *usability* across many settings. The two are inter-related. The solution-focused approach originated in the world of psychotherapy, and this is a world which has an ever-strengthening evidence base (Cooper, 2008). However, psychotherapy is only ever going to reach a relatively small number of people, and the vast majority of helping professionals work in other roles, which frequently feel round in shape when confronted with the square pegs of therapeutic approaches. In contrast, solution-focused practice has a shape shifting quality which gives it a very high usability quotient. One of the reasons for this is that there are two ways of using the approach. It can be used as a fully structured approach, in planned sessions, and elements of it can also be utilised in more opportunistic ways within the unplanned conversational contexts in which many helping professionals frequently find themselves.

It was in the second of these ways that I was using the approach in the three examples given above. However, even as a social worker based in a duty team, in which the work was fast-moving and often responding to crisis, my very first use of the approach the day after that introductory training course was in the first, more planned way. I undertook the first of a series of solution-focused sessions with a family, while visiting them in their home, to avert the need for one of their children to be received into care, and this was where I began to discover the usability and usefulness of the approach. However, while a first session can be succeeded by one or more follow-up sessions, it is not infrequently the case that only one session takes place, and this can be useful in its own right. Often it cannot be known in advance whether another meeting will be wanted, or possible, or needed. So a solution-focused practitioner treats every session as if it might be the last and, in this way, is led to make full use of the one opportunity that might be available. But that opportunity might be even more fleeting than one offered by a full session. In more unplanned and unpredictable situations, each moment might offer an opportunity that can be grasped by a solution-focused practitioner. And it is often in those moments, when just one question can lead to a shift in thinking, an injection of purpose, or a beginning of a forward movement, that the power of the solution-focused approach is most evident.

To summarise then, the use of the solution-focused approach may be possible *on any occasion when a helping professional is talking to someone*, whether it has been premeditated or is used on the spur of the moment, whether in a crisis or more planned work, whether it is a one-off meeting or one of several. And when it is used, it is likely to be useful. The formal evidence base for the approach is growing fast, as I shall make clear in the final chapter. Its usefulness will also be evident in the many real-life case examples to be found in the preceding chapters. The majority of these are from my own social work, counselling, coaching and supervision practice, but there are also examples I have come across in the work of teachers, nurses, housing support workers and therapists. Professionals in these roles and in any other job that exists within the helping professions can attest to the useful part that solution-focused practice plays in their work with the people they serve.

What this book sets out to do is to provide a comprehensive guide to any professional who wishes to use solution-focused practice, whether in a planned way or by taking the moment-by-moment opportunities afforded within their everyday work-based conversations. I have structured it so that the approach unfolds in a similar way as on my introductory training courses, which means that the reader will be shown the whole approach first, before being taken through it step by step, until the components of the approach are put back together again into the typical structures of first and follow-up sessions. This will lead, by the end of Chapter 8, to a comprehensive knowledge of the full range of solution-focused questions and a firm understanding of how they are used together to carry out a solution-focused piece of work. From this vantage point, it will be possible to see how to use elements of the approach outside of planned, full sessions, and in this the reader will be assisted by a number of case examples throughout the book and by suggestions contained in the final two chapters. I also believe that for those practitioners whose role might not usually be thought of as encompassing the use of structured sessions, it is possible to create a context in which the solution-focused approach can be used more fully. I will share some thoughts on this in the last chapter.

Solution-focused therapy was first developed in the US, by an inspired group of therapists in Milwaukee, and its development can be traced in the books of one of the group's leading members, Steve de Shazer (1985, 1988, 1991, 1994). His partner and the other leading originator of the approach, Insoo Kim Berg, began her series of mainly co-written books about applications of the approach with various client groups or for different tasks in the early nineties (Berg, 1994; Berg and Miller, 1992; Berg and Reuss, 1997; Berg and Kelly, 2000; Berg and Steiner, 2003; Berg and Szabo, 2005). Berg also co-wrote the book *Interviewing for Solutions* that has most clearly set out to be a generally applicable step-by-step guide on how to use the approach as developed by the original group (de Jong and Berg, 2008).

As the solution-focused approach has travelled beyond Milwaukee, it has been developed in a number of different ways. I believe that the present volume is the first of its kind in setting out step-by-step the version of solution-focused practice that is presented among its pages, in a way intended to make it accessible to professionals in any helping context. This may reasonably be called the BRIEF version, after the group of therapists in London with whom I trained and later worked and whose influence I make plain in the first chapter. This group has done a tremendous service to solution-focused practice and to helping professionals more generally, in developing a version whose simplicity has increased its applicability across such a wide range of helping contexts. Having long been the mainstream way of approaching solution-focused practice in the UK, this is now becoming increasingly influential beyond these shores.

As I was being first exposed to this version of solution-focused practice, back in 1995, I became gradually more excited, convinced by its usability and usefulness, and equipped to start using it. My best hopes are that by reading these pages you will experience similar effects.

Acknowledgements

Solution-focused practitioners tend to focus on the future, present and recent past, but my acknowledgements need to start almost 30 years ago, when I began working at the Young People's Unit in Macclesfield. It was there I was first exposed to the brief therapy ideas that heralded the solution-focused approach, and I am grateful to Sue Wright in particular for turning me on to them. When I started learning how to use the solution-focused approach in earnest, I was a social worker in Derby and I need to thank a number of people who helped me immeasurably then, my manager, Wendy Purgavie, my colleagues, Adrian Pugh, Phil Lewis and Margaret Hinchcliffe, and the rest of the Reception Team. Thanks also to the Leicester Family Service Unit, for facilitating the beginning of my solution-focused training career and for being the place where I met Paul Hackett. My own learning accelerated when I attended the MA in solution-focused brief therapy at the University of Birmingham, so thanks to Bill O'Connell and my fellow students, to Carolyn Emanuel in particular. Thanks also to Rob Black, Darius Evans, Sue Young and Yasmin Ajmal, who have all been inspirations. A big thank you to Judith Milner, for getting this project off the ground in the first place, and to Heather Fitton, Marie Devine, Rob Rave, Clare Thormod, Ylva Olsson, Clinton Whitehouse, Nick Bohannon, Tim Sanders, Glyn Robbins, Andy Wilson, James Clossick, Dave Harper, Liz Spilsbury, Arabella Howell, Jennie Caminada, Jim Bird Waddington and the staff at Caer Las, and to everyone else who has contributed to the writing of this book.

My development as a solution-focused practitioner and trainer owes most to the input of BRIEF and of Chris Iveson in particular. I have acknowledged Chris as the origin of some specific ideas in a number of chapter endnotes, but this does not really do justice to the extent of his influence. This acknowledgement should perhaps be seen as a general endnote to the whole book. By the same token, if I were to look down I would see that Chris and his BRIEF colleagues, Harvey Ratner and Evan George, were standing on the shoulders of Steve de Shazer, Insoo Kim Berg and the other original solution-focused brief therapists in Milwaukee, to whom go my deep respect and gratitude.

The authors and publisher would like to thank the following individuals and organisations for permission to reproduce copyright material:

American Psychological Association for permission to reproduce an extract from S. Gable and J. Haidt, 'What (and Why) Is Positive Psychology?' in R. F. Baumeister and D. K. Simonton, *Review of General Psychology* (2005);

HarperCollins Publishers Ltd for permission to reproduce an extract from J. Franzen, *Farther Away* (2013).

1

Introduction

Simplicity is probably a really good place to start.

Andy Flower

Andy Flower, the England cricket coach, was responding to a question on the 'Today' programme (BBC Radio 4, 30 November 2011) about the best piece of advice he had been given to help bring about success, and not just in sport but more widely in life. So here to start with is a simple idea from Nancy Kline, a different kind of coach, which invariably informs the beginning of my training courses, group work sessions and team meetings:

> People think better throughout the whole meeting if the very first thing they do is to say something true and positive about how their work or the work of the group is going. (Kline, 1999, p. 107)

I hope it is not stretching things too much to see this interaction – you reading these words that I am now writing – as a form of a meeting. If this is the case, then we can put Kline's hypothesis to the test.

Activity: Pleased to notice?

If there is someone nearby, ask them to help you with this. What they need to do is to ask you the first question, give you time to think, to come up with your answer, then ask you the next question, and so on. If you are on your own, you can simply ask yourself the questions. Here is the first question:

What have you been pleased to notice about how you've been working recently?

And the second question:

What else have you been pleased to notice...?

This question then becomes the third question, then the fourth, and so on. Keep going until you have come up with five answers or for five minutes, whichever comes first.

I hope you were able to say, or think, something true and positive about how your work is going, and that Nancy Kline is right, because in this case you will be thinking better as you read the rest of this introductory chapter. Personally, I think she is onto something. However, if you did not happen to have anyone nearby to ask you those questions, it might not have been such an easy activity. And here we can have a first glance at what the solution-focused approach is all about, thinking about it in as simple a way as possible. Solution-focused practice is a talking-based activity, engaged in to be useful in some desired way, and one of the main activities of a solution-focused practitioner is to ask questions, intended to help the talking go in such a way that it does become useful. Now, being in a position to ask someone questions puts one in a potentially very influential position. To illustrate, let me ask you another question, and please, after you have read it, do not read on for a good few seconds. Here it is:

What did you have for your most recent meal?

Hang on. Do not read on for a few seconds yet...

I am going to assume that you did pause for a few seconds after reading the question, and I am going to assume that it is, therefore, likely that you brought to mind the meal you most recently had. I am going to further assume that you were not thinking about this until you read the question. So what happened? Well, I imagine it was my question, followed by the pause to give you time to think, that caused you to think of your most recent meal.[1] Having heard, or read, a question, the normal response is to start thinking of an answer, and in fact it is very hard not to. Solution-focused practice takes advantage of this straightforward idea, and the most simple way to think about the approach is that the solution-focused practitioner tries to find potentially useful questions to ask the person they are working with, a useful question being one which leads to the person being asked having useful thoughts or answers. I do not imagine that thinking of a recent meal will ordinarily be very useful, but consider if you asked this question of someone you are working with who is finding life hard at the moment, and who you last saw a week ago:

What have you done that's helped you to get through this week?

It is not hard to imagine that this question might help a useful thought or two to come to this person, and that they might voice one out loud:

I've just been taking each day as it comes.

Having heard this answer, you could follow it up with another question, and again it is not hard to imagine other useful thoughts and answers forming in response:

What have you been doing to get through each day? What did you do yesterday for example?

And that, in a nutshell, is the process we are going to be expanding upon for the rest of this book – one in which one person helps another to come up with thoughts, ideas and answers that turn out to be useful for them. Now, coming up with potentially useful thoughts and ideas clearly requires thinking, and thinking can be a difficult thing to do. This is why I said if you did not have anyone nearby to help you by asking you those questions in the first activity, it might not have been easy. Because thinking is hard, it is often helpful and sometimes necessary to have another person to help us to do it, someone who will keep us to task, who will not let us off the hook. And this, in another nutshell, is the job of a solution-focused practitioner, which we will be expanding on in the rest of this book – to ask questions, listen to the answers and then ask further questions, to help people think and talk in such ways that turn out to be useful for them. I will be going on in this chapter to open up these nutshells a little, to provide a clear overview of what you can expect within this book and of what you can hope to get out of it. I will include in this a brief account of my own route into the solution-focused approach, which will help to explain and put into context the particular version to be found here. First though, let me address the question of who the book is for. Put another way – who might be able to use a solution-focused approach?

Setting out what solution-focused practice consists of in the most general and simple way as I have done above makes the answer to these questions clear. The solution-focused approach can be used by anyone whose job involves talking with people in order to help them to make changes in their lives, to move on in some way, to resolve problems or to achieve goals. The people who developed the approach were therapists, but therapy is only one activity of many that involves purposeful talking aimed at change. Therefore, if you are a nurse, doctor, social worker, occupational therapist, teacher, counsellor, mentor, psychologist, health visitor, coach, youth worker, management consultant, family support worker, substance misuse worker, young people's advisor, residential worker, housing support worker, probation officer, youth justice worker speech and language therapist, physiotherapist, teaching assistant, foster carer, complementary health practitioner, or in any other health, social care, educational, coaching or organisational development role, then this book is likely to be relevant to you. My apologies if I have missed anyone out, as what was guiding me in compiling that list was bringing to mind the various people who have attended my training courses in solution-focused practice in the past 15 years or so, and who have been able to make good use of the approach.

I had my own first brush with the newly developing solution-focused approach while working as a nursing assistant in an adolescent psychiatric unit in the mid-1980s. A seed was sown at that time which was to come to fruition a decade later when I was first trained in solution-focused practice. In between these times, I qualified as a social worker, which I was fortunate enough to do at the University of Sheffield, the fortune being to do with two factors in particular. One was the school's commitment to equip students in the skills of structured models of social work practice, with their favoured approaches being typically short-term, goal-focused and behavioural in nature (Reid and Epstein, 1972; Hudson and Macdonald, 1986; O'Hagan, 1986; Corden and Preston-Shoot, 1987; Scott, 1989). Entering my profession when there was an ever-increasing emphasis given to assessing people, this input at Sheffield helped me to retain the belief that my role also included helping people to change. The second aspect of my social work education at Sheffield that I valued in particular arose from its research tradition of client studies (Sainsbury, 1975; Fisher, 1983). It might be hard to credit now, in this more consumer-oriented age, but seeking the views of people on the receiving end of services was a radical activity when it was pioneered in social work in the 1970s (Mayer and Timms, 1970) and 1980s. These two factors, a focus on practice models and associated skills needed for effecting change with people, and a commitment to being guided by the views of the people using or receiving services, have influenced me ever since, and in particular in my attraction to and developing use of solution-focused practice.

I attended my first course in solution-focused brief therapy in 1995, at a time when I was struggling to find a model of practice that could be used within the busy, often crisis-driven social care setting in which I found myself. In the last chapter of this book, I will relate how on my first day back at work after this four-day course I was able to use a solution-focused approach with a family of five that was close to breakdown. One of the great advantages of the solution-focused approach is its flexibility, which arises in part from its simplicity, both of which features make it an eminently usable approach, way beyond the confines of the therapy room, in social services and elsewhere (Shennan, 2008). The version of solution-focused practice I was trained in emphasises the simplicity of the approach, and it is important that I say a little about this, not only as a means to a clearer understanding of what this book is about but also because it will allow me to pay some dues. First though, I want to just clear out of the way some issues of terminology, concerning the people who use the solution-focused approach, the people they are using the approach with, and the approach itself.

We have already seen how wide-ranging the group of people is who can and do use this approach. While I will sometimes talk about *solution-focused practitioners*, given their use of *solution-focused practice*, I have decided, for the sake of brevity and also given that the people listed all use the approach as part of their work, to use the word *worker* as shorthand for them. In terms of the people the workers are working with, a difficulty is that they might be patients or clients or service users or students or supervisees or other designations, depending on who their worker is. *The person being worked with* is probably the most accurate descriptive expression, as it applies across the board, but it is rather long-winded and so I shall use the word *client* as a conveniently brief though not ideal shorthand. In terms of the approach itself, I said above that I was trained in *solution-focused brief therapy*. This label reflects the fact, also mentioned earlier, that the people who developed the approach were therapists. More specifically, they were *brief therapists*, as they followed a certain approach to therapy that I will allude to in thumbnail historical sketches in Chapters 4 and 5. Hence, when they were developing the solution-focused approach in the 1980s, for them this was a way of doing brief therapy, and indeed the brief therapy they had been using was enormously influential in their developments. However, as already indicated, the approach has long since mushroomed into many other contexts besides therapy, and so in common with many others, I now use the more inclusive expressions *solution-focused practice* and *the solution-focused approach*.

Let me now sketch what has led to the version of solution-focused practice presented in this book. The original solution-focused brief therapists were based in Milwaukee in the United States, and one of the leading members of the group was Steve de Shazer, who was responsible more than anyone else for the dissemination of the approach, in part through the regular appearance of his books (de Shazer, 1985, 1988, 1991, 1994). There were many articles also coming out of Milwaukee (de Shazer, 1984; de Shazer et al., 1986, being especially influential), and this literature began to arouse the interest of practitioners around the world, including three social workers/family therapists working together as a team within the National Health Service in London: Chris Iveson, Harvey Ratner and Evan George. They were among the first to use the solution-focused approach in the UK (George, Iveson and Ratner, 1990) and became hugely influential in its development here when they began to run training courses having set up on their own as the Brief Therapy Practice. As well as using and teaching solution-focused practice, this team also took on a developmental role, and by the time I attended my first course with them in 1995, their own distinctive version of solution-focused practice had already taken much of its shape (George, Iveson and Ratner, 1995, 1999; Iveson, George and Ratner, 2012).

When I worked with the team, from 2004 to 2010, its name had been shortened from the Brief Therapy Practice to BRIEF. The 'BRIEF version' of solution-focused practice, which I have contributed to in my turn (Shennan and Iveson, 2011), is probably the predominant one in use in the UK and informs the practices presented in this book. Sitting squarely in the solution-focused tradition established in Milwaukee in the 1980s, its distinctive features come in particular from a development of the focus on simplicity and minimalism. This focus has always been present in the approach, with Steve de Shazer drawing on the principle attributed to the 14th-century philosopher William of Ockham: 'What can be done with fewer means is done in vain with many' (1985, p. 58). BRIEF took on the task of sharpening Ockham's Razor (George, Iveson and Ratner, 2001), and a streamlined solution-focused process has been the result. This process will be unfolding in front of you as you read through this book, though the simplicity will already have been evident from the activity presented at the beginning of the chapter and my subsequent commentary.

Having said a little in general terms about some characteristics of the approach, let me take the opportunity to say very clearly a couple of things the approach is not. It is often thought by people taking a cursory glance at it that solution-focused practice is about 'being positive'. Related to this is an idea that solution-focused practitioners do not allow space for clients to talk about their problems, or minimise or even deny the problems clients have. However, these are misconceptions. First, take another look at the questions in the activity at the beginning of the chapter. 'What have you been pleased to notice about how you have been working recently?' does not carry an assumption that the person being asked has just had a nice and easy time at work, without any problems. There may well have been problems, and one of the answers to the question might relate to being pleased about how they have been handled or coped with.

My clients often talk about their problems during their sessions with me – many of them are seeing me after all because they have severe difficulties. What determines whether or not these sessions are solution-focused is how I respond to the problem talk – Chapter 7 in particular is focused on this issue. An important aspect of this response is to listen to the client as they talk about their difficulties, for as long as they need to do this, and to show the client they are being listened to, for example, by acknowledgement of what they are saying. It is equally important not to try to make the client feel positive, or to see that things are not as bad as they had thought. Clients need to be fully accepted where they are, in solution-focused practice as much as in any other approach. No, the essential characteristic of solution-focused practice lies elsewhere, in its focus on difference and change, and on what is wanted in this respect by the client. This will be laid out clearly from Chapter 2 onwards.

Let me now anticipate a crucial distinction a solution-focused practitioner always needs to be aware of, which will be coming to the fore later, by talking about the expected outcomes of this book and of the process that I hope will take you towards those outcomes. Starting with the outcomes, let me suggest first that there are two ways of using the solution-focused approach. One is to use it as a whole, in a planned fashion, on a session-by-session basis. This requires a grasp of how solution-focused sessions are structured, which in turn requires a grasp of the overall solution-focused process, in other words how the individual questions asked by a solution-focused practitioner are organised into a coherent whole. So one of the outcomes of this book is that by the end of it you will have a clear understanding of this process and a sound knowledge of how solution-focused sessions are structured. The second way to use the approach is more opportunistically, in unplanned ways within everyday conversations, by extracting aspects of the approach or asking individual solution-focused questions. For example, after I first trained in solution-focused practice as a social worker, I would at times be able to sit down with a family and use the approach in a planned way, going through a whole session and then arranging to meet for a follow-up. At other times however, I might be meeting a client in a crisis situation, where the context was not right for a thoroughgoing solution-focused session, but I found that I could (usefully) use, for example, the type of question mentioned earlier: 'What are you doing that's helping you to keep going?' So the second thing that will come out of your reading of this book is an awareness of the different types of solution-focused questions, many of which you will be able to use at various times with your 'clients', even when you are not in a position to put them together into the whole process.

In terms of this second outcome, I should add that solution-focused practitioners tend to think carefully about the wording of their questions, because all questions have assumptions embedded within them and so convey messages to the people on the receiving end of them. However much we like to think of ourselves as not making assumptions about people, once we start asking questions it is inescapable that we do. For example, the questions I asked earlier conveyed my assumptions that you have eaten a meal and that there would be something you had been pleased to notice about your work recently. If I had asked instead the closed question, 'Is there anything you've been pleased to notice about your work recently?', then I would still have been making an assumption, but this time that I thought maybe there was and maybe there was not something you had been pleased to notice. I would be most surprised if the latter were the case, so this is not a message I would want to convey. Solution-focused practitioners are far more likely to make the confident assumptions that are found in open questions, which often begin with 'What...', than to ask closed questions. So I recommend that, as you are learning these questions, and perhaps trying them out, you stay close to how they are worded in these pages. This may feel awkward at first, but so does speaking any language that is new to us, and learning to talk in a solution-focused way is not dissimilar to learning a new language. And, in just the same way, fluency comes with practice.

Finally, what process will be followed in order to achieve these outcomes? In the pages to come will be a mixture of description and explanation of the approach, together with numerous illustrative case examples, usually in the form of transcripts of actual solution-focused sessions with accompanying commentary.[2] Interspersed throughout will be activities, many of which have been designed simply to encourage and guide the reflecting that you will be doing while you read in any case, with a small number suggesting you try something out with a partner. I recommend that you have a go at these if you can, as they are likely to add to your learning. The major case examples and the activities are tried and tested in that I have used them on my training courses over the years, where I have also been able to sharpen my presentation of the approach, always simplifying where possible. So what follows is my current and most up-to-date way of conveying what solution-focused practice is and how to do it.

In Chapter 2, I will help you to continue to discover the overall solution-focused process by using an example of my work that has proved remarkably effective in this regard in recent years.[3] Chapters 3 to 7 will see the process broken down into its constituent parts, before it is put back together again in Chapter 8. Chapter 3 will consider the starting point of the process and, therefore, its most essential aspect, which is a focus on what the client wants from the work to be done. The articulation of what the client wants creates a direction for the work, towards this desired outcome, and from this point the solution-focused practitioner will be asking questions that, again thinking of the approach most simply, fall into just two groups. Chapter 4 will consider the future-focused aspect of the approach, whereby the worker helps the client to describe in detail the realisation of their desired outcome, while Chapter 5 will examine the focus on what is working and on how the client has managed to have parts of their desired future in place already. Scaling questions are amongst the most useful techniques available to a solution-focused practitioner and are both an integral part of the overall process and usable in a stand-alone way. I will give a detailed account of how to use scaling in Chapter 6, which will show how it provides a bridge between the future focus and the focus on what is already working. Chapter 7 will look at ways of responding in the most difficult situations, such as when a client has rated themselves at the lowest point on a scale. The main focus in all these chapters, and of the whole book, is on how to do it, though I will also allude briefly in some to the development of the approach, to provide some historical context and a more informed understanding of what a solution-focused practitioner does.

By Chapter 8 we will be ready to put the pieces back together again, to look at using the whole approach on a session-by-session basis. The structures of first and follow-up sessions will be laid out in some detail and an extended example given to show a piece of work from start to finish. Even if you consider that you would only be using bits of the approach in an unplanned way, it is important to be clear about how it all fits together, as then you will be more likely to be using the parts that you do use in a way that is actually solution-focused. By the end of Chapter 8, the process and all the questions and techniques that contribute to it will have been covered, and you then have the job of working out how to apply it in your context. Chapters 9 and 10 are intended to help you in this task. I will draw on my own experiences in this, going right back to 1995 when I came to the end of my first course in solution-focused brief therapy, remembered that I was not a therapist, and had to work out how to apply what I had learned to my statutory social work role. It was an exciting and invigorating task, though not always straightforward, and I hope that what I have to share, about what I did then and about applications and adaptations I have made since, will be useful for you in whatever context your work takes place. The answers to the frequently asked questions listed in Chapter 10 will also include information about the evidence base for the approach, but I can summarise this for you here – it works!

One last note – I have been an enthusiast for the solution-focused approach since I undertook that first course in 1995. I am not writing this book as an impartial observer, but as someone fully immersed in the solution-focused community, who has invested a great deal in learning, using and disseminating solution-focused practice. At the same time I know it does not fit for everyone and there is no reason why it should. It may be that you will not be sure for some time whether it is an approach that is right for you to use, until you are well into or have even finished this book. There are many approaches out there that have good evidence bases (Cooper, 2008), and if ever I compare solution-focused practice with other ways of working, it is only to use the contrast to help explain what a solution-focused practitioner does and does not do. It is not to say it is better, just different. Similarly, books such as this often begin with a list of the values that underlie an approach, and I have deliberately steered away from this. This is in part because the values of solution-focused practice, for example of respect for the client, self-determination, transparency, openness and partnership, are shared with many other approaches, so to list such values would not help the reader to discover what is distinctive about solution-focused practice. In any case, the values are implicit in what the solution-focused practitioner does. There are no values other than those you can see. If I am as clear about what the solution-focused practitioner does in what follows as I hope to be, then the values will speak for themselves.

Reflections

At the end of each chapter I will be posing some questions to help you to reflect on what has been covered and on your own progress through the book. For this first chapter:

- What has interested you so far in what you have picked up about the solution-focused approach? What else?
- What assumptions are embedded within the above questions?
- You probably brought some pre-existing ideas with you about solution-focused practice, before beginning the book. How has what you have read so far fitted with these ideas? Has anything surprised you?
- From what you have read, what are you looking forward to in what is to come?

2

The Solution-Focused Process

These questions are…difficult to answer and, therefore, very much worth asking.

Jonathan Franzen (2013)

Introduction

Unlike most models of helping, the solution-focused approach did not originate in theory. It was developed by practitioners who spent countless hours practising and many more hours engaged in the 'disciplined observation' of their practice, trying to work out what worked and discarding those elements that appeared not to (de Shazer, 1988). So, since its earliest days, solution-focused practice has always been a pragmatic approach that is best grasped by seeing it done and by doing it. As we shall see again and again throughout this book, solution-focused practitioners' questions come from what they hear their clients say, rather than from theories they carry around with them in their heads. It is not possible to learn how to do solution-focused practice from reading books containing theories about people, about why they have problems and about what therefore needs to be done to help to resolve those problems. Unlike the majority of helping approaches that have originated in the world of psychology, counselling and psychotherapy, solution-focused practice is not based on such theories. This poses a challenge for anyone setting out to write a book aimed at helping people learn how to do solution-focused practice. However, although the approach is not based on theories about people, it does have a clear process which guides practitioners through their solution-focused conversations. What is required is to see this in action.

This process will emerge clearly from a carefully chosen transcript of part of a solution-focused conversation. Although every conversation that ever takes place is a unique event, an advantage of solution-focused practice is that the process is transferable across the many contexts in which it is used. Whether one is carrying out a series of one-hour sessions, as in counselling for example, or talking more briefly with a patient by their bedside, or with a school student during break, or offering consultation to a colleague, the process is fundamentally the same. There is no preconceived programme to follow, only certain types of questions to ask, and a few solution-focused questions asked during a conversation lasting a few minutes can be as valuable as a therapy session lasting close to an hour.

The transcript

The transcript here is of a section of a solution-focused counselling session I undertook with Michelle who I had first met two weeks previously. Michelle had contacted the clinic where I was based on the recommendation of another mental health professional she was seeing, who had done a training course in solution-focused practice at the clinic. What you will read here is the first few minutes of the second session. There is a typical structure for an initial solution-focused session, or conversation, and another typical structure for a follow-up session. Once you have a grasp of these structures, and of how the work flows from a first meeting to a second and perhaps beyond, then you will have a good grasp of the solution-focused process.

The reason for using this particular extract is twofold. First, you will 'see' the beginning of a follow-up session and how my questions begin to create the structure for this session. Secondly, you will 'hear' Michelle talk, with great interest, about what took place in the first session and therefore about how the beginning of a solution-focused piece of work is structured. Putting the two together – what you see of the follow-up session and what you hear Michelle saying about the first session – will take you a long way towards working out what the solution-focused process is all about.

Activity: Discovering the solution-focused process

As you read through this first extract, be continually asking yourself what you are discovering about the solution-focused process so far.

Guy: So, what's been better?

Michelle: Erm ... I don't know really. I guess a bit of everything.

Guy: Ah-hah?

Michelle: Yeah, a little bit of everything I guess.

Guy: Yeah? Ok. What things then, what things have been better?

Michelle: Er ... erm ... ha! ... I think I'm more positive, because I had to go away and think about what you were saying last week, 'cos I'm like that, and then I suddenly got the questions that you were asking, which I didn't get before. So I suddenly got what you were asking, how will I know when I've turned the corner?

Guy: Yeah?

Michelle: Yeah, it was a simple question but I wasn't getting it (*laughs*).

Guy: Ok, it sometimes needs a bit of thinking about, yeah?

Michelle: Yeah. And, erm, yeah I guess it will be when I, erm, get a job and ... maybe get a house and just move on, do everyday things like everybody else. But it's ok. It's not so bad.

Guy: Yeah. So you've been doing some thinking since the session about how you'll know that you've turned the corner.

Michelle: Yes, yes, oh yeah, you've got to do your homework! (*laughs*).

Guy: Ok, ok. So what was that like? What was the effect of getting the question and doing that thinking?

Michelle: Ermm ...

Guy: How was it useful to you?

Michelle: Because nobody had ever asked that question before, so I guess I was just looking for a corner to turn, but not knowing what to look for when I got around there. Or maybe I have moved on, and I just hadn't realised I'd moved on. So when I put, sat there thinking, well I have moved on a little piece, because I'm here and I'm in Brighton ...

Guy: Yep.

Michelle: I guess I just don't know how to move on, erm, you know, like the whole picture?

Guy: Yeah.

Michelle: Because I'm just, I've been stuck in one place for so long, so, I guess it's the actual moving on bit that's quite difficult ...

Guy: Yeah, sure.

Michelle: ... that I don't really understand.

Guy: Yeah, yeah.

Michelle: So yeah, so I think it has helped me. I think it has helped me. Because the question was never put to me or I'd never thought of it myself, erm, but suddenly when you, when you understand the question I guess you understand where you're going to be going to or where you want to be going to, or want to be getting out of it, or... so, yeah.

Guy: Ok. So you've been doing some thinking then, some thinking about that question, and you've been feeling a bit more positive, did you say, yeah?

Michelle: Yeah, yeah, I guess so.

Guy: Tell me a bit more about that, how do you know? What have you noticed about yourself?

Michelle: Erm... well I didn't have to ask every fifth person how to get here today and I took a totally different route, which was an easier route.

Guy: Ok.

Michelle: Erm... the fact that I know what I want in my head now is good whereas last time I didn't know – I knew I wanted to be happy, I knew I wanted to move on, I didn't know how, I didn't know why... erm, I just know things now, I just know, I know that I want to be able to get a job and be able to get up and go to that job everyday without suffering with deep depression where I lose the job. I know that I want to own my own home in time and I know that I, you know, I want to do everyday things, and I haven't been doing those ev..., not even the everyday things, I have not been doing them until, erm, last time I saw you. And now I do everyday things.

Guy: Yeah? Such as?

Michelle: Erm, the shopping, erm, walking, because normally I hide in my car and drive everywhere in my car. And I've probably walked a good ten miles.

Guy: Really? Woo...

Michelle: Yeah, because I walk everywhere, or catch the tube if it's too far. I don't sit in my car anymore, hiding.

Guy: Ok, so over the past couple of weeks since we met, you've been doing plenty of walking, and shopping, and, yeah...

Michelle: Yeah (*laughing*). I do the shopping on my own now, which is really neat.

Guy: What difference is that making to you, Michelle?

Michelle: Loads.

Guy: Yeah?

Michelle: Loads, yeah, because I guess this is what independent people feel like, when they just get up and think you need to go and get the shopping instead of ... I wait for one of my family to come with me and do the shopping, so to do it on my own is really really neat.

Guy: Right.

Michelle: Yeah, it was really good. Such a small step for every other person and a big step for me *(laughs)*.

Guy: Right. And how did you take that step?

Michelle: Erm, well, I was just thinking, where do I want to be? And I kept thinking about the questions that you asked, where will I want to be and how will I know when I get there? Well I'm not going to get there, sitting down, doing the same things that I was doing. So I just decided that I would start doing simple things that everybody does and I would start from the bottom, like going shopping on my own, and going to the shop first, because I never go to the local shop and if I do it's in the car.

Guy: Um-hum.

Michelle: And erm ... I just, we're here once and once only, and ...

Guy: Yeah. So you've taken some steps, having thought about where you want to be, you've taken some simple steps, in a sense ...

Michelle: Yes.

Guy: Yeah? So you've been walking to the shops?

Michelle: Yes, yeah.

Guy: Yeah, ok. How's that been feeling, doing that?

Michelle: Erm, it was really scary at first, but I don't know what I was so scared of really, you know, because I've done it and there's nothing scary about going to the shop. But it was really really scary *(laughs)*.

Guy: So, how did you get through the scariness, to actually do it?

Michelle: I had to talk my way through it. It took me four attempts to erm ... I got past the front door but it was getting past the car, and erm ...

> ### Activity: What the solution-focused worker does and does not do
>
> The conversation has been going for just over six minutes at this point, so let us pause and take stock. What has been happening so far? Make a list of what you see me doing on one side of a sheet of paper and what it occurs to you that I am not doing, on the other side.

General overview

What we have seen unfolding above in a more extended way is the process touched upon in Chapter 1 – on the most general level, I am engaging in two main activities: asking questions and listening to Michelle. So the first thing I want to underline is that the solution-focused approach is *a question-based approach*. The solution-focused worker tries to find useful questions to ask, rather than answers or advice to give. What sorts of questions are asked, and when, will take us further into the solution-focused process, and we will return to that shortly, having first looked more closely at the second activity – listening.

The questions come clearly off the page, but how can you tell that I am listening, just from reading this dialogue? You might think it would be easier to discern this if you could see me and my client together, so that you could see me making eye contact, and nodding, and saying 'um-hum' and 'ah-hah' (which are not transcribed here, in the main) and so on. But even if you could see me doing these things, and even though they would generally be seen as good practice in showing that one is listening, they would not be sufficient evidence of this. I could be looking at Michelle, nodding and saying 'um-hum', and, as far as anyone knows, be thinking about what to have for lunch, or that this is a case of depression and running through ideas about this.

The only sure way of being able to tell if someone is listening is when they start to talk back, and if what they say is connected to what has been said to them. In the extract above, you will notice that I occasionally repeat or summarise what Michelle has said.

Ok, so over the past couple of weeks since we met, you've been doing plenty of walking, and shopping, and, yeah…

I could not have given this accurate summary of Michelle's words without having been listening to her. So, added to the two major activities of asking questions and listening, we can add a third solution-focused activity, which is what the worker says back to the client. This *saying back* includes echoing and repeating certain words of the client, showing appreciation, acknowledging difficulties and summarising more formally at the end of sessions. The latter is to some extent a residual activity left over from the practices of giving compliments and setting tasks that have historically been (and still are for some practitioners) an important part of the solution-focused approach. In the version of solution-focused practice being presented in this book, their use has been considerably reduced. While summarising is still useful, as a means of showing that you have been listening, reinforcing for the client what they have said and for bringing conversations to a close, in my practice I see it as supplementary to the main activities of asking questions and listening. I shall be saying more about summarising in the closing stage of a session when looking in more detail at session structures in Chapter 8.

So, hearing their words echoed, reflected back and summarised will show the client that they are being listened to. The other way in which the worker's talking in response to the client will do this is when their *questions* connect to what the client has just said. For example:

Michelle: It was a big step for me.

Guy: How did you take that step?

How could I have asked that question, without having been listening to what Michelle was saying? This is an example of what I said earlier, that the worker's questions come from what the client is saying, rather than from theories in the worker's head. This means that solution-focused practice calls for very close listening on the part of the worker. Moreover, these two major activities, listening and asking questions, are absolutely connected and entwined with each other. The above example, where I asked about Michelle's 'step', is a relatively straightforward one. More difficult is when a client talks at more length and the worker has to choose which part of what the client has said to ask about. Being clear about the solution-focused process will help the worker in making their choice. Another helpful idea comes from the American solution-focused therapist Eve Lipchik, who wrote about 'interviewing with a constructive ear' (Lipchik, 1988b). When we listen with a constructive ear, we are listening, among other things, for the person's strengths, skills and abilities, for what they are doing that fits with their hopes and aspirations, for how they are managing to cope with and get through difficulties they are experiencing, for exceptions to those difficulties, and for how they would like things to be. And what we listen for, and therefore hear, determines what we ask. Near the beginning of the session, Michelle said that she thought she was 'more positive'. She then reflected at length about the first session, and this lone word 'positive' might easily have been swallowed up by Michelle's reflections. However, having been listening with a constructive ear, I had heard this word and retained it in my mind, knowing that it was a part of what Michelle was saying that I was likely to want to return to and ask about.

Initial summary: What we do

So, here is our first, very general overview of what a solution-focused practitioner does:

*   Asks questions
*   Listens, with a constructive ear
*   Echoes, appreciates and summarises

And, when being purely solution-focused, this is *all* that will be done. In Chapter 9, I will touch on how the approach can be used partially, alongside other activities, but for the most part I will be sticking strictly to solution-focused practice, pure and simple.

Activity: Asking, listening and summarising

Interview a colleague for five minutes about what they plan to do this evening or weekend. Ask questions that show you are listening by including words used in your colleague's previous answers. Summarise what you have heard using the exact words that your colleague used to describe their plans.

The solution-focused process

This list of three activities is only the beginning of the story. In the extract above, I am asking lots of questions, and Michelle is reflecting on other questions that were asked in the first session. These questions are not being asked randomly but are being determined by the solution-focused process. What can we discover about this process from this particular example?

Starting with what the client wants

Starting with the questions that Michelle refers to from the first session, she first mentions 'how will I know that I have turned the corner?' The phrasing is Michelle's own, but she has remembered the thrust of the questions in the first part of the first session beautifully. It becomes even clearer how finely tuned to the process Michelle has become, however hard she found it to answer the questions in the first session, when she reflects further a few minutes later: 'I kept thinking about the questions that you asked, where will I want to be and how will I know when I get there?' A teacher of solution-focused practice could hardly have put it better!

So, the process begins in the future, at the endpoint of the work in fact, and an endpoint that is determined by the client. And this brings us to the central defining feature of any solution-focused piece of work. Whether it is taking place in a five-minute conversation or in a series of one-hour sessions, the most essential characteristic of a solution-focused piece of work is that it has a direction to it, and the direction that you want the work to be heading in is towards the client's hoped-for outcome from it. This direction begins to be created when the client is able to articulate something that they 'want to be getting out of it', to use Michelle's words. So, the business of solution-focused practice is begun as soon as the worker asks the client what they want from the work to be done, from the conversation that is to take place. There are many ways of asking this, and the 'getting down to business' question that I asked Michelle was 'what are your best hopes from coming here?'

Michelle's immediate answer was 'moving on'. She wanted to be moving on in some way, having felt stuck for a long time. So, in the space of a few seconds and a few words, a direction for the work had been created. Everything that I would do from that point onwards should in some way be connected with Michelle's hoped-for outcome of moving on. Another way of thinking about this process is to see it as one of contracting. By asking the client what they want from the work, the worker is asking if they want to do business. By articulating a desired outcome, the client is simultaneously saying yes, I want to do business with you, and a contract has been arrived at, with the worker implicitly agreeing to work with the client towards their desired outcome.

Though the question and answer – 'What are your best hopes from this?'– 'I want to be moving on' – might make this seem like a very straightforward process, it is often anything but. As you are reading this, questions might be occurring to you about asking someone you are working with what they want, such as what to do if what they want appears unattainable. Let us not be concerned with this further here, as the whole of the next chapter will be devoted to this part of the process. Suffice it to say, for now, that for a conversation to be described as solution-focused, it needs to be directed towards an outcome that the client is wanting from it.

Describing what is wanted in detail

To those familiar with the notion of SMART goals (there is no consensus about exactly what the acronym stands for, though it is broadly 'specific, measurable, attainable, relevant, time-sensitive' (Doran, 1981)), 'moving on' might appear rather vague to serve as a desired outcome. Yet the initial contracting was only the first part of a twofold future orientation of the work. As Michelle had put it so well, 'where will I want to be and how will I know when I get there?' The second part ('how will I know') involves the specification of the hoped-for outcome. In the first session, I went on to invite Michelle to suppose that when she woke up the next morning, she *was* moving on, in just the way that she wanted. The sorts of questions that followed – 'What would be the first thing you would notice about yourself?' 'How would you know?' 'What differences would you notice?' – are intended to help the client to *describe* their desired outcome in as much concrete detail as possible. This description is often labelled as the client's preferred future (Iveson, 1994), and we will be exploring this aspect of the solution-focused process in detail in Chapter 4.

Michelle's reflections, in the transcript above, indicate how she really struggled to find answers to these questions, and how I struggled to find ways of helping her to answer. This was a fairly typical example of her answers to the future-focused questions of the first session:

> Erm... I don't know. I don't know, I couldn't answer that question. I really don't know, er, I've no idea how I would know that I was moving on. I don't know, I couldn't answer that question I'm afraid.

The extent to which Michelle answered 'I don't know' is actually quite unusual in this particular context. Most people, with the help of solution-focused questions, are able to describe a preferred future in some detail. A couple of points are worth making. First, 'I don't know' is not an uncommon answer to solution-focused questions in general, which should not come as a surprise as they can be very searching, novel and hence difficult questions to answer. Note how Michelle said at one point, 'nobody had ever asked that question before'. In fact, it is an answer that, at first at least, should be welcomed. If someone 'knew' the answers, straightaway, to all the questions that a helping person asked them, then it would appear unlikely that they needed the help in the first place, or that it was helping them. 'Knowing' the answers in this way might suggest that the questions are not provoking the client to think differently, in which case it would be questionable whether the talking would make any difference. The second point to be made here is that, however often someone says 'I don't know', we do not need to panic. Certainly, it is not the worker's job to answer the question for the client. Consider what happened for Michelle after her first session. She went away, thought about the questions she had been asked, which she had not been able to answer there and then, and came up with answers in her own time.

So, to return to our exploration of the solution-focused process, the first part of it is a focus on the future, broken down into these two steps:

* What is the client hoping for from the work?
* How might the client know that these hopes have been realised, and what differences might this make?

Describing progress towards the preferred future

The next part of the process can be seen clearly in the way I was structuring the second session with Michelle from its outset. The very first question asked – and the transcript starts at the very beginning of the session – is 'What's been better?' What does this question tell us about the continuation of the solution-focused process? It is a dynamic question, concerning movement and change, which is immediately signified by the word *better*. It is a different question to, for example, 'What's going well?' I am assuming that Michelle will have been making some movement towards her desired outcome for the work, and I want to signal that this is what I am interested in, above all, at this stage.

We referred earlier to the way a piece of solution-focused work flows from conversation to conversation. Now it can be seen that the starting point of an initial solution-focused conversation is to look forward, to what the client is hoping for from the work and how they will know that they have achieved this, while the starting point of a follow-up conversation is to look back, at the period since the previous conversation and to help the client to talk about *progress* they have noticed during that time.

So we can now add the third step of the solution-focused process:

• What progress is the client making towards their hopes from the work?

However, we do not need to wait for a second conversation to ask about progress. Usually, all three steps of the process will be taken during an initial conversation, which might indeed be the sum total of the work, as it is not unusual for solution-focused practice to take place in a one-off meeting. A technique frequently used to elicit progress is known as scaling (Berg and de Shazer, 1993), and I introduced a scale about 20 minutes into the first session.

> If we have a scale, Michelle, from 0 to 10, and 10 is that you were moving on exactly as you want to, 'and 0 was that you'd never moved on one millimetre, you've not done anything', yeah? The complete opposite of 10. What point on the scale are you at, would you see things now?

Constructing a scale in this way, especially one where the client is unlikely to rate themselves as at 0 ('and 0 was that you'd never moved on one millimetre, you've not done anything'), enables the client to start talking about progress they are already making towards their desired outcome, even when they might have felt at the outset of a conversation that they were making no progress at all. Michelle had complained of being completely stuck, and it turned out that she was already at a 3 in this first meeting.

Now, the reason I asked this scaling question was not to assess the progress Michelle was making. If there is any assessing taking place, it is being done by Michelle herself. The actual number was irrelevant to me, the significance of any answer above 0 being simply that it enables some potentially very useful questions to be asked.

Activity: Numbers as prompts for questions

What questions might you consider asking in response to Michelle's answer of 3?

It would not be surprising if the first idea that presented itself was to ask about 4. It is quite common for those who are new to the approach to ask first about moving up the scale – people want to help others to make progress after all. When we *do* ask about higher up the scale, then focusing on only one point up does make a lot of sense. However, our attention will be directed first to the difference between 0 and 3, and we will remain interested in this for a considerable time. There are a number of ways of asking about this difference, which can be divided mainly into two types: questions about how the client has got to 3 and questions that invite a description of 3, in comparison to 0. We commonly start with the second kind:

> 3? Ok, so what are the differences that are making it 3 now, compared to 0?

Notice how I have asked about differences in the plural. I want to help Michelle bring as much of her progress to mind as possible, and will be prepared to ask repeatedly, 'What else puts you up at 3?' The importance of *detail*, and of helping the client to continue adding to their accounts of progress in as simple a way as possible, will be referred to again and again in this book. The conversation continued to focus on progress, as I also asked Michelle about what she had done, and about the qualities she had drawn upon, to move from 0 to 3. Eventually, I moved up the scale, in the following way: 'How might you know that you've moved just one point higher?' This returned Michelle to the consideration of a preferred future, though one that was closer to where she was at present. Nevertheless, she still found thinking about the future difficult, and the answer 'I don't know' returned to centre stage! Scaling questions, the most flexible friend of the solution-focused practitioner, will be the subject of Chapter 6, where we will see some of Michelle's answers to these questions.

Summary: The solution-focused process

We have now set out the whole solution-focused process. To recap, it is made up of three main stages, which can be represented by these questions:

- What is the client hoping for from the work (or from the discussion or conversation)?
- How might the client know that these hopes have been realised, and what differences might their realisation make?
- What progress is the client making towards their hopes from the work?

Or perhaps there are three and a half stages, with the next, half-stage, being:

- And what might be some small signs of further progress?

And that, give or take some summarising back to the client by the worker, is it. But as Steve de Shazer, one of the two main founders of the approach, often said, 'It's simple, but it ain't easy!' (de Shazer and Berg, 1997). Conceptually, it is simple, which I believe is one of the great strengths of the approach. But being simple to understand does not make a process easy to carry out in practice, and working in a solution-focused way can be a hard discipline. So we need help in sticking with it, and being clear about the overarching process is essential in guiding us when in the midst of a solution-focused conversation. If you are feeling stuck, it can be useful to ask yourself:

- Is this heading somewhere?
- Does the person I am talking to have a desired outcome from this?
- Is it clear what that is, however generally framed it might be?

Then, assuming that the answers to these questions are yes, you can remind yourself that there are basically only two areas of interest to ask about – the preferred future and progress that is being made towards that future.

Constructing questions

There remains the task of constructing particular questions within the two areas. Fortunately, as well as there being an overarching process, there are a number of features of the approach that, if assimilated and borne in mind, will assist in forming individual questions. Many of these will be covered elsewhere in this book, but in the final part of this chapter, let us consider a few that can be seen in the work with Michelle.

Getting straight to the point and being focused

We have already commented that 'What's been better?' was the very first question asked in the second session, while 'What are your best hopes from talking with me here?' is often the first question asked in an initial conversation. Solution-focused practitioners will get straight on with the business of what the client wants, or what progress they have made. A preliminary relationship-building phase is not considered necessary, though of course a relationship will develop, simply through the conversational process. The example here is from a relatively leisurely counselling session. Many professionals who use a solution-focused approach do not have the same amount of time in their conversations, hence the value of getting straight to the point, creating an immediate focus for the conversation, and maintaining a focus throughout.

Including the client's words when constructing questions

The task of constructing questions that connect with the client's last answer is aided by utilising the client's own words. Just as the worker is not drawing on theories inside their head, they are also not looking to draw upon their own language, but rather to work in the client's language. This can be seen at several points with Michelle, including right at the start.

Michelle: Yeah, a little bit of everything I guess.

Guy: Yeah? Ok. What things then, what things have been better?

Using plurals and asking 'what else?'

Granted, it would have been ungrammatical to have asked 'What thing have been better?' in the singular, but it is useful to 'think in plurals' as a general rule. If we assume that there will always be more that the client has noticed, or done to make progress, or is good at, then we will keep asking for more, thereby encouraging the client to continue thinking and extending their awareness of themselves as able to make progress. We can signal our intention by framing a question in this plural way and then continue by using the question 'What else?' Another example given above was: 'What are the differences that are making it 3 compared to 0?'

Directing the client's attention to their life outside of the session

In some talk-based helping approaches, such as those originating from psychodynamic theory or from the person-centred tradition, the worker focuses the client on what is happening within the conversation, for example on their feelings during it or on what is happening in the relationship between them. In solution-focused work, we are always focusing the client on their life outside. When Michelle said that she had not understood the future-focused questions at first, but that now she did, I wanted to direct her attention to the effects this understanding had had on her actual life since: 'So how was it useful to you?'

Allowing oneself to amend questions, while in the process of asking them

Constructing questions is not easy, and there is no reason to suppose that you will always find the 'best' or most useful question straightaway. Sometimes it is not until you hear a question out loud, or notice the client's reaction to it, that you realise that there is probably a different way of asking it that might be more useful. The question above, 'So how was it useful to you?', was a third attempt, after 'So what was that like?' and 'What was the effect of getting the question and doing that thinking?'

Moving from the general to the specific

What happens over and over again in any solution-focused conversation is that the worker will be helping the client to develop a general answer into more specific details, in particular, concrete details. We all speak in generalities – the question 'How are you?' typically being followed by something like 'Fine, thanks'. The person being asked does not usually expect that the person asking wants a lot of fine detail. There is no reason to suppose that a person being asked questions in a solution-focused conversation will be thinking any differently. It is the worker's task to ask questions that invite concrete detail. Fortunately, there are lots of ways of doing this. A couple of examples came in response to Michelle saying she was more positive – 'How do you know?' 'What have you noticed about yourself?'

Keeping it simple and minimal

There are a host of reasons for keeping our questions simple, short and to the point. One is based on our belief that change arises from the client's answers, not from the worker's questions. We therefore want the client to be focused on their answers rather than on our questions as far as possible, and for their answers to take up as much of the space as possible. The shorter our questions, the more space will be available for the client. The two-word question below, for example, was all that was needed to prompt Michelle to expand on the everyday things she was now doing, and left her more space to do so:

> *Michelle*: And now I do everyday things.
> *Guy*: Yeah? Such as?

Asking how the client gets through, not into problems

When I asked Michelle how it felt walking to the shops, I meant after she had done so, and I was assuming that it would feel good to Michelle (this itself was a cardinal error – a useful rule is never ask a question you think you know the answer to). However, Michelle heard a different question, about how it felt trying to do it in the first place, which had been really scary. What guided me next was the 'both/and' thinking of a solution-focused practitioner (Lipchik, 1993). It had been scary *and* Michelle had done it. I was, therefore, interested in how Michelle had done it, especially as it had been scary, not in why it had been scary in the first place or what lay beneath Michelle's fear – 'So, how did you get through the scariness, to actually do it?'

Outcome of the work with Michelle

The work with Michelle lasted for three sessions in all, taking place over a period of six weeks. In the third session, Michelle indicated that her progress had been consolidated, but then she did not turn up for a fourth session planned to take place four weeks later. I therefore never heard in any detail what happened after those three sessions. However, about a year after the end of the work, the professional who had suggested to Michelle that she came for the solution-focused counselling contacted the clinic to refer another client of hers, as it had been so helpful for the person she had recommended to come a year before.

Conclusion

The work done with Michelle constituted a typical piece of solution-focused practice, and three was the average number of sessions for my clients at that time. During these sessions, I had:

- asked questions
- listened with a constructive ear
- offered summaries.

The particular questions asked had first helped to establish a *contract* for the work, based on Michelle's hopes from it, which were to be 'moving on', and had then helped Michelle to describe:

- her preferred future – what 'moving on' would look like and the differences it would make;
- the progress she was making towards this, and how she was making this progress.

I was guided in my construction of questions by my knowledge of a number of features of the solution-focused approach, some of which I have set out above. In the following chapters, I will break down the process of listening and asking questions in more detail and continue exploring the features of this fascinating and empowering approach.

Reflections

- In setting out the solution-focused process, I have described what a solution-focused worker does. In the activity after the transcript, I asked you to note what I was not doing. What does it appear that a solution-focused worker does not do, perhaps in contrast with many other helping approaches?
- How does the solution-focused process fit with your own preferred ways of working with people?
- In which of your work roles and responsibilities can you imagine, at this stage, utilising the process?
- How might applying some of the principles guiding the construction of solution-focused questions affect your work, whether or not you were to apply the solution-focused process in its entirety?

3

Contracting

Beginnings have to be made for each project in such a way as to enable what follows from them.

Edward Said (1978)

Introduction

As Edward Said suggests, beginnings are crucial, and a good beginning will set the tone for all that follows. If the essential characteristic of any piece of solution-focused work, whether it consists of a five-minute conversation or five one-hour therapy sessions, is that it is aimed in a particular direction, that is, towards the client's hoped-for outcome from the work, then a lot depends on how we set about establishing this direction at the outset. The solution-focused practitioner is helped immeasurably in beginning the work by keeping in mind what I see as the fundamental solution-focused assumption: if someone is talking to you, they must want something to come from that. A second useful idea is to see the process of asking someone what they want as one of *contracting*.

Having introduced these ideas, much of the rest of the chapter will be given over to two examples of contracting, the contrasting nature of which will bring out many of the issues that arise during the process. Both these examples are with adult clients attending sessions voluntarily, so I will also look at contracting with children and with mandated clients. Finally, I will discuss some general points about the questions used during contracting and common responses they receive.

The solution-focused assumption

There are a number of assumptions a helping person can make when someone has come to them for help, perhaps boiling down to only two if we think about this situation in the most simple way. It could be assumed, perfectly reasonably, that if someone is seeking help from somebody else, then there must be something wrong – some problem that they would like to resolve, to disappear or to ameliorate. We could call this *the problem-focused assumption*. On the other hand, it seems equally valid to assume that if someone has gone to somebody else for help, then they must want something to come out of this – they must be hoping to achieve some different future state of affairs. We could call this *the solution-focused assumption*. While both assumptions appear to be valid, choosing to operate according to one rather than the other will lead to completely different opening questions. Holding the problem-focused assumption at the forefront of our minds might prompt us to ask something like: 'What's the problem that has brought you here?' Whereas, operating instead on the solution-focused assumption – the person has come so they must be hoping that something will come from this – will lead us to ask about what that hope is. This solution-focused assumption can also be made even where the person did not choose to come for help but was told or made to go somehow. In this case, they can still be seen as choosing to talk, and so the solution-focused worker will assume that the person wants something to come from their talking. In other words, the worker is assuming that the person has come for a good reason, which is a respectful assumption to make about anyone. The value of making this assumption will be readily apparent in the second of the examples below.

Establishing outcome-based 'contracts'

So, in solution-focused work, it is towards an outcome that we want to help the person turn their thoughts – something they are wanting to be different about themselves, as a result of the work to be done. Note the final part of the previous sentence, which indicates that it is not about their hopes in a general sense, but their hopes from the work. If I were to be asked what I was hoping for at any one time, the promotion of my football team to the next division of the league would usually be high up my list, but that is not something I could reasonably expect to be achieved by my talking to a professional helper. So it is never just 'What are your best hopes?' but always 'What are your best hopes from this?' This immediately limits the possible answers and will help to keep them in the realm of the possible.

This beginning of the work can be compared to what happens when you hail a taxi[1] and the taxi driver stops and asks you the most important question a taxi driver could ever ask you: 'Where do you want to go?' You answer, 'The station please', and the taxi driver says, 'Ok, in you get'. This conversation has taken only a few seconds, but it has determined the whole journey (unless you were to change your mind en route and ask the driver to go somewhere else instead – which the people we are working with are also at liberty to do at any point, but we need to start by heading somewhere). Furthermore, once the taxi driver has asked you, 'Where to?', this has put you in complete control of the destination of that journey – the driver cannot go anywhere until you have said where you want to go. The getting-down-to-business question in a solution-focused piece of work is of similar importance, and the destination is determined by the client in a similar way.

Returning to the taxi analogy, once the driver says 'Ok, in you get', an implicit contract has now been established between you and the driver, the driver's side of this being the commitment to take you to your desired destination. It is useful to view the process between the solution-focused worker and client at the beginning of a piece of work in the same way. Once the client has been able to articulate a desired outcome from the work, and as long as this falls within the legitimate remit of the worker, it is as if a contract exists between them, that they will work together towards this outcome.

Example 1: Sonia – A variety of questions

Let me now illustrate this by turning to the first of our two main examples, which will show that there are many ways of wording questions to a client about a hoped-for outcome. This is the beginning of an initial session with a young woman I saw whom I shall call Sonia, which shows many of the issues that arise during the contracting process. Sonia had been referred by Elaine, a young person's advisor who had herself received some solution-focused training. Elaine knew from this training that I did not need to be given any background information, and all I knew at the outset was that I would be working with a 21-year-old woman who was willing to be seen. The transcript begins a couple of minutes into the session, after I have said a few words by way of introduction and explanation.

> *Guy*: What are your best hopes from coming here?
>
> *Sonia*: My hopes are ... it's just that I've got a few problems with anxiety. We've got mental illness running in our family, right. My Dad's mentally ill, he's like paranoid schizophrenic and what I want to achieve is that, you know, I've always had this fear that I might end up like him. I don't know why but, it's like since I've got pregnant I've had really bad depression and one of those things is just like, I don't know why, I can't explain it. I'm really, really scared that I might end up like him because of my circumstances, because I'm in a hostel at the moment, I'm involved in Social Services, my daughter's on the child protection register, and things aren't going that good, and I feel really stressed and there's so many things that I feel that I can't explain to myself. I feel scared of everything when I think of the future. There's times that I really want to get my own flat but when I think about getting my own flat I just feel scared ...
>
> *Guy*: Yes, sure.
>
> *Sonia* : ... that I'm going to be on my own and who's going to be there. Like, I've got a partner, the baby's Dad, but things between me and him are not going well.

Just because you ask someone what they are hoping for from seeing you, this does not mean that they will be able to talk about this straightaway. Here is a young woman with a lot of difficulties to contend with, and it is reasonable to suppose that her problems and difficult living situation will currently be at the forefront of her mind. So it is perhaps likely that she will talk about this at first, whatever she were asked. In response I have simply listened and not interrupted Sonia. There is nothing about being solution-focused that means a client is not allowed to give an account of their problems. Clients are free to talk about whatever they wish or need to talk about. It is the worker's questions that define a conversation as solution-focused, rather than the client's answers. Sonia has paused, and so now I will ask my next question, not about any of the problem material that Sonia has introduced, but once again about what she is hoping for from coming. As you will see, there are many ways of asking this.

> *Guy*: Right, ok. (*pauses*) So how would you know that coming here, coming here and seeing me, how would you know it's been useful to you?

Sonia: Because it will, in a way, I've been to counselling before but, like, Elaine has referred me to you and she said that you're very good, and I think it will help me, you'll help me explain, you'll explain to me what I'm going through and why I'm going through it, because I just need some reassurance that I'm OK in my life and that it's normal to feel the way I do.

Here I want to make the crucial distinction between *outcome* and *process*, alluded to in Chapter 1. The aim is to help the client to look beyond the work and into their life after the work is done, and to alight on what it is that they would like to be different about themselves at this future time – in other words, on their desired *outcome from* the work. It is not uncommon for a client to respond, as Sonia has done here, about the *process of* the work, a process that they would like to happen, or think might be necessary, or think would help. Any explanations by me would be part of a process that would happen between me and Sonia, albeit an unlikely one in this case, given that such explanations are not part of the solution-focused approach. However, the important point here is not how likely or unlikely a process is to happen, but that it *is* a process and not an outcome. Whatever the process mentioned, the solution-focused worker's thoughts and curiosity will always move beyond it and towards outcome. If Sonia had paused here, I might then have asked her how she would know that having explanations had proved to be useful for her – what is she hoping that explaining would lead to? As it is, there is no pause and Sonia continues.

Sonia: ...because sometimes I feel like, I have really strange feelings and I think coming here will help me control my thoughts as well because I think a lot, I'm stressed a lot...

Most of what Sonia has said so far has been in the present and past tense, while I am looking to orientate her towards the future. Sonia's comment about controlling her thoughts *is* a future-based one, though it sounds more like an expectation than a hope. I will say more about the distinction between hopes and expectations later in the chapter. In any case, the comment is superseded somewhat by Sonia's continuing answer.

...and it's just nice to talk to someone and tell them how you feel, without that person judging you and it takes the stress off as well, but, you know, I just like having someone to talk to when I'm low and when I'm depressed, so that someone can help me, it's just help, I just want help.

Guy: So if this does prove to be helpful, what would tell you, what would you notice about yourself that would tell you that this has proved to be helpful?

In saying that she wants someone to help her, Sonia is giving another process-related answer, and my follow-up questions are intended to take Sonia beyond the help to the outcome she hopes will result from it. Note the shift in the wording of the questions, from the earlier 'How would you know this has been *useful*?' to 'What would tell you that this has been *helpful*?' This is simply following Sonia's own use of language. She repeated the word *help* three times in quick succession at the end of her last answer, so 'What would tell you that this has been useful?' would have just missed her and the language that she is using. The solution-focused worker is always trying to construct questions that closely connect to the client's answers, and using actual words contained in those answers is an important aspect of this.

Sonia: I'll feel really relieved that I've spoken to someone about how I feel and that person understands and I'd like to continue coming more often. I feel relieved now because you feel like a very understanding person and I've been to counselling before and it hasn't really helped much at all…

When helping professionals are first exposed to the idea that in solution-focused work they will be asking lots of questions, and questions that appear, at first glance, not to allow people to talk about their problems, some worry about the impact this might have. Here I have asked the same question in three or four different ways and otherwise simply listened. And what Sonia has just said indicates this has been fine for her.

…I went for two years for family counselling, me and my Mum and Dad, but that didn't help, and I went to counselling when I was pregnant, it didn't seem to help at all. But, now, when I can get things off my chest, when I feel better about it, if I can walk out of the room smiling, then I'll know that I feel better now and I'd like to come again, you know.

Guy: OK, so just suppose that this does help in that way and just suppose you do go out feeling relieved, and smiling, what difference are you hoping that that will make, a bit later on?

A shift in the conversation has now taken place, in which Sonia is beginning to follow my invitation to look to the future. The questions can be thought of as invitations to think about a desired future, which Sonia has been politely declining by continuing to talk about her problem past and present. Now though, she has started to look to the future, to the end of the session at least, when she would like to be smiling, feeling better and wanting to come again. My task is to help Sonia to think further into the future than this, away from the session and firmly into her life beyond it, which led to my follow-up question about the difference she was hoping this would make later on. The 'contract' is close to being established.

> *Sonia*: Yes, well obviously you can't make a difference in one day, but I wish that, when I do come, I don't feel anxious. I hope that I can get help with feeling anxious all the time, because my heart's always going bang bang bang, for some reason, I don't know why, and I hope that I can get help with my worries and stresses.

And now for the first time, Sonia is talking about a future difference in herself that she hopes will come from the work – to feel less anxious, or at least not to be feeling anxious all the time. This is, however, a problem-related outcome, to have moved away from something – her anxiety – rather than towards something. It would not be enough for the taxi driver simply to be told that you would like to travel away from here. It is better to contract around reaching a desired state rather than removing a problematic one.

> *Guy*: So if you were to start to feel a bit less anxious, what would you be feeling instead?
>
> *Sonia*: I just want to feel happy. I was happy, a generally happy person but I've had depression and since then I haven't felt the way I did when I was 16, 17. I just want to feel that way again, when I didn't have so much on my mind. My mind was always clear.

I might have taken a shortcut and, confident that people who do not want to be anxious want to be calm, could have decided that the contract was about developing a capacity for calm. However, the word *calm* would then have come from me and not Sonia; so rather than deciding on the destination for her, I simply asked Sonia another question, which elicited the idea of *happy* instead. And now the way is clear for a future-focused conversation about Sonia having revived her capacity for happiness.

Summary: A variety of contracting questions

I said above that there are many ways of asking about hoped-for outcomes. In this example, I used some common forms of the question, always fitting them into what Sonia had been saying:

- What are your best hopes from coming here?
- How would you know that this has been useful?
- If this is helpful, what would tell you?
- What would you notice about yourself that would tell you that this has been helpful?
- What difference are you hoping that this will make, at some point later on?

Summary: Client responses

Sometimes a client will respond about a hoped-for outcome straightaway, but we saw a number of other ways in which people sometimes respond first:

- by talking about their problems;
- about the process of the work rather than its outcome.

Then when a client begins to talk about an outcome they want, this is often framed initially in a problem-related way: 'I wish that...I don't feel anxious'.

I will discuss these opening questions and the responses to them in more detail later in the chapter, but now I want to turn to my second illustrative example. Another common response, and only to be expected given that 'What do you want?' can be a hard question to answer, is 'I don't know'. Indeed, this is a very common answer across the board in solution-focused conversations, which are full of difficult questions. There are several 'I don't knows' in what follows, and we will see a number of potentially useful ways of responding.

Example 2: Mandy – Trusting the client

Mandy, aged 18, had been referred for solution-focused work by her social worker, and it soon became apparent that she was not very keen on the idea. I asked her a little about herself and learned that she was in foster care, had recently completed a hairdressing course though was not interested in pursuing this as a career, and was unsure about what she wanted to do instead.

Although Mandy seemed ambivalent about being there, she was still there, so I continued to hold in my head the solution-focused assumption that she must want something to come from it. The usefulness of this assumption will now become apparent, as it put the onus on me to find a way of talking and of asking questions of Mandy that would help her to work out what her motivation for coming was. By holding this assumption you are trusting in the client that they will have an answer, and this is what keeps the solution-focused worker going.

Guy: What are your best hopes from coming here, Mandy?

Mandy: (*after a 5 second pause*) I don't know, I really ... I don't see there's a hope for anything really, I don't know, I don't really – I don't like counselling and I don't like therapy. I don't think it helps, me. So, I'll just see the outcome really. I'm not really hoping for anything.

The first part of Mandy's answer might seem to pose something of a difficulty at this stage. She does not like counselling or therapy and does not think that they help, yet that is what is on offer here. This returns us to the important distinction between *hopes* and *expectations*. We are asking the person about their hopes, what they would like to happen, rather than their expectations, what they think is likely to happen. If someone has had therapy before and it has not helped, which can reasonably be surmised to be the case with Mandy, then it would be entirely sensible of them not to expect it to help on a future occasion. Yet they can still hope. And it may be that this is a more useful outlook. As the golfer Colin Montgomerie once said, after losing a tournament that he should perhaps have won:

But expecting to do something is dangerous in golf. It is always harder when you are expected to do something rather than just hoping. I should have just hoped.

So having heard Mandy's first answer, in addition to my solution-focused assumption, I now have a second thought in my head – that she does not expect anything much will come from the work. It is important that I first show Mandy that I have heard her, by saying something that acknowledges and appreciates her position. And yet she is still there, so I will also continue to assume she is there for a good reason and would like something to come from this and go on to ask her another question about what this might be. Mandy has assisted in the construction of my next question by the second part of her answer, 'I'll just see the outcome...'.

> *Guy*: Ok, so you haven't got any great hopes for this. Ok. You're willing to sort of see what the outcome is. Ok. So if the outcome of this is in some way useful to you, you know, if it was, what would, what would you notice?

Notice my tentative and low-key approach, 'in some way useful', and the repetition of the word 'if'. Tentativeness is a useful stance for a solution-focused practitioner (Thomas and Nelson, 2007, p. 6), and here it helps me to respond appropriately to Mandy's ambivalence. It is one of the ways by which I am trying to get alongside Mandy, trying to find a 'fit' (de Shazer, 1985) with her. Watch how this tentativeness, hedged around by lots of 'ifs' and 'maybes', continues in what follows.

> *Mandy*: (*after a 6 second pause*) I don't know (*laughing*). I really don't know. I don't really – probably when, if there is an outcome, or if something there was changed then I'd be able to notice it, nearer that time, but at the moment I really don't know.
>
> *Guy*: Ok, so what do you think? If there was an outcome or a change that happened, as a result of this, that was ok for you, that was even perhaps useful for you, what do you think it might be? (*pause*) What would you hope it would be?

I caught myself asking the question in such a way that might have suggested I was asking about an expectation – 'what do you think it might be?' – so I followed up to emphasise that I was asking about something desired – 'what would you hope it would be?' – rather than something expected.

> *Mandy*: What would I hope it would be? Um... (*a 7-second pause*) At this moment I don't know.
>
> *Guy*: Have a guess...
>
> *Mandy*: Hum (*sighs*).
>
> *Guy*: ...maybe.

Mandy: (*6-second pause – shrugs shoulders, shakes head and smiles*) Don't know, don't know, my mind's blank, so...

I have responded in a number of ways to Mandy's successive 'don't knows':

- Pausing – Mandy has said a couple of times that she does not know 'at the moment'. It is useful always to hear the answer 'I don't know' as having this qualification attached, even when it is not actually said. It is an answer in the present tense after all, so what else could it mean other than 'I don't know right now, right this second?' This does not mean that an answer might not come soon afterwards, as long as the client has the time and space to think. Therefore, it makes sense to pause and allow the client that time and space.
- Softening the question – Asking 'what do you think?' is intended to convey to Mandy that she does not have to be certain. She might not *know* what would be different if the work ended up being useful, but she could have *ideas* about this. I want to convey that she can hold any answers she gives lightly, and she will not be held to them for ever after. The direction of the work is always provisional and can shift at any point. The additions of 'have a guess' and 'maybe' serve the same purpose.
- Persisting – I am asking fundamentally the same question, albeit reworded to fit Mandy's words and the developing conversation, in a gently persistent manner.

I now continue to do this, and also acknowledge that it is not an easy question, giving Mandy permission not to know while at the same time encouraging her to continue thinking.

Guy: Ok, just take your time, take your time, because – in some ways it might seem like a straightforward, I don't know, it's just a little question but it's a big question and it's not an easy question. So take your time, but er, so maybe, you know, maybe this won't help, ok, and maybe just if somehow it was helpful, for whatever reason, if it turned out to be helpful, by whatever, by some outcome, something was to change – what might that be? What change might you notice that would tell you 'blimey, hang on, it was actually helpful, going there'?

Mandy: (*after a 9-second pause*) To tell you the truth I really don't think I need to change anything or anything needs to come out of me coming here, but erm... if anything maybe I can stop being insecure...

Guy: Yeah?

Mandy: ...and a bit more confident and that's it really...

Guy: Ok

Mandy: ...and nothing else.

Guy: Ok, ok, so just really, just about stopping, maybe, to stop being insecure, a bit more confident, ok, and nothing else really. Ok, ok, ok. So, well can I ask you some questions based on that? Is that ok?

Mandy: Ok.

So now there is a contract, and having sought permission to continue asking questions, as Mandy has not found them easy so far, I will now invite Mandy to describe a future in which she has the confidence that she wants. Given my persistence, some people might wonder whether Mandy has given this answer in the end just to get me off her back, and whether more confidence is something she really does want. The solution-focused worker's position on this is always to take people at face value and to accept their answers as they are given, at least where they are not in an assessment role. Being doubtful about a person's answers is likely to lead to questions which convey that doubt, and disbelieving people is a sure way to losing their cooperation. If Mandy said that she wanted to be more confident simply to please me and to put an end to my interminable questions, then it is unlikely that she would have shown much interest in talking about a more confident future, whereas she went on to do so for the next 25 minutes of the session.

Contracting with children and young people

Where a child is wanting to talk to someone, there is no fundamental difference in the contracting process. The solution-focused assumption can be held in just the same way – if they want to talk, then there must be something they want to come from that. Frequently however, a conversation intended to help a child will not have been instigated by the child themselves. I doubt there are many conversations over the breakfast table where a child tells their parents that they are coming with them to see the social worker/CAMHS[2] worker/family support worker/counsellor whether the parents like it or not! And pastoral conversations with children in schools, whether about social, emotional or behavioural issues, are in the main convened by members of staff. It will be useful to look at a typical school-based scenario, as this will offer some general lessons about contracting with children.

In schools, certain members of staff with a pastoral responsibility will be available to see a child perceived by other members of staff to have a social or behavioural difficulty. It may be that if a child is sent to see someone with a pastoral role, then that person could start by asking the child what their best hopes are from seeing them. An alternative that is more likely to enable a solution-focused conversation to develop in this context would go something like this:

> Mrs Smith has asked me to see you as she would like you to be more settled in school, and she hopes that our talking together might help this to happen. Is that something you would like too?[3]

An answer of 'yes', even if a half-hearted one, or a 'maybe' is sufficient for a contract for a conversation to have been established. Becoming 'more settled' in school is a wonderfully general frame that is likely to fit most pupils, and can be individualised once the conversation shifts to a detailed preferred future. The main difference here compared to the rest of the chapter up to now is that the worker, as a member of the school staff, has an *agenda* for the conversation. The staff would like the child to be more settled, and they have a responsibility to this child as well as to others who will be affected by the child's behaviour. In the cases of Sonia and Mandy, while I had a responsibility to do the best job I could, I had no agenda of my own for the work. That is, my role did not include any requirement to try to facilitate any particular type of outcome, whereas a school staff member is required to help a young person become more settled in school and to meet certain parameters with their behaviour.

Contracting with externally mandated clients

The above school-based example also differs from Sonia and Mandy in the level of voluntarism involved. Sonia and Mandy went to see a solution-focused worker voluntarily, and while Mandy was referred by her social worker and appeared ambivalent about being there, at 18 years of age she could have simply refused to go. With children it is a little different, and it can be useful to see them as 'involuntary clients' (Berg and Steiner, 2003, pp. 14–15). Where someone is seeing a worker not from their own volition but, for example, because of a court order, a contracting process can be followed in just the same way:

> *Worker*: What are your best hopes from the time you'll spend here?
>
> *Mandated client*: What do you mean? It wasn't my idea to see you in the first place. Why should I have any hopes from it?
>
> *Worker*: Sure. I appreciate that this wasn't your idea, and that you are here because of the court order. And maybe nothing useful will come of this for you. As you do have to come here though, and for the next six months too, I hope it can be useful to you somehow. If it were to be, how would you know?
>
> *Client*: I don't know. I don't see how coming here and talking to you would be useful for me.
>
> *Worker*: Well, maybe it won't be. (*Pause*) If it is though, if for some strange reason this did end up being useful to you, from your point of view, what would tell you that?
>
> *Client*: Oh, I don't know. I suppose if it means that you lot lay off me after this...
>
> *Worker*: And what difference would that make to you?
>
> *Client*: It means I'd be able to get on with my life for one thing...

The worker is helped by making the fundamental solution-focused assumption. In this case, the client has to be there but does not need to talk, so the worker is choosing to assume that the client is talking for a good reason – they must want something to come from that. And being able to get on with their life, in a way that would enable the authorities to 'lay off' them, sounds like a good basis for a solution-focused contract.

Having looked at these various examples, let us take stock and reflect on some of the features of the contracting process – first about the questions asked and then about the responses that these questions sometimes elicit.

Contracting questions

We have seen that there are many different ways of wording a question about what outcome someone wants – many solution-focused equivalents of the taxi driver's 'Where to?' There are also many ways of asking questions that appear similar but, on closer examination, do not actually direct the client towards an outcome. Consider, for example, the question 'What do you want to change?' This might seem to be asking about an outcome, a self changed in some way, but it is actually focusing more on a problem the client wants to change. A more solution-focused question using the word *change* would be: 'How would you know that you'd made the change you want to make?' Many other questions end up being about process rather than outcome – 'What do we need to do for this to be useful for you?' being an example. A similar and commonly asked opening question in many helping contexts is: 'How can I help you?' As well as being about process rather than outcome, this also 'centres' the worker (White, 1995), suggesting a dependency on the actions of the worker that is at odds with the client-centred thrust of the solution-focused approach.

Two solution-focused teams in particular have devoted a considerable amount of time to this aspect of the approach. By becoming clearer in their thinking and practice about the difference between process and outcome (Chris Iveson, personal communication), the London-based team, BRIEF, has been of considerable service to the wider solution-focused world. On their training courses in the mid-nineties, the question 'What needs to happen for this to be useful for you?' was favoured (George et al., 1995), but this led to a degree of ambiguity between what might need to happen in the work and what might need to happen in the client's life outside the work. Their development of the *best hopes* question (George et al., 1999) was a breakthrough, though even this can be interpreted as being about process – 'My hopes are that you'll advise me', for example. The BRIEF team suggests that asking about someone's best hopes *from* the work rather than their hopes *for* the work takes care of this (Ratner, George and Iveson, 2012, p. 69), though in my experience this can still be heard as a process question. However, there are still plenty of differently worded questions which can be used to follow up and clarify the intended meaning, as we have seen.

As an aside, if the question 'What are your best hopes from this?' sounds a little strange to you, then this might not matter as much as you think. A Swedish social worker, Jörgen Andersson, once told me he was keen to follow BRIEF's lead, but when he translated their *best hopes* question word for word into Swedish, it sounded strange. He was wondering how else he might translate it, and I told him that it sounded strange in English too. He contacted me a few weeks later, saying he was now translating it literally and it was working well!

Another team whose careful thinking about the beginning stage of solution-focused work has helped the field is SIKT in Malmo, Sweden. In an excellent article, available on their website, they talk about establishing a 'common project' rather than contracting (Korman, 2004), but the similarities are clear. Their typical initial outcome-seeking question is: 'What needs to be different in your life today, tomorrow or the day after tomorrow – something small – for you to feel or think that it was useful having talked with me today?' A common project is summarised as having three essential properties:

- something that is important to the client – it needs to be something that *they* want;
- realistic in their current life situation;
- ethical – something that lies in the legitimate remit of the worker.

Client responses

Problem talk

It is common for clients to talk first about their difficulties, even when asked about what they want, as we saw with Sonia. As well as problems being at the forefront of many people's minds, there may well be a cultural expectation at work here, that problems are what to talk about when seeking help. At these times it is important for the worker to listen and to show they are listening, though without being sidetracked by asking for more detail about the problems. Rather, the solution-focused worker will continue to ask about what the client wants, though their questions should be seen as invitations rather than as demands for the client to think about a desired outcome.

Process rather than outcome

People often think about a process that might happen in the work, before thinking of the outcome they hope that process will lead to. Sonia, for example, hoped that the worker might explain to her what she was going through and why. Other examples include when a client asks for advice from a worker or says that they just want to talk. These are all things that would be happening between the client and the worker during the work, and they do not say anything about what the client is hoping the work might lead to. It is therefore important to always be asking yourself if you have just heard a desired outcome or a process answer. If process, the next step is to go beyond this to outcome: if that process were to take place, how would they know that it had been useful?

'I don't know'

You have to be prepared for the answer 'I don't know' at any time in solution-focused work, not only during contracting. You are asking potentially hard questions, and it is to be expected that someone will not have answers straightaway. It is incumbent on the solution-focused worker to help the client to continue to think and be able to come up with answers. We saw how I did this with Mandy in a number of ways, including pausing, softening and rewording the question. This is not always easy, and the urge to rescue the person by asking something else or, worse still, suggesting an answer can get in the way. Harry Korman of SIKT suggests counting mentally to six as a way of keeping oneself silent, to allow the client the time to think (Korman, 2004). During the contracting process, it is useful to remember the solution-focused assumption: the client is there – they will have an answer. Trusting that this is the case – trusting the client – becomes easier with experience and practice.

Unrealistic hopes

A common worry of beginning solution-focused practitioners is that the client might respond with unrealistic hopes. In reality this does not often happen, especially when it is made clear that strictly circumscribed hopes are being asked for, hopes which relate to the work:

Worker: What are your best hopes from this?

Client: That I win the lottery!

Worker: Sure, I could do with winning it too! I'm afraid I haven't got the numbers though, sorry. No, what I'm meaning is, what are your best hopes from this, from your talking with me?

Once clear that they are being asked about their hopes from talking, people do tend to respond with the sorts of things that talking can help with. A similar situation occurs when the person wants something that the worker is not able to offer. If you say to the taxi driver that you want to go somewhere 200 miles away, they might say they do not go that far, but may tell you who will, or point you in the direction of the coach or train station. For example, a person asking a counsellor for benefits advice may be referred on to the local Citizen's Advice Bureau. On other occasions, an outcome that initially sounds unrealistic, or irrelevant in a certain context, may not be if reframed in a particular way:

Counsellor: What are your best hopes from our work together?

Client: I need to get a job.

At this stage, the counsellor might say that this is something they cannot help with, and so ask 'What else?', or alternatively respond in this way:

Counsellor: So if our work together led to you being more able to do what you need to do to get yourself a job, that would make this useful?

Sometimes an answer that sounds like an unrealistic desired outcome, or one that is undesirable to the professionals involved, is actually a process answer in disguise. Amongst the most difficult situations faced by a children's duty social worker (DSW) is when parents at the end of their tether ask for their child to be taken into care. There are good reasons for not acceding to such a request, and social workers are obliged to help children stay with their families where possible, but a straight-out refusal can cause conflict and a raising of the stakes. A solution-focused approach can open up other possibilities:

DSW: What are your best hopes from contacting us?

Parent: That you take Freddie into care.

DSW: Well, the situation must be pretty dire for you all to have got to that point. If we were able to do that, what difference are you hoping that it would make?

Parent: That someone could drum some sense into him, because we can't.

DSW: And how would you know that that had happened?

Parent: He wouldn't be so impossible to have in the house (*lists a lot of things that Freddie would no longer be doing*).

DSW: What difference would that make?

Parent: Things would be back to normal I suppose, there'd be a better atmosphere at home.

DSW: Ok, sure. Well, to be honest it's not very often that we end up taking a young person into care. My manager tends not to agree to that. I can see that you desperately need some changes to happen, though, that will take some working towards. We'd be keen to work with you and Freddie, to help these to happen. Would you be interested in that?

If the parents say no, the only way forward is for Freddie to go into care, then nothing has been lost by this dialogue, and the social worker's department would have to follow whatever procedure they have for such situations. In my experience, parents often do agree to the offer of such family meetings, which should be unsurprising, given that what most parents do 'really' want is to have better atmospheres at home and children with whom they can get on. This is typically the *outcome* to which they hope that the *process* of local authority care would lead towards.

Broad starting points

While the hoped-for outcomes of both Sonia and Mandy were framed as feeling states or qualities, contracts can also form around something the person wants to be doing ('moving on', 'becoming settled in school') or thinking differently ('I'd like to be thinking more positively'), or be about relating differently ('We'd be getting on better'). All these examples are of very broad, generally-stated outcomes, and it may be objected that they are, therefore, too vague to be useful. On the contrary, at this stage of the solution-focused process, it is a positive advantage for the outcome creating the direction for the work to be articulated in general terms. The more specific it is – 'I'd like to get a job as a plumber, working Monday to Wednesday'; 'I'd like my son to eat his greens'; 'I'd like to be more relaxed on aeroplanes' – the more hemmed in the conversation can become, whereas hopes such as a capacity for happiness or moving on can open up greater, potentially infinite ranges of possibilities and differences in someone's life, and also more easily point someone to progress already being made. The specifics come next, when the client is invited to describe the realisation of their broad hopes in detail, as we will be seeing in the next chapter.

Conclusion

When you try to put into practice what you have learned from this chapter, even in the apparently simpler contexts, you might well come up against the truth of that maxim of Steve de Shazer's 'It's simple but it ain't easy!' Establishing what someone might want, or find useful, from talking with us can indeed be a tricky process. It helps to be clear that we are asking about *outcome*, to make this clear in our questions, and to be aware of the range of possible responses to these questions. It also helps, in my view, to think about the process as simply as possible. All we are doing, in essence, is beginning a conversation with someone by helping them to think about what they want rather than what they do not want, to look forwards rather than back. And looking forwards usually helps us to see where we are going.

Reflections

- Is the fundamental solution-focused assumption a reasonable one to make?
- What effect would keeping this assumption near the forefront of your mind have on your work?
- Asking clients about their hoped-for outcomes from the work to be done establishes a direction for the work. Does helping work need to have a direction?
- Bring to mind a person you are currently seeing, who you could imagine using the solution-focused approach with. How, specifically, might you go about establishing what they want from their work with you? Would it make sense to ask them about this? If not, who, if anyone, should determine where the work is heading?
- What are your best hopes from reading the rest of this book?

4

Description I: The Preferred Future

Tomorrow to fresh Woods, and Pastures new.

John Milton, Lycidas

Introduction

Once there is a contract for the work and the client has been helped to look forwards to where they want the work to take them, the worker will typically start to help them to describe, in rich, concrete detail, how they will know they have arrived there and the differences that arriving there will make. Such a description has come to be termed the client's *preferred future* (Iveson, 1994), the future in which their hopes from the work have been realised. Solution-focused practitioners believe that describing such futures is a helpful step in bringing them about. Before reading further then, you might want to carry out this activity, just in case they are right!

> **Activity: Your preferred reading of this chapter**
>
> Ask yourself (or have someone ask you): How might you notice you were at your best while you are reading this chapter? Bring to mind as vivid a picture of this as possible. What else might you notice about yourself? What else? And if someone else were to notice you being at your best while reading this, how might they be able to tell?

A little history of the preferred future

Two of the main precursors of solution-focused practice were the *brief therapy* approach that was developed in Palo Alto, California, from the 1960s (Weakland, Fisch, Watzlawick and Bodin, 1974; Watzlawick, Weakland and Fisch, 1974) and the work of the innovative psychiatrist and hypnotherapist Milton Erickson (Erickson and Rossi, 1979; O'Hanlon, 1987), which influenced the future-based aspect of solution-focused work in particular. The emergence of brief therapy at the Mental Research Institute (MRI) in Palo Alto was a significant moment in the history of talking therapies, which hitherto had been dominated by psychoanalytic approaches. These latter approaches were based on the notion that problems had deep-rooted causes within the individual psyche, and so therapy was typically long-term, often lasting a year or more. Nowadays, there are almost as many brief therapies as there are therapy modalities, most of which having developed brief versions of themselves, but the MRI brief therapy was brief by design from the outset. This was in part due to the MRI therapists' different ideas about problems, seeing them as situated in the interactions between people (Watzlawick and Weakland, 1977) rather than as arising from deep within the individual. Another primary means of ensuring brevity of treatment, and the one we are most interested in here, was the setting of clearly defined and concrete goals (Watzlawick et al., 1974, p. 112). As de Shazer later (1988, p. 93) observed, without determining how the client and therapist would know when the problem is solved, 'therapy could reasonably go on forever'. Both de Shazer and his partner, Insoo Kim Berg, began as brief therapists, and, in their shift from the problem-focused brief therapy of the MRI to their solution-focused brief therapy, took this clear goal-setting practice with them.

So, determining criteria for the end of the work contributed to a future orientation, but this was only a part of the story. Probably the greatest influence on Steve de Shazer was the methods of Milton Erickson, one of these being the 'crystal ball technique' (de Shazer, 1985). This involved inviting the client to imagine a future in which their problem was solved and then to look back from that future and explain how they had solved it. This technique came to be regarded by de Shazer 'as a precursor of a solution focus, in that it was an early attempt to systematically focus the client on solutions rather than on problems' (Molnar and de Shazer, 1987, p. 350). So, as well as being the place where goals were set, the future was somewhere where solutions – ways of achieving these goals – could be found. In this search for solutions, the crystal ball technique came to be replaced by the *miracle question*, which took up a central place in the approach as its value became increasingly appreciated.

The origins of the miracle question are disputed (Lipchik, Derks, Lacourt and Nunnally, 2011), but my favourite account is one of serendipity. Insoo Kim Berg was working with a client who was struggling to answer a question about change happening, because 'It would take a miracle'. In a moment of inspiration, Insoo replied, 'Ok, well suppose a miracle did happen ...', and the client became unstuck and able to answer (Norman, McKergow and Clarke, 1996). The question became formalised and eventually used routinely in virtually all first meetings, framed along the following lines:

> Just suppose that, when you go to bed tonight and go to sleep, a miracle happens, and the problems that brought you here today have gone, just like that. But you're asleep, so you don't know that the miracle has happened. So, when you wake up in the morning, what will you notice, that will tell you that this miracle has happened?

With increasing use, this opening question set in train a succession of follow-up questions, all serving to help clients describe a life without the problem, hence a life in which they no longer needed to attend therapy. It was seen in part as a process of goal-setting (de Shazer, 1988, p. 5) and also as a way of finding (hypothetical) solutions (ibid., pp. 92–96).

Though the miracle question is still widely used, several developments have taken place that have led to the future-focused practices described in this book, in particular at BRIEF in London. First, the more clearly the BRIEF therapists helped their clients to describe the differences after the miracle, the more finely detailed these descriptions became, and 'it became increasingly difficult to see the "miracle day" as a goal or even a set of goals' (Shennan and Iveson, 2011, p. 286). Instead, what the therapists were seeing were 'entire (preferred) ways of being, located within a hypothetical future', and so the BRIEF workers began to use the term *preferred futures* (Iveson, 1994) instead of goals. Second, as the team began to see the importance of the initial 'contracting' question,[1] they noticed a discontinuity between asking what someone *wanted* from the work and then defining a miracle in relation to the *problems* they had brought to it. Hence the stated effects of the miracle shifted to the client's hopes having been realised:

> *Client*: My best hopes? To become more confident I guess.
>
> *Worker*: Ok, well imagine a miracle happens tonight ... and the miracle is that you have the confidence you want ...

Third, the idea that a miracle was required to enable a client to describe in detail the differences they were looking for came under increasing scrutiny (Prosser, 2001; Hanton, 2011, personal communication in 2001). Inspired by their attachment to the minimalist principle of Ockham's razor, the BRIEF team began to experiment by inviting clients to describe their preferred futures without the use of a miracle as a means of getting there:

> Suppose you wake up tomorrow to find that you have the confidence you want, what's the first thing you'd notice about yourself?

What they found was that, in the vast majority of cases, people were able to make the shift into their desired tomorrows without needing to imagine a miracle. So the miracle question, though it paved the way for our future-focused descriptive practices of today, now plays only a very occasional role, usually when someone is so stuck that they are finding it hard to imagine a different tomorrow. For example:

> *Worker*: Suppose when you wake up tomorrow, you find that you're able to get on with your life, in a way that's right for you. What's the first small sign you'd notice?
>
> *Client*: I don't know. I just don't see how that will happen.
>
> *Worker*: What do you think, what might be the first thing you'd notice?
>
> *Client*: I don't know. I don't know how to do that.
>
> *Worker*: Ok, well don't worry about how you're going to do this. Imagine a miracle happens tonight, and does it for you. So you're there anyway, you're able to get on with your life as you want to. What's the first difference you'd notice?
>
> *Client*: Well, I suppose I'd feel like getting out of bed...

What the miracle can do in situations like this is help the client around the seemingly insuperable obstacle of 'What to do?' to 'Suppose it's done'. By sidestepping the stuckness, temporarily at least, the client can be freed to describe a different tomorrow, which in its turn can go some way towards helping them become unstuck. This is, of course, the situation in which the miracle question was originally developed. Having sketched this historical development, let us turn to our present-day practices of helping people to describe detailed preferred futures.

Describing preferred futures

Solution-focused practice is not alone in having a future orientation, but what sets it apart from other approaches is its focus on *description*. In other approaches, the establishment of a goal is typically followed by a focus on the means of getting there, either through asking questions – 'What do you need to do to achieve that? What would help?' – or by the provision of advice. In contrast, the solution-focused practitioner invites the client to imagine that they *are* there and simply to describe what this would be like. It is the ends not the means that receive the attention in solution-focused work, in its future aspects at least – we will see in the next chapter that we do become interested in the client's means of achieving existing progress. In terms of future progress, the client is left free to determine their own means of making this, in their own time, outside of the work. The more detailed the descriptions of the ends, the more able clients seem to be to come up with the means.

Preferred future descriptions: Practice principles

A number of practice principles prove invaluable in enabling the emergence of detailed descriptions. These include:

* concretising;
* maximising client choice in framing their answers;
* sequential descriptions – from the first small signs onwards;
* building on the client's answers;
* what would be noticed rather than what would no longer be;
* widening out and zooming in;
* tangible and observable;
* from the perspectives of others;
* making interactional.

I shall illustrate these principles with the help of more transcript of Sonia's first session. To do this, I will break off from the transcript at a number of points to explain how one or more of these principles was being applied. We saw in Chapter 3 that Sonia was wanting to become less anxious and more happy. This is how I invited her into the next stage of the work:

So just suppose you wake up tomorrow and you do feel that way again, you feel happy in the way that you'd like to, and anxiety is not a problem for you – what's the first thing you'd notice about yourself?

Concretising

One of the virtues of inviting the client to imagine that the changes have happened upon waking up tomorrow is that this sets up an actual concrete situation in which the client can be helped to notice these changes. In this case, the time and place have been determined – the time Sonia wakes up and the place she will be waking up in tomorrow morning. Just asking 'What would you notice about yourself if you were happy and not anxious?' would leave Sonia floating in the air, and, not tied to any specific time and place, the question can be harder to answer. I will continue to look for opportunities to concretise throughout the description, and we shall see other examples later.

Maximising client choice in framing their answers

I have asked Sonia what she would *notice* about herself. The advantage of using the word *notice* is that it is neutral with regard to the main aspects of our experiencing – namely our thoughts, feelings and actions. If I had first asked Sonia how she would be feeling or what she would be thinking or doing, then *I* would have been directing her to that particular dimension of her experience. By using *notice* I am allowing Sonia to choose the dimension in which she would first discern that her hopes had been realised. In this sense, the question is minimally directive and maximally open for the client to make her own choices.

A sequential description

All questions convey messages, and by asking Sonia about the *first* thing she would notice, I am conveying the message that I will then be interested in the next thing, and the next thing, and then the thing after that. Helping the client tell a story of their day, from waking up onwards, is a helpful way of structuring the questions, for the worker and the client, and asking for the first thing both signals this structure and is the first step in building it. It also adds to the concretising described above – having been invited to consider herself in a specific time and place, Sonia is encouraged to focus on what she would notice 'right there and then'. A further benefit of asking about the first signs is that it encourages clients to think small, and small details are very much what we are looking for.

> *Sonia*: Oh, I'd notice that – when you're not anxious, your head's kind of clear, you've got a clear head haven't you?

Guy: So you'd have a clear head?

Sonia: I'd have a clear head. I wouldn't be thinking so much about my problems. Because problems make you anxious. When you don't think you're not anxious, are you? That's the way I see it.

Guy: So what might you be thinking about tomorrow then, if you woke up feeling how you'd like to?

Building on the client's answers

As the solution-focused worker is always wanting to formulate questions so that they follow directly from the client's answers, this frequently means having to select which aspect of a diverse answer to pursue. In order to do this, it is important to keep in mind whereabouts in the process one is and the purpose of the questions being asked at that point. Here, my intention is to help Sonia to describe herself tomorrow having realised her hopes from the work, and the parts of her last answer in which she is doing this are: 'I'd have a clear head. I wouldn't be thinking so much about my problems'. I therefore chose to let pass by Sonia's speculations about the effect of thinking about problems and construct a question in response to one of the first two sentences.

What would be noticed rather than what would no longer be

As is usually the case, there were numerous options available, but my attention was drawn to the beginning of the second sentence, 'I wouldn't...' When asked what would be different if things were better, it is common for a client's first answers to be about what *wouldn't* be happening. When someone answers in this way, they are really making a statement about a current problem. This is understandable given that problems, especially ones significant enough to lead someone to be talking to a professional helper, will usually be at the forefront of the person's mind. The solution-focused worker's task then is to help the person to think differently, about what they would notice in place of the problematic thought, feeling or behaviour. If I may be allowed a pre-digital age metaphor, it is like developing the negative into the actual picture. This is such a crucial aspect of a preferred future description that I would go as far as to say that whenever a client responds by saying that something would not be happening, then the ONLY question to be asked next is about what would be happening instead. And here we can stay in the client's frame. If they say they would not be doing, thinking or feeling something, then the worker matches this in their next question, by asking what they would be doing, thinking or feeling instead. Part of what makes these descriptions useful is the new possibilities they evoke for the client, and this requires replacing the absence of the old with the presence of the new.

> *Sonia*: I wouldn't be thinking about next week or next year, or when am I going to get my flat, I'd take each day step-by-step. I wouldn't think about negative things, the way I do now. I'd just be more into taking more care of my little girl, more into taking care of myself and getting into my hobbies and interests as well, and not letting my relationship get the best of me really. Just an outgoing person who doesn't take life too serious. That's the way I was before.
>
> *Guy*: Ok, so you'd notice a lot of differences about yourself then (*Sonia* – yeah), if you woke up with a clear head tomorrow (*more emphatically,* yeah). So you'd be more into taking care of your little girl (yeah, yeah), more into taking care of yourself (yeah), more into interests and hobbies (yeah, yeah), and not letting your relationship get in the way.
>
> *Sonia*: No, yeah. And not letting any problems get in the way. I've become so sensitive if someone says no to me I just burst out crying whereas before I wouldn't care. I don't know, I don't know what it is.

Widening out…

The solution-focused practitioner aims to help the client to describe the differences that the realisation of their best hopes would lead to as widely as possible. The more the description moves across all the areas of a person's life, the more possibilities arise for making changes and the more opportunities occur for observing changes taking place. It is often not possible to predict in advance where desired changes will begin to show in someone's day-to-day life, certainly not for the worker, and usually not for the client either, so it makes sense to cover as many bases as possible. Hence the worker, having elicited description in one area, might go on to ask 'Where else might these differences show tomorrow?' or 'In what other areas of your life would you notice the effects of more confidence (or whatever the client's hoped-for outcome is)?' or simply 'What else? What else would be different tomorrow?' In this instance, Sonia has *widened out* the description herself, by spontaneously listing a number of areas of her life where she would notice differences.

A digression about summarising

In Chapter 2 we talked about some of the ways a solution-focused worker will respond to a client's talking, other than by asking the next question, for example by 'echoing', 'appreciating' and 'summarising'. Although summaries are frequently offered at the end of a conversation, they are often useful in the midst of one too. Recapping at certain points, and using the client's own words in doing so, helps to bolster an emerging description and to ensure that it continues to be built on the client's words. It can also punctuate a shift, in this case into the *zooming in* that is to come next. So as Sonia articulates her list, I note it down and, realising that this will provide a potentially helpful structure for the rest of the preferred future description, decide to ask about each area in turn. First though, I summarise and, by staying close to Sonia's words, show her the importance I am ascribing them. I am also intending to show that I am listening closely and that I want to check with Sonia that I have heard her correctly, thereby giving her the chance to correct me, to edit or add to her words. This example also shows how recapping can amplify for the client the force of ideas she has shared. As Sonia hears each item on her list reflected back to her, she becomes progressively more enthused by what she hears she has said.

Guy: OK, so taking care of… what's your little girl's name?

Sonia: Mo.

Guy: And how old is Mo?

Sonia: Six months.

Guy: OK, so what's the first thing you'd notice yourself doing with Mo, then, if you did wake up tomorrow with this clear head and…?

Zooming in

Having summarised the areas of Sonia's life which would be affected by the realisation of her best hopes, I begin to ask about each in detail, starting with the first one mentioned, taking more care of her little girl. Notice how I concretise first. Since I had launched straight in earlier with Sonia's hopes from the work, I know little of the factual details of her life, such as her daughter's name, for example. In solution-focused work, there tends not to be a preliminary getting-to-know-you stage, as there is no need for one. What workers need to know in order to ask their questions can be filled in along the way. *Personalising* descriptions by asking for names of significant others is another aspect of concretising. I then return to the *first small signs* principle, in this case the first thing Sonia would do with her daughter in this different tomorrow. There is always this type of interplay between widening the description and then zooming back in to examine certain parts of it in greater detail. It is like turning around a telescope, looking through first one end and then the other.

> *Sonia*: I think it's like, I do play around with her a lot, I take great care of my daughter, but I think I'd be more into the playing instead of thinking it's boring half the time. Sometimes, when you're a mother and you're on your own bringing up the baby, sometimes you don't have the energy to play with the baby. You do want to play with her, I do play with her, I do stimulate her, but there's sometimes I just think, oh I need a break.
>
> *Guy*: So tomorrow, what would be different tomorrow?
>
> *Sonia*: I think I'd have more energy.
>
> *Guy*: More energy.
>
> *Sonia*: I'd have more energy for the baby.
>
> *Guy*: So what's the first thing you'd notice between you and Mo, given that you had more energy? What's the first thing you'd do?
>
> *Sonia*: The first thing I'd do, oh my God, all my attention would be on her, 24/7. Like sometimes now she'll be there next to me and she'll be laughing, or you know, making baby noises and I'll just look at her and say 'alright'. I'm not saying that I'm not a good mother (*Guy* – sure). My daughter, you should see her, she's so stimulated, she makes so many noises, she's so tall as well and she's so chubby. You know, I do take care of her but I want to pay more attention to her. I feel like I'm not doing enough.

Tangible and observable

Preferred future descriptions are enriched by the inclusion of all aspects of the person's experiencing – how and what they are thinking and how and what they are feeling as well as what they are doing. Pichot (2009) calls for a balance between what she terms cognition, being and behaviour questions in this respect. Having said this, the solution-fo-cused practitioner will always err on the side of questions about what the client will notice themselves actually doing, which helps a description to become more tangible, more concrete and hence more vivid and real. Emphasising behaviour in this way increases the likelihood that the client will experience their preferred future as doable, and that they will recognise aspects of it actually happening. These two effects of preferred future descriptions – an increasing sense of an ability to make desired changes together with an increasing likelihood that even the smallest changes will be noticed – can create a positive feedback loop, the latter feeding the former, thereby leading to more changes and so more changes being noticed and so on.

Here, Sonia has said that she would have more energy, an answer that one hears frequently – achieving what one wants is so often accompanied by an upsurge in energy. It is, however, an entirely abstract notion, hence the follow-up questions: 'What's the first thing you'd notice? What's the first thing you'd do?' Another useful way to elicit concrete and observable descriptions is provided by the question: 'How might that show?'[2]

Sonia's response here is interesting in that it requires that I make a significant decision about which part of Sonia's answer to follow. She had said that, if she were happier and had a clearer head, she would be 'more into taking care of (her) little girl', and now she has said that she *does* take care of her and stimulate her. The solution-focused worker will always be inviting descriptions either of the preferred future or of progress towards this future, or, put another way, times when it is happening already, and will always be considering when to shift from one time frame to another. So an option here would have been to ask about how she takes care of her daughter already. However, on hearing Sonia's last comment, that she is 'not doing enough', I decided to continue into the future and to invite small, concrete detail.

> *Guy*: So what would she notice about you then? I know she's only six months but...
>
> *Sonia*: She'd notice me change. When I wake up in the morning I wouldn't wait until I was awake and then give her her milk. I'd wake up straightaway to do it, you know. Sometimes when you just wake up and hear the baby cry you think 'baby, go asleep again', you know?

From the perspectives of others

Asking what someone else would notice or how they would know the person was in a particular feeling state are examples of 'relationship questions' (de Jong and Berg, 2008) or 'other person perspective questions' (George et al., 1999). This type of question betrays solution-focused practice's roots in the family therapy field, where such questions might be termed *circular* (Selvini, Boscolo, Cecchin and Prata, 1980). They are invaluable in eliciting tangible and observable detail, as how could someone else know that you were happy, let us say, other than by such details, by what they saw or heard you do or say and by how you did or said this. Having the client draw on the perspectives of a range of significant others can add immeasurably to the richness of a description, and to the range of possibilities for action that a rich description can call forth.

Guy: You'd wake up straightaway.

Sonia: I'd wake up straightaway. That's what I can see myself doing, if I didn't have my depression.

Guy: Ok. So what would be … just suppose you woke up straightaway, just like that … What would be the very first thing you'd do after you'd woken up straightaway?

Sonia: Woke up? Just go and make her milk.

Guy: And after that?

Sonia: Then, you know, I'd change her nappy, I'd play with her. I'd play with her, give her a bath, like I usually do, but I'd play with her more. It's like, I wouldn't give up on her sometimes and I'd be much more patient if she starts crying and I don't know what the reason is. I think not being anxious would give me the energy to be patient with the baby.

Activity: Constructing questions

Which part of Sonia's answer might you follow with your next question?

Which word(s) might you build a question around?

What question might you ask?

It is not that there is a right question to ask, or only ever one part of an answer to follow. There are, however, some general criteria to bear in mind when constructing questions, and I have noted the importance of keeping in mind where one is within the process and the purposes of the questions that have just been asked. At this stage of the conversation, my aim is to help Sonia describe herself having energy early tomorrow morning, in the finest, most concrete detail possible. The detail is becoming more specific – she would *play* with Mo more and be more *patient* with her – and

I decide to utilise one of these words, choosing the playing, remembering that Sonia also mentioned playing with Mo more a few answers earlier. I now need to find a question that encourages even more specificity.

> *Guy*: Ok, so you'd play with her more and be more patient with her – and how would you play with her? What sorts of things would you play?
>
> *Sonia*: Oh, I'd sing to her, I'd read books to her, I'd make her stand up, I already do, I do a lot, but I feel I'd do more than I do right now. I'd play with her, I'd make her feel she's walking around everywhere.

One way of determining whether a description is sufficiently specific is to ask yourself: can you actually see it happening in your mind's eye? To picture a parent playing with her child requires the adding in of more specific information, and it is this that Sonia does once she is asked *how* she would play with Mo.

> *Guy*: And what difference would that make to you, if you were playing with Mo more?
>
> *Sonia*: It would make me feel good because my baby's happy and I'd be happy as well.

'What difference would that make', alongside 'What else?', is one of the most commonly used questions in solution-focused conversations (Shennan and Iveson, 2008). It can be thought of as a widening question, which, following a sequence of zooming-in questions, can then launch a client off in a different direction. It can also elicit many more future possibilities. In a sense it treats every answer as a process answer (see Chapter 3), as a means towards an end, with the difference that means might make being the end, which can be the means towards another end, and so on, theoretically ad infinitum. Any specific means might turn out not to be possible, or not to be of interest to the client, whereas the difference it would make might well be desirable, and achievable in other ways. A third positive effect of asking what difference doing something would make is that it can increase the motivation to do it, and this can be imagined happening for Sonia, as she reflects on the likely effects of playing more with Mo.

> *Guy*: And what about Mo? Would she enjoy that do you think? You playing with her in that way?
>
> *Sonia*: I'm sure she would. She loves it when I play with her like that.

Guy: How would you know she was loving it then? How do you tell she does when you play with her like that?

Sonia: She'd be laughing, and squealing, you know. And she'd look up at me when I walked her around, and be smiling.

Interactional

One of the advantages of eliciting such fine detail in these descriptions is that the more detail there is, the more likely it is that the client will later be able to notice some of it actually happening. And as well as looking out for differences in themselves, if clients are assisted to become aware also of differences they might notice in someone else, then they can look for evidence of change happening with that other person as well. Added to this, people often want others to change, as well as themselves. In fact, some people come with the belief that it is only others who need to change! Of course, we influence other people around us all the time, and so we can effect changes in others. Actually, it is impossible not to do so. One of the fundamental assumptions of the solution-focused approach has always been that one small change may be all that is needed, as a small change can lead to larger changes (de Shazer et al., 1986; O'Hanlon and Weiner-Davis, 1989). A change in one part of a system will affect other parts of that system. We will come across more interactional questions in the concrete interactional sequence below.

Preferred future descriptions: Worker positions

Let us turn now from specific practice principles to some of the more general positions the worker endeavours to adopt for the development of these future-based descriptions, which can be seen in the work with Sonia shown so far.

Non-directiveness

The idea of being *non-directive* is most closely associated with the work of Carl Rogers (1951) and the approach now usually known as person-centred counselling or therapy (Mearns and Thorne, 2007). While there are overlaps between the person-centred and solution-focused approaches (Hales, 1999), I want to be clear that I am using the idea in a particular way within solution-focused practice. In this context, non-directive refers to the *direction* and *content* of the work, in that this should be directed, as far as possible, by the client. The solution-focused worker is clearly directing the *process*, by choosing which questions to ask. However, in part by asking open questions, often starting with 'What...?', the worker is allowing the client to choose how to answer. Following the practice principle of *maximising client choice* described above is another way in which a solution-focused worker aspires to a position of non-directiveness.

Non-instrumentality

Linked to the idea of non-directiveness is non-instrumentality. As well as the client determining the direction and content of the work, the solution-focused worker wants to allow the client the maximum choice in what to do after and as a result of the work, if anything. To this end, the worker tries to keep out of the client's way. So, in this case, I was not trying to get Sonia to do anything or suggest that she do anything. The influence of any suggestions of mine might have limited Sonia's ability to generate possibilities for herself. By continuing only to invite descriptions of possibility, I was aiming to be non-instrumental and neutral about any future actions Sonia might take.

Opening up possibilities and working in the subjunctive

Another reason for not suggesting that a particular action be taken is the difficulty of knowing in advance what this should be, for, as the mythologist Joseph Campbell has said, 'Your path is created in the moment of action' (quoted in Nelson, 2010, p. 278). The worker's aim is to elicit various possibilities, rather than to fix with the client a predetermined path towards a specified target. Solution-focused practice is sometimes mistaken for an action-planning approach, and we will be underlining how it differs in this respect when we look at scaling in Chapter 6.

Working in the subjunctive mood, by using lots of ifs, mights and maybes, can encourage possibility. This has involved a shift in practice from earlier solution-focused days, when a typical future-focused question might have been: 'What will be different in your life when the two of you are getting along better?' (O'Hanlon and Weiner-Davis, 1989, p. 72). The idea then was to subtly 'influence client's perceptions in the direction of solution' (ibid., p. 80). Preferring to allow the client to develop their own perceptions in their own way and time, and realising we can never know for certain what we will be doing tomorrow, I began to replace *when* by *if* and *will* by *would* and later, as even *would* suggests certainty, by *might*. This shift is more congruent too with the non-directive and non-instrumental positions, as well as with the possibility-based one. Evoking possibilities means asking about the many things that might happen rather than the one thing that will.

Activity: Worker positions

Read through Sonia's unfolding preferred future description again and look for ways in which I was developing and maintaining positions of non-directiveness, non-instrumentality and possibility.

Summary of the worker's task: Scenes from a preferred future

We can summarise the worker's task in eliciting these future-focused descriptions by the use of a film analogy. Describing the preferred future can be likened to the telling of a story, typically of the client's next day, from waking up onwards. Given the amount of concrete and observable detail elicited, it is useful to see this story being told through the medium of a film, with the worker helping the client to be its writer and director. Certain parts of the client's day become scenes in the film, with each scene being fleshed out by the detail of the client's answers. Imagining the amount of detail that one can see and hear when watching a film – every movement and sound made from one moment to the next – can be a useful guide to how much detail to encourage with your questions.

The worker's job in this respect is twofold: first, to help the client to consider a wide range of scenes through which their preferred future is shown, and to move sequentially from one scene to the next; and second, to help the client detail each scene, to 'thicken its description', to borrow the language of narrative therapy (White, 1997).[3] Within the solution-focused literature, this has been described as 'widening and deepening' (Tohn and Oshlag, 1997), though given the psychoanalytic connotations of the word *depth* in therapy (Davis, 2003), *detailing* may be a better fit for the worker activity here.

Activity: At your best

All you need for this exercise is a willing interviewee and a few minutes some-where where you can talk. Your task as the interviewer is to invite your partner to describe themselves being at their best tomorrow, in as much concrete detail as you can elicit. Begin by inviting them to imagine they have woken to find themselves at their best, then ask what is the first thing they would notice about themselves that would tell them that. And then what is the next thing...Tip: Keep on concretising, asking what your interviewee will be doing at various times of the day tomorrow, where and when, and what they and others would notice about themselves while engaged in those activities, if they were at their best. Interview for five or ten minutes, or just keep going until you have gone through the whole day.[4]

Concrete interactional sequences

I used a part of Sonia's story to illustrate some principles which underpin the construction of individual questions. Given that every individual question should connect with every preceding answer, it follows that every question should connect with the previous question too. Therefore, the skill of constructing individual questions needs to be accompanied by an ability to put questions together into certain sequences. One such I have called the 'concrete interactional sequence', which has proved invaluable in developing detailed scenes within a preferred future. I will illustrate this with the help of an extended transcript.

Yolande, aged 15, is hoping to be happier and to get on with people better, in school and elsewhere. The interactional nature of the sequence below, which takes place in the middle of the preferred future description, emerges from my opening question onwards. Notice too how the later questions continue to focus Yolande on the interactions with her mother. Before the fleshing out of the scene, however, I *concretise*, so that Yolande can determine where and when the scene will take place.

Guy: And after school, who'd be the first to notice that you were happier?

Yolande: My Mum.

Guy: Where and when would you first see your Mum after school?

Yolande: When she comes in from work.

Guy: What time would that be?

Yolande: About half past six.

Guy: And when she comes in at half past six, whereabouts would you be? Where would your Mum first see you?

Yolande: I'd be in my room, but if things were better, I'd go downstairs when I heard her come in.

Guy: So when she comes in, what's the first thing she'd notice about you that would be a sign to her that you were getting on better and had had a happier day at school?

Yolande: That I was downstairs. Because when I'm not talking to her, when we're not talking, we've had an argument or something, I just stay in my room. I hear her come inside but I just don't say nothing.

Guy: Ok. So a sign to your Mum that you were happier would be ... you'd be there when she came in? You wouldn't stay in your room?

Yolande: Yeah, I'd go downstairs and I'd be there, yeah.

Guy: Ok, you're downstairs, your Mum's come in, you're there, just think about it very, very small now, as she sees you, what's the first thing she'd notice about you, the very first thing, the smallest thing?

Yolande: That I'd said hello.

Guy: Ok, and the next?

Yolande: I don't know, I'm not her!

Guy: Have a guess!

Yolande: Hmmm ... that I'd seem happier, that I've had a good day at school. She'd be able to tell probably, without me telling her, yeah.

Guy: Would she? Yeah? She'd be able to tell that you've had a good day, without you telling her?

Yolande: Yeah.

Guy: How would she tell? What would she notice?

Yolande: I'd be awake. If I've had a bad day at school then, for some reason I'm really tired when I go home and I just need to sleep. So if I'm awake then it means that, I've either got a lot of coursework to do, or I've had a good day at school.

Guy: Ok. Would your Mum be pleased to come in, to find you downstairs, awake, saying hello to her ... ?

Up to this point, I have been focusing Yolande's attention on what her mother might notice about her, and this question now signals a shift in the sequence to encourage Yolande to consider possible differences in her mother. It seems reasonable to suppose that Yolande's mother will be pleased, and that this will be a useful lens through which Yolande might view her, but first I check this with Yolande. A simple alternative would be 'What would you notice about your Mum?', though the neutrality of this might not quite fit the positive nature of Yolande's answers so far.

Yolande: Yeah.

Guy: Yeah, ok. So how would you know she was pleased? What's the first thing you'd notice about her?

Yolande: Hmmm...I don't know. I'm always upstairs when she comes inside...I don't know (*reflecting to herself*) what does she do when she comes home? She comes in, goes in the kitchen...I don't know. (*laughs*) I don't know after that.

Guy: What do you think? What would you notice about her, given that she was pleased?

Yolande: Hmmm...Oh, this is a hard question, I don't know. I don't know these things about her, she's just there. I don't know. She'll, hmmm...I don't know, I don't know how to answer...come back to that one afterwards.

Guy: Well, would you notice straightaway she was pleased or would it take a while to notice?

Yolande: Hmmm...She always looks the same, it's kind of hard to tell.

Guy: So can you tell more by how she looks or how she sounds, that she's pleased?

Yolande: She always sounds the same as well.

Guy: And you can tell that she's pleased?

Yolande: Yeah.

Guy: Yeah? How can you tell?

Yolande: I've lived with her all my life.

Guy: Yeah, you have! What would happen next, then? After you've said 'hello'?

Yolande: She might say, 'you alright?' And she'd be like, 'Make us a cup of tea'. If I'm not talking to her I'd just ignore that she said that.

Guy: And tomorrow, supposing you're happier, and you've gone downstairs to say hello to her?

Yolande: I'd make the tea. Then she might start moaning about work. Or I guess she might say something good about it. If she felt better.

Guy: Ok, so suppose you got this pleased response, it's hard to describe how, but you'd be able to tell. What would happen next?

Yolande: I can't tell you, I don't know.

Guy: What do you think? What do you think might happen if...?

Yolande: Oh, I don't know! I can't do all this thinking!

Guy: Can I just say, you're doing a really good job, especially for someone who finds questions hard, you're doing a good job at answering them. So what else might happen in the evening? What else would be different if you were getting on better with your Mum?

It is my job to help Yolande do the difficult thinking that might make a difference, and complimenting someone who is finding the work tough going – as long as done genuinely – frequently helps in this regard (Iveson et al., 2012, pp. 107–108).

Yolande: She'll cook!

Guy: She'll cook.

Yolande: Yes. She's a bit lazy with cooking. Don't tell her I said that.

Guy: Would you like that? What's your favourite thing that she cooks?

Yolande: I don't really mind. She's kind of good all round.

Guy: Ok. And as well as cooking, what else?

Yolande: I don't know, cooking's a good start!

Guy: Yeah?

Yolande: I don't know, she'd just be...no, I don't know.

Guy: She'd just be?

Yolande: I don't know, I don't know, I'm trying to think of the word and I just couldn't think of one.

The hard work involved for Yolande here is typical for a solution-focused conversation, as is the persistence on my part that is needed to support that hard work. The difficulty is to be expected, welcomed even, for answers coming easily might suggest there is insufficient difference going on for new possibilities to emerge. In this case it may be that the hard thinking paid off, for when Yolande returned two weeks later, she was able to list 25 ways in which she and her Mum were getting on better with each other.

Handling difficulties within preferred futures

The next piece of transcript from the session with Sonia will serve two purposes. First, it will show how a client can be helped to consider how they might handle difficulties arising within their preferred future. Remember, a preferred future is not defined as a perfect future in which all problems have gone, but as the future in which the client's hopes from the work have been met. In Sonia's case, having the capacity for happiness she wants and not finding anxiety a problem do not mean she will no longer have to deal with any difficulties. The transcript starts about 20 minutes further into the session from where we left it earlier, and Sonia is talking about being more assertive with her partner. As you read through the transcript, notice how I help Sonia to consider how she might handle difficulties arising from this. The second purpose this transcript will serve I will leave slightly more mysterious for now. The discussion is mainly in the future still, but there is something else that Sonia says that is somewhere else in time, and it is the sort of client comment that a solution-focused worker needs to hear and make a mental or written note of. See if you can spot what I am referring to.

> *Sonia*: I'd feel more assertive if I was happy and able to say 'no' properly. Sometimes my boyfriend calls me late when he's working a twelve-hour shift, and Mo's sleeping and I feel tired. But if we were both happier I don't think he'd get offended by me saying, 'Is it alright if I get my sleep now?'
>
> *Guy*: So if you were to be assertive and say no, what difference would that make to you?
>
> *Sonia*: Then, I wouldn't feel guilty about it if I was happy, and I feel that my boyfriend would be more understanding, and he'd say 'Ok, get your sleep, and I'll talk to you whenever'.
>
> *Guy*: Ok. Is it a possibility that at first he might not quite get it?

Having heard about the difficulties in their relationship, I wondered whether it would be this easy, so I decided to check this out with Sonia. This is an example of 'toughening up the preferred future',[5] where a worker invites a client to imagine difficulties arising and their response to this.

Sonia: Yes, that's what I'm worried about.

Guy: So, supposing you gave that a go, and your boyfriend didn't quite take it the way you wanted him to, and yet you were still feeling assertive, like you could deal with it. What would you notice about yourself then?

Sonia: Well, I would just explain to him, 'I'm bringing up the child, and you have to understand that I find it difficult to sleep in the daytime, and if I get a good night's sleep, I can concentrate'. Because when I had depression I couldn't sleep all night, and it's only like, recently I've started to sleep well, and I'd like to continue sleeping well, you know. I used to panic in the night. But, now that I can get my sleep, I'd like to sleep, and I'd say to him, 'Don't be offended by what I'm saying, but I just want to get my sleep, and that's it'.

Guy: So you'd explain it to him.

Sonia: I'd explain it to him clearly. But I hope that just because I said I don't want to talk to him – sometimes he's the type of person who doesn't want to see me the next day because of that.

Guy: Ok. Suppose that happens and yet you're still feeling assertive and full of energy...

Sonia: Well, then I'd just tell him, 'You're making a big deal out of nothing. If you don't want to see me, that's fine, I can do other things to keep myself busy'. And that's what I'd do, instead of running after him all the time!

My last intervention above shows clearly the both/and position (Lipchik, 1993; see Chapter 2), which is useful to adopt when inviting a client to imagine handling difficulties in their preferred future: 'Suppose BOTH that this problem happens AND that your hopes from the work have been met'. This conveys a message that it is possible to handle the difficulty and helps the client to come up with their own ideas about how to do so, as happened with Sonia above. I shall return to the second reason for showing this transcript in the next chapter.

Using future-focused questions outside planned contexts

The detailed examples above are from planned solution-focused conversations. Many opportunities also arise for using similar questions in ways that cannot be predicted in advance. The knack is to be alive to such occasions. I was at an 'accommodation panel' meeting, called because Mrs Perryman had asked the social services department where I worked to take Steve, her teenage son, into care. Such a panel meeting was part of the department's standard response to such a request, to try to avoid 'accommodating' a child in part by offering a social work service instead. Mrs Perryman was impressing on my manager, the panel chair, just how bad the situation was, and in return, Steve talked about the problems as he saw them:

> When I arrive home, I always find my Mum waiting to have a go at me, and Dad just ignores me, and...

Up to that point, my manager had been doing most of the talking to them, so I decided to intervene, assuming I had nothing to lose:

> Can I ask you something? I'm not sure what you'll make of this...

Steve paused and both he and his Mum turned towards me, so I quickly carried on:

> *Guy*: Supposing things at home were how you both want them to be – Steve, when you next get home, what will you notice?
> *Steve*: She won't be going on at me.
> *Guy*: What would your Mum be doing instead?
> *Steve*: Leaving me alone.
> *Guy*: Mrs Perryman, what would you notice?
> *Mrs Perryman*: I don't know. That we were able to sit round a table and talk...

They soon returned to problem talk, with Steve talking about being unhappy. I saw another opportunity:

> *Guy*: I guess you'd rather be happy?
> *Steve*: Yes.
> *Guy*: So how would you know you were feeling happier?
> *Steve*: I don't know.
> *Guy*: Who'd be the first to notice?

Steve: My mates.

Guy: How would they know?

Steve: I'd have cheered up.

Guy: How would they know that?

Steve: What a **** stupid question!!

This was not a planned solution-focused 'session', and I had not really had the go-ahead from Steve, or his mother, for the sorts of questions I had started to ask, so Steve's reaction did not surprise me. However, my questions had interrupted the blame-based talk and perhaps produced a glimmer of possibility to work towards. By the end of the panel, Steve and Mrs Perryman had agreed to my visiting, so that we could 'sit around a table and talk'. I was involved for the next few months, using a lot more solution-focused questions in my social work with the family, and Steve remained living at home. What this example suggests is that when someone is complaining about a problem, the chance to ask future-focused questions often presents itself. If you hear the person as saying something is happening that they do not want to be, then it is a logical step to ask what they want to be happening instead.

Another unplanned use of future-focused questions in my statutory children's social work indicates the potential usefulness of these questions outside the strictly solution-focused process and also helps to clarify when we need to go beyond this process. Gita's son, Sunil, was on the child protection register, and I became the responsible social worker. Gita made clear to me her unhappiness about the situation she was in:

I don't want Sunil to be on the register! I want to be a normal Mum!

It struck me that following up her positively stated desire might serve several purposes. It would show that I was taking her and her desires seriously, it would be a good way to start to get to know her, it would be useful to me in beginning my assessment, and it might also be useful to Gita in helping her to think about and even in making some required changes.

Guy: You want to be a normal Mum, with Sunil's name off the register. Sure. Can I launch into a few questions about this? It would be a good way for me to get to know you a little, to find out how you want things to be.

Gita: Yes, ok.

Guy: So, suppose when you wake up tomorrow, you find that you're exactly the Mum you want to be, and also, when it comes to it, the case conference is happy for Sunil's name to come off the register, what's the first thing you'd notice about yourself tomorrow morning...?

The conversation that ensued was indeed useful in the ways I had hoped, but it is important to note that, while I was incorporating some solution-focused ideas, here I was necessarily stepping beyond the solution-focused process. My overriding responsibility was to Sunil and his safety, rather than to have a conversation that ended up being useful to Gita according to what she wanted from it. If we could work together to achieve both, then that would be all to the good, but it was important for me to be clear where my priorities lay. That was why I invited Gita to imagine not only that she was the Mum she wanted to be, but also that the conference would be satisfied regarding Sunil's safety. In situations of concern about a child's safety, a parent's hopes can be worked towards only when they fit within the boundary of safety for the child. What this example clarifies for us is that to be able to undertake a fully solution-focused piece of work, we need to be in a context where it is possible to be guided solely by what the client wants. However, when the direction for the work is determined by a worker's statutory responsibilities, it may be possible to pay attention also to the client's hopes from the work and thereby to incorporate solution-focused questions.

Reflections

- A process of action planning is future-focused in that it involves setting goals and targets. The future is approached differently within the solution-focused approach. What would you say the differences are?
- What might you see a worker do that would suggest they were taking positions of non-directiveness, non-instrumentality and possibility?
- How might you fit the practice of inviting detailed descriptions of preferred futures into your own work roles and tasks?
- Bearing in mind the final section of this chapter, can you think back to a recent moment in your work when an opportunity to ask questions about a preferred future presented itself?
- How might it be useful for the people you work with to be helped to describe their preferred futures?

A part of the answer to the first reflective question is that no attempt is made to plan or work out how to get to the client's preferred future, the focus remaining instead on evoking possibilities through wide descriptions of differences which zoom in on small details. In the next chapter, it will start to become clearer why there is no need to plan what to do in the future, as we realise that the client not only already knows what to do but is already doing it.

5

Description II: Instances

One change always leaves the way open for the establishment of others.

Machiavelli, The Prince

Introduction

In this chapter we turn our attention from preferred futures to the other pillar of the solution-focused approach – its focus on progress that is being made towards these futures, and on times when any parts of them are already happening or have happened. At the heart of the original shift from a problem-solving approach to a solution-focused practice was the increasing attention given to what people were doing that was working for them in some way, and to the notion of *exceptions* in particular. Helping people had traditionally been based on finding out what their problems were and then acting to resolve them, usually by first working out what was causing the problems. Steve de Shazer, Insoo Kim Berg and their colleagues turned this approach on its head by taking the simple yet revolutionary step of finding exceptions to the problems instead and helping them to happen more often.

In the version of solution-focused practice presented here, the language of exceptions has been largely supplanted by the language of *instances*. As our work is organised from the outset around what the person wants from it, and not around the problems they bring, it makes sense to think about times when what is wanted is happening, rather than times when the problem is not happening. It is useful to retain the idea of eliciting exceptions, as a tool to use on certain occasions, and with this in mind and given the importance of exceptions in the development of a solution focus, I shall begin this chapter with a brief historical account. Having then traced the move from exceptions to instances, I shall pose the question of how to elicit such instances, so that we can then have conversations with our clients about them. One way is simply to ask. My earliest memory of consciously attempting to be solution-focused in my work dates back to 1993, when I was working with a family where the constant fighting between two brothers was driving their single mother to distraction. Feeling stuck, I was ready to try something new and, coming across the idea of exceptions in a newly published book (Cade and O'Hanlon, 1993), this seemed like an idea I could try. I asked the boys if they could think of a time when something had happened which might have caused them to fall out with each other, but where they had managed not to and had done something else instead. They could, or at least one of them could, and he told me of such a time. I tried but failed to remember what the book said to do next. All I could think to do was to say 'Great, keep it up!', realising that this sounded a little lame.

What I went on to learn was the importance of follow-up questions and of building sequences of questions (Lipchik, 1988a), which help people to describe in detail instances of what they want actually happening in their lives. So, as well as considering how to elicit those instances, we will also set out the sorts of questions that prove useful in developing conversations about them and some of the sequences and structures in which these questions can be placed.

A little history of the focus on what is working

In the previous chapter I described how the BFTC team incorporated the goal focus of MRI brief therapy into their developing solution-focused approach. To trace the development of the focus on what is working in solution-focused practice is to see how the BFTC turned another of the MRI's ideas on its head. MRI brief therapists do not see problems as being deep-rooted within the individual but rather see them as arising from people's attempted solutions to ordinary life difficulties, solutions which are not working (Watzlawick et al., 1974). In a nutshell, the MRI therapist's job is to find out what is not working and then to intervene, to help their clients do something different, that does work, to resolve the problem. The MRI therapist's job, in other words, is to initiate change.

To see how the alternative practice of asking about exceptions to problems emerged, we need to begin with the BFTC's development of the so-called Formula First Session Task:

Between now and next time we meet, we want you to observe, so that you can tell us next time, what happens in your (life, marriage, family, or relationship) that you want to continue to have happen. (de Shazer and Molnar, 1984)

This task was designed by Steve de Shazer and Elam Nunnally of the BFTC for one particular family, who 'appeared rather hopeless and described their situation in very vague terms' (de Shazer, 1985, p. 138), and it had a startling effect on the family and hence on the team. The family returned for their second session having 'turned itself around' and able to describe positive changes in concrete, behavioural terms. The team began to give this task to other clients and found that not only did it frequently have a similar effect but that the positive occurrences reported had often been happening *before the therapy started* (Kiser, 1995, p. 132, emphasis added).

This last finding in particular set in train a process whereby the BFTC team started to see their role more as helping change to continue rather than as initiating it (de Shazer, 1988, p. 5), and this shift was supported by their experience in another case. A client who, in a first session, had been describing a problem as deep-rooted and seemingly intractable mentioned, almost as an afterthought, improvements in the three days leading up to the session. The team decided to focus on these improvements rather than on the intractability, and the work was successfully completed in three sessions. They began to call improvements that had happened before the work had started *pre-session change* (Weiner-Davis, de Shazer and Gingerich, 1987).

In the above examples, the clients engaged in 'change talk' either after an end-of-session task from the previous session or having spontaneously mentioned change themselves. The team was committed to the idea that having clients talk about change led to change in their actual lives outside, but their research indicated that most clients did not spontaneously talk about change in this way. They would do so, however, when asked about changes by the therapist (Gingerich, de Shazer and Weiner-Davis, 1988). Given the observations of positive change happening before the work had started, such questions were brought forward from second to first sessions. The team then found that 'almost all problem patterns have exceptions' and that asking about pre-session change and exceptions 'frequently resulted in eliciting client-change talk' (ibid., p. 29). The search for exceptions began to take place earlier and earlier in the first meeting, and so, in another nutshell, the therapist's job had been reversed and was now focused on finding out what *is* working and then helping the client to do more of this. The solution-focused therapist's job, in other words, was to facilitate the continuation of change. It looks such a simple switch on paper, yet it has been revolutionary in its impact on ways of helping people to make changes in their lives.

From exceptions to instances

Revolutionary as the switch was, asking about exceptions meant that there was still an orientation within the work towards problems. Asking someone about times when they did not feel insecure, for example, keeps the notion of insecurity alive. However, the increasing emphasis on preferred futures enabled a further practice shift away from problems, by focusing, for example, on parts of the preferred future that are happening already. The version of solution-focused practice being described in this book takes us further away still, as it organises our work from the beginning around what the person wants rather than around a problem and defines preferred futures by the realisation of what is wanted rather than by the absence of problems (Shennan and Iveson, 2011, pp. 286–287). So, once it has been determined that more confidence is what is wanted instead of insecurity, *instances* of confidence can become the subject of enquiry, and the idea of insecurity can just fade away.

Eliciting instances

If we are to have conversations with people about instances, then how do we find out what these instances are? How do we ascertain the times and events that will be the subjects of these conversations? Some ways of doing this have already been mentioned, but I find it useful to group them in the following straightforward fashion:

- listening – with a constructive ear;
- asking directly;
- using scaling questions.

Listening with a constructive ear

The third of these will be the subject of the next chapter, so here I will be focusing on the first two, beginning with listening with a constructive ear. In Chapter 2, we saw how solution-focused practitioners train their ears to hear anything their clients say they are doing that fits with how they want things to be, and the usefulness of that will be apparent here. It is not uncommon to hear people say, as they describe their preferred futures in fine detail, that some part of them is happening already, especially if one is listening with a constructive ear. In fact, this is one of the very good reasons for inviting wide and detailed descriptions – the more the detail, the greater the chance of someone alighting on something they are already doing. And it can be encouraging to find that one is already doing some of what one wants to be doing.

Activity: Listening for instances

Look back at the last extract from the session with Sonia in the previous chapter (pp. 69–70), which was used as an example of handling difficulties in a preferred future. Read it through again, this time with the visual version of your constructive ear, and try to spot the instance that is buried in there.

It was probably easier seeing it on the page than hearing it when Sonia was actually talking, though when you have trained your ears to be constructive, phrases such as Sonia's 'Recently I've started to sleep well' tend to jump out at you. As soon as I heard this, I wrote Sonia's comment down, exactly as she said it. I did not want to interrupt her flow as she talked about being more assertive with her boyfriend but knew that this was the sort of statement, an *instance* in our terminology, to ask more about at a later, appropriate moment.

Activity: Asking about instances

Imagine you are in my seat, and that you want to ask Sonia about her statement that she has started to sleep well. What are you curious about? What ideas for follow-up questions does your curiosity lead you to? Make a note of some questions that you might ask. Writing them down will encourage you to consider how you might actually word them.

Questions to follow up instances

There is never just the one question that is the right one to ask, and always many options. The context of the work, the flow of the conversation, the responses and words of the client, and the style and preferences of the worker will all affect and influence what is asked. However, there are certain types of questions that the worker will usually draw upon, about what led to the instance, the differences it has made and about its possible future effects.

Questions about what led to the instance happening

These include questions such as:

- How did you do that?
- What did you do that helped that to happen?
- What else did you do that helped?

All questions contain embedded assumptions, and a powerful one at work in these is that Sonia is an active agent in her life, who is able to effect change by her own actions. Other questions can be asked about what led to Sonia starting to sleep well, such as 'What was different that enabled you to sleep?' and 'What else helped?', though these are more neutral with regard to Sonia's own part in the change. Questions that assume the client's part are seen as 'indirect compliments' (Berg, 1994, p. 59), as they help clients to compliment themselves through their answers. This can be more useful than direct compliments, which, apart from potentially sounding patronising, can stop a conversation in its tracks. 'Well done' will typically be followed by 'Thank you' and then a full stop, whereas asking a question keeps the client thinking and the process moving forwards.

> *Guy*: You mentioned that recently you've started to sleep well.
>
> *Sonia*: Yeah.
>
> *Guy*: I'm wondering how have you managed to do that?
>
> *Sonia*: I don't know.
>
> *Guy*: What have you done that's helped you to sleep?
>
> *Sonia*: Oh, I read a lot of books on changing my thought patterns. I read a lot of psychology books like – you know the *Five Areas Approach*, have you heard of that?

Guy: I've never heard of it.

Sonia: I read books on that, and Carl Jung or something, his name is.

Guy: Oh, yeah.

Sonia: Yeah, I read books on childhood behaviour, and I read special books on how to deal with your parents not being well. So I read a lot of books and I do meditation as well. I meditate a lot.

Guy: Ok. And when did you start doing meditation?

Sonia: Well, when I had my depression.

Guy: So, ok, and that's helpful?

Sonia: That's really helpful...

I shall resist the urge to suggest having a Carl Jung book by your bed if you are having trouble sleeping, and simply observe that Sonia was a most resourceful young woman! Shortly after this, I set up a scale to continue eliciting instances, and this provided the framework for the rest of the session.

In the previous chapter, I issued a cautionary note against action planning. By asking 'How did you do that?'-type questions, note that we are not trying to work out a strategy for the client to repeat as part of an action plan. The intention is rather to shift 'the client's attention to thinking that they took control over a situation in a manner beneficial to them' (Lipchik, 1988b, p. 4), thereby increasing the client's sense of themselves as able to take control. I will return to this issue again in the next chapter.

Some useful questions have been imported into the solution-focused approach from its close relative, narrative practice (White and Epston, 1990; White, 2007). In contrasting the two approaches, Bill O'Hanlon (2001) once suggested that while the quintessential solution-focused question in response to a client success is 'How did you do that?', the narrative practitioner would be more likely to ask 'Who are you to have done that?' White (1991) borrowed the terms *landscape of action* and *landscape of identity* from the psychologist Jerome Bruner (1986)[1] to distinguish between the two types of question. Identity-related questions include:

- What did it take?
- What skills or qualities did you draw upon to make that change?
- What does that say about the sort of person you are?

Where 'How did you do that?' indirectly compliments actions of the client, and identity questions compliment their qualities, a third type of question compliments the thinking behind changes made:

- How did you think to do that?

There is a nice example of this type of question and the useful responses it can produce in the extract that follows. The worker also asks a *checking question*, one of the small number of occasions in a solution-focused conversation when a closed question, inviting a 'yes' or 'no' answer, is called for.

Checking questions

Before asking questions about what led to an instance happening, it is important to be sure that it is actually an instance, in other words it needs to be a part of the person's preferred future. This is often self-evident, but at other times it can be checked simply with questions such as

- Is that something you want to continue to happen?
- Are you pleased about that?

Moreover, before asking 'How did you do that?', it is also worth checking whether 'that' was hard to do or not. If it was easy, then the question is unnecessary and will fall flat or, even worse, sound 'solution-forced' on the part of the worker (Nylund and Corsiglia, 1994).

How Alex managed to stay calm

Alex, aged 12, has been struggling to keep his temper, and this has been making it hard for him to get on with his sisters and with other young people at school, from which he has been suspended. I am meeting Alex for the second time and hearing that he has managed to be a little calmer.

> *Alex*: ... even when my sister has been rude to me, I've tried to ignore her and I go and tell Mum, instead of having a whole lot of argument and a whole lot of shouting.
>
> *Guy*: Really? So there's been times when she's been rude to you and you've been ignoring her?
>
> *Alex*: I've ignored it and I've just told Mum instead.
>
> *Guy*: Ok. So was it hard to do that? Was it hard to ignore it?
>
> *Alex*: A bit, but I still told Mum, without losing my temper.
>
> *Guy*: Ok. How did you manage to do it?

Alex: I just thought to myself...When she said, 'Oh Alex, you need help', and stuff, I said, 'Yeah Lorna, I do need help' and I just sort of agreed, 'Yeah Lorna, yeah, I do, yeah'.

Guy: Ah, so you just agreed with her.

Alex: Yeah.

Guy: How did you get that idea, to do that?

Alex: Um...I got it off a TV programme.

Guy: Off a TV programme? Which one?

Alex: *My Wife and Kids.*

Guy: Well, what a fantastic idea. So how was that helpful to just agree with Lorna when she said that?

Alex: Well, it's been helpful because in a way it's a bit funny to me because I know it's not true what's she saying, and I know that I'm the one who's doing the right thing, and it feels a bit better instead of having to get angry and lose my temper with her.

Questions about the effects of an instance

The future-focused question 'What difference would that make?' has its progress-focused counterpart in 'What difference has that made?' Asking this question can help the client to assess a change they have made. In the words of the systemic theorist Gregory Bateson (1972), is it a 'difference that has made a difference'? When the difference *has* made a difference – and positive changes frequently do – there can be a strong reinforcing effect, as we saw in Chapter 2 when Michelle had started walking and going shopping on her own.

Guy: What difference is that making to you, Michelle?

Michelle: Loads, yeah, because I guess this is what independent people feel like...to do it on my own is really, really neat.

Notice that I asked the question in the present continuous tense – 'is that making?' – which implied that the difference was not a static event but was continuing to happen. This question also enables the client to trace the effects of one particular instance, thereby opening up a range of other positive changes that have taken place. Asking about differences in the plural can enhance the widening effect.

Client: We've been talking a little more recently.

Worker: What differences has that made?

Client: Well, I've not been dreading arriving home so much – almost looked forward to it some days in fact. It's also meant that John has been helping me a bit with what to do about Robbie. We're going to go and see the head teacher next week. It feels like a bit of the weight is off my shoulders.

Worker: And what difference has that made?

Continuing with this question, which can be done for as long as the client thinks of further differences, creates a very simple 'chains of difference' sequence.[2] The more differences that are brought into the client's awareness, the more they will be able to think of themselves as able to make changes.

In the previous chapter, I described the practice principle of 'maximising client choice in framing their answers', by, for example, using the word *notice* to allow the client to choose which aspect of their experience to describe first. The word *difference* serves the same purpose here, as it does not direct the client to their thoughts, feelings or actions, but allows the client to decide how to answer initially in their own way. After questions of this most open type, the worker can follow up more specifically:

- What difference did that make/has that made/is that making?
- How has it made you feel?
- What has it enabled you to do, or to do more of?
- What effect has that had on how you are thinking now?

The questions suggested so far have asked about the client's own perspective, and these can be supplemented with other-person-perspective and interactive questions, to further enrich the descriptions of differences.

- What do you think Mo has noticed about you since you've been sleeping better?
- What effect has it had on things between you and Mo?
- How has she responded?
- Who else has noticed that you're sleeping well, and what do you think they've noticed?

Questions about the possible future effects of an instance

Having traced the effects thus far, attention can be given to differences that might continue into the future. Once again, this is not in order to create an action plan for the client to follow, but to facilitate the description of more possibilities. The following question could trigger further potentially useful future-oriented sequences with Sonia.

- Suppose you continue sleeping well, what other differences might you notice?

Instances emerging within a preferred future: An illustration

The following sequence shows how a solution-focused conversation can shift gradually, and at times seamlessly, from a description of a preferred future into changes that are already happening. Colin wants to regain his confidence and a sense of stability, after years of being in and out of psychiatric hospitals. When I ask who else might notice that this was happening tomorrow, Colin mentions an older cousin he is very close to, and then immediately mentions positive changes he has been making already. I decide at first to continue with the preferred future, which Colin has been describing in fine detail. There is always a choice to be made when instances are heard, about whether to ask about them straightaway, or to make a note and come back to them later, as happened with Sonia. As you read the first part of this extract, consider what questions I might have asked if I had followed the instances as soon as they were mentioned.

> *Colin*: I might see my cousin, Frank. We were brought up together... What I've been doing which has been quite refreshing recently is, and has helped me feel myself is, I've been able to listen to the news in the morning – I've had something to talk about – and he's interested to listen to what I have to say about things and I'm interested in what he says.
>
> *Guy*: So he's probably already seen some changes in you, recently?
>
> *Colin*: I think he might have, yeah, maybe.
>
> *Guy*: So tomorrow then, what's the first thing Frank might notice about you, if you were right back to your confident self?

Colin: He notices when I'm alert and I'm sort of, like, he asks questions...we would have a discussion about what's in the news, what's been taking place, give his views, hope for me to give back mine...

Guy: Right. And how would he know that you were feeling relaxed and assertive, that you were really aware of what you were doing tomorrow. What would he notice about you?

After mentioning his alertness in the present tense, Colin continued in the future conditional – 'would'. I chose to continue in Colin's preferred future (I might have missed the present tense of 'when I'm alert') in which he had said earlier that he would be relaxed, assertive and aware.

Colin: Because – he tries to wind me up...and if I can...before my breakdown, I'd tell him to sit back and he'd laugh. So I'd go 'Hold on, wait a minute, what are you saying?' He'd wind me up, and I was usually very sure and could cope with people teasing.

Guy: So he'd try and wind you up, and you'd respond in a certain way?

I have heard Colin say how he used to be in the face of his cousin's teasing, and I am checking how he would be tomorrow, with his regained self.

Colin: Yeah, I'd be very sharp with him and then he'll laugh and know I'm ok.

Guy: He'd know that you're ok. Would he like that? You being sharp with him?

Colin: Yeah. When I was younger, we had a close relationship. I'd play with him and his mates and I was always confident, ready to join in. I was very, kind of, alert, with people.

Guy: So, confident, and alert, that's part of how you'd be tomorrow?

Colin: Yeah. That would be, yeah, me feeling more confident, yeah.

Guy: What would the effect be on your relationship with your cousin, the way you were together, of you being back like that again?

Colin: It's come, it has come along quite a bit. He's introduced me to a lot of his friends and they're very considerate and they kind of like, listen and respond, and the conversation goes somewhere and you feel like you've done something, and there's that whole clarity comes back.

Guy: So you've noticed a change in the way you've been getting on with his friends?

Colin: Yeah, and other people. And I felt that, with him being interested in me, and asking lots of questions about things, where I may have said, 'I don't want to talk about it' and sort of shied away, now I'm answering a lot of the questions.

Guy: So what are some of the other positive changes that your cousin will have noticed about you recently?

In his last couple of responses, Colin has been stating more and more strongly the changes he is already making, and he has now clearly left tomorrow in his thinking and is focused on these changes. I am following Colin's flow.

Colin: I've cut down my drinking, he's noticed that.

Guy: Ah-ha. So you...

Colin: I wake up early, and I don't waste my day.

Guy: Ah-ha. So you're getting up earlier again now than you were doing?

Colin: Yeah, I don't, obviously I don't have anything to do, but I get up, and I look for something to do, and it's coming, and I'm starting to appreciate getting up early, what it means to get up early, and I'm starting to appreciate actually being alive, you know? Meeting people and having, you know, positive conversations with people.

Guy: How have you managed to make these changes, to start doing this?

Colin: Erm... it's been difficult. It was like, 'You've got to, like, take stock of yourself and decide what it is you want to do'. Which isn't easy. But time is going and you can live in this sort of cloud of what could have been, what should have been, better to just enjoy each moment.

Guy: So it was a difficult step to take, to take stock and do this. So how, so what did you do to help yourself to start to make these changes that you've made?

Colin: Well, erm, I've spent time talking to people, listening to people, erm, thinking of other people – my sister's been ill, and I've been visiting her. Putting others' needs first is quite refreshing, not give myself such a hard time. I put a lot of expectancy on myself when I was younger, I'm trying to enjoy what I'm doing at the moment more now.

Guy: Ok, so what other changes have you made? You said that you're not wasting your day. So what else are you doing now that you're...?

Colin: I'm going, well, I've enrolled for a computer course. I'm looking for something else to focus on. I've been trying to learn Spanish, I did a course in that. Erm, started to read a bit...

Guy: Right. So, you've become very active, yeah, you've been doing a number of things. How's that been helping you to move on, to become more yourself again?

Colin: Yeah, well, it's new interests that I've developed, keeping kind of fresh optimism and at the same time doing it with my own particular tastes, my own particular way of doing it. I've had a lot of people steering and guiding me and I think that's taken away a lot of the sense, the essence of who I was as a person. Now I think I've started to regain that essence...

Colin had three sessions over a two-month period, and in a later session he contrasted this solution-focused work with his other experiences within the mental health system. He valued the attention given in the solution-focused work to his 'own particular way of doing it'. Coming across him again over five years later, I learned that Colin was in full-time employment, his frequent stays in hospital having ceased after our work together.

Asking directly for instances

Although we will often hear instances when we listen constructively, on many occasions we will need to ask direct questions to elicit positive changes. In first meetings, scaling questions provide an excellent means of doing this, as we shall see in Chapter 6. A simple alternative, after having helped a client to describe a preferred future in detail, is to ask:

- Tell me about any of this that you've noticed happening recently, even the smallest bits of it.

Although she never used the word *instance*, Eve Lipchik was probably the pioneer with regard to such instance-seeking. In her 1988 article on putting together sequences of solution-focused questions, she gave examples of 'exception sequences' (Lipchik, 1988a), with problem statements by clients being followed by questions such as 'When doesn't that happen?' and 'When is that just a little bit better?', whereas a statement of something that is wanted would be followed by:

- What is different about those times when that happens already?
- When does that happen?

Lipchik suggested persistence in the face of negative answers:

- Not even a little bit, sometimes? (Lipchik, 1988a, p. 107)

Lipchik was also credited by her colleague, Michele Weiner-Davis, as being the first BFTC team member to follow up the miracle question with questions such as

- Is something of this miracle happening already? (Malinen, 2002)

In short, whenever a client has been able to articulate something of what they want, the option of inviting them to relate times when any of this is already happening is always available. The focus in this section has been on introducing instance-seeking in first sessions after the articulation of what is wanted. In follow-up sessions, the search for instances is begun immediately with the question 'What's better?', as we saw with Michelle in Chapter 2. I will explain how these sessions are developed in more detail in Chapter 8.

Asking about instances outside planned contexts

There will be many occasions when questions seeking out and following up instances can be utilised outside of planned sessions. Whenever you hear a person you are working with mention a positive occurrence, an opportunity might well present itself. Remember that you may need to check first that something you see as positive is seen in the same way by your client, with a question such as: 'Is that something you want to continue happening?' However, as Eve Lipchik once warned, although practitioners 'must ask direct questions about positive differences' they 'cannot rely on client report only' (1988b, p. 7). Opportunities to be creative in looking for instances in the absence of client self-report arise when working as part of a team, for example in group care contexts. A housing support worker[3] tended to find herself stuck in problem talk with Catherine, a vulnerable person with a history of homelessness and mental health problems. The worker found a way out of this by making enquiries of her colleagues before meeting with Catherine, encouraging them to think of even her smallest achievements, and was then able to replace the problem-generating 'How are you?' with, for example, 'Oh my gosh, I heard you caught the bus this morning, and walked over from the supermarket. Great, well done'. The worker described the effects in this way:

> It's almost changing her way of thinking and her mindset and letting her see that she can have a future, because I don't think over the years that she's thought it's possible. We just build on things like going to the GP, taking her antibiotics, having a haircut or a bath, and I do find by doing that it's getting more positive. Tomorrow, we're viewing a flat! Possibly moving into it Thursday. We'll see. There's a long way to go, but that's a massive step for Catherine.

Workers who spend time with their clients on a day-to-day basis will also be able to see for themselves 'achievements' of their clients, and once again the key to making use of a solution-focused approach is to be ever-ready to ask questions about what has been observed. For example, a nurse in an in-patient unit was able to say to a recently admitted patient:

> You told me yesterday that you wanted to cut down your smoking and not be chain-smoking, and I've noticed that you've not had one for a while, but I see you've got some. How have you managed that?

Documenting change: The use of lists

The last two means of developing conversations about instances and achievement that we will look at in this chapter both draw on the influence of narrative therapy. Narrative practitioners have developed elaborate uses of documentation since the approach's beginnings (White and Epston, 1990), and creating lists is one of the simpler examples of this (Morgan, 2000, p. 97). This has made them suitable for use in the solution-focused world, where they have been developed by the BRIEF team amongst others (Ratner et al., 2012, pp. 109–111). Writing down instances and achievements has proved useful in a number of ways. The search for instances can be a testing one, with the question 'What other changes have you noticed?' twenty minutes and twenty changes after the first was mentioned being potentially difficult to ask and hard for the client to answer. However, it is potentially one of the most useful. Recording the answers as they emerge, so that they are visible to the client as well as to the worker, is both encouraging and reinforcing. Seeing the list increasing encourages the process of thinking to continue, and writing down each change, achievement or sign of progress can reinforce the positive effect the answer had when occurring to the client in the first place.

Setting a target number of items for the list at the outset also helps to keep the client thinking. In this way, Yolande, who we encountered during her first session in Chapter 4, was able to list 25 ways she was getting on better with her mother by her second. This technique has had an enormous impact on the level of detail elicited within solution-focused conversations, as can be seen in a comparison of case examples from BRIEF from almost 20 years apart, where in the later example, with the help of a list, a young man could come up with 50 things he had done to help him to 'go straight' (Shennan and Iveson, 2011, pp. 290–291 – we will meet Ben again in Chapter 8).

Another example of the utility and versatility of lists comes from the work of a teacher coach[4] who, impressed by the use of lists on a solution-focused training course, left saying that she would try, on one of her training days, to have a school come up with a 100 things they do well. Sometime later she emailed me in triumph to report that she had succeeded, with a junior school, and attached a photograph to prove it: 'There were only thirty people attending and they loved it. Several said it was the activity that meant the most to them in the whole day'. The photograph showed a strip of paper, several feet long, pinned to the wall, covered with the list of a hundred things and a picture of a silver trophy drawn proudly alongside.

Focusing on change: Sparkling moments

Here we need to give another nod to narrative therapy, for its evocative vocabulary of 'sparkling moments' (Freedman and Coombs, 1996), which encourage us to break down reports of positive change into its smallest building blocks. People commonly first report change in a generalised fashion:

I've been a bit more assertive.

The solution-focused practitioner's task is always to help talk move from the general to the specific, and one way to do this here would be to ask for a recent example of increased assertiveness, a moment when this was evident. The client can then be invited to examine themselves at this moment as closely as possible, from their own perspective and from the perspectives of anyone else who was present. As the character John Bubber said in Stephen Frears's 1992 film, *Hero*, 'We're all heroes if you catch us at the right moment'.

Focusing on a moment: An illustrative sequence

Natalie's difficulties with her mother had been longstanding and had contributed to periods of homelessness. Now Natalie was trying to put her life back together, and improving her relationship with her mother was a part of her preferred future. In response to some instance-seeking questions, she mentioned she had managed to be calmer and more patient recently, and that her mother would have noticed this. The question 'When might your Mum have noticed this do you think?' uncovered an important recent moment.

> *Natalie*: There was a conversation we had yesterday. We were talking about some stuff, and ... I just told her how I'd been feeling and stuff, and then ... At first she was, like, trying to explain to me why she used to act the way she did, and I just listened but I also, I tried to explain that I understood what she was saying and maybe why she said things, but how it still sort of affected me, yeah. And we just talked.
>
> *Guy*: So you did a mixture of explaining things to her and listening to her.
>
> *Natalie*: Yeah.
>
> *Guy*: Ok, so what are you pleased to recall about the way you spoke, the way you explained things to her?
>
> *Natalie*: I'm pleased that I finally ... (*at this moment she became tearful*) ... I'm pleased that I'm finally ... I've finally been able to communicate how I feel, because that's something that I used to find very hard.
>
> *Guy*: This is a big thing that you did yesterday, yeah?
>
> *Natalie*: Yeah. I didn't even realise how big it was until now, until I'm speaking about it. Because I never used to be able to speak to my Mum about a lot of things, I always found it hard to speak to her about things. So ...

Guy: So it was a big thing to communicate how you felt to her.

Natalie was realising how big this moment was for her, and I was simply trying to show that I had heard this. And having heard it, I continued to help Natalie focus on this moment with my next question.

Natalie: Yeah.

Guy: Ok. So what else are you pleased to remember about how you did that?

Natalie: I'm pleased that, erm, I wasn't angry, or I wasn't, like … I didn't feel like I lashed out at her or anything. I just, I was just able to express myself, without like, and I felt relieved afterwards, I felt … just … much better, more positive, yeah.

Guy: Ok, what did that lead to? What effects did that have?

Here I was following Natalie's move into 'afterwards' by asking about the effects of this instance.

Natalie: Well, today, I felt a lot different at work. I feel like, yeah, I don't feel so tense.

Guy: What have you been feeling like instead?

Natalie: I don't know, I haven't really thought about it. I've just been doing my work, and … I feel happier, like positive, yeah …

Guy: Ok, and going back to yesterday, what do you think your Mum noticed about you, the way you were being with her?

Having followed Natalie beyond yesterday's moment, I took her back into it, so that she could consider her mother's perspective.

Natalie: I don't know, I'm hoping that she felt pleased, happy that we had the conversation, yeah.

Guy: Um-hum? Have you noticed any signs already that she does feel like that?

Natalie answered a different question than the one I had asked, about effects on her mother, and I was happy to follow this up.

Natalie: Erm, not yet, because I haven't spoken to her, since yesterday, so …

Guy: So how would you know when you do speak to her? How would you know that she does feel pleased?

Though I have moved into the future, this will soon provide a path back to yesterday's moment.

Natalie: Gosh, that's a hard question … I guess maybe the way that she deals with me, the way that she speaks to me … she's protective all the time, and doesn't give me space. I don't know how to explain it …

Guy: So, what small signs might you notice with your Mum, from this point, if she was to be dealing with you how you wanted her to, and less protective maybe?

Natalie: Maybe, like, allowing me to make decisions sometimes, and if we have conversations and maybe I do come to her and speak to her about my decisions, or what I want to do, then, she'll support me, and if there are things she doesn't agree with, she'll let me know, but not in the way that she used to do, not where it's so like, you have to do this, that sort of stuff, yeah.

Guy: Um-hum, ok, so allowing you to make decisions and perhaps supporting you in things you'd like to do, that you'd talked to her about.

Natalie: Yeah.

Guy: (*now taking the path back to yesterday*) Ok. So were there any signs yesterday with your Mum, in how she responded to you, that were, sort of promising signs that that might come about, in terms of how she reacted to you?

Natalie: Yeah, there were, there were signs.

Guy: What signs were there?

Natalie: Erm … she was listening a lot more.

Guy: Um-hum?

The *um-hum* with the questioning tone acts as a minimal 'What else?'

Natalie: She wasn't, like, constantly, like, just talking, talking, talking and not letting me have, say anything. She was actually listening and, when I was speaking, and, yeah … It made me feel like, like my views did count, like, what I'm saying isn't wrong. There are things that I do know, and, erm, yeah …

Guy: Ok, so she was listening to you, while you were talking.

Natalie: Yeah.

Guy: And what else did you notice in your Mum, that were promising sort of signs, that it will go the way you want it to?

Natalie: Erm, gosh, erm ... (*Lengthy pause*) I can't think of anything else, apart from, yeah ...

By asking 'What else?' until Natalie says she cannot think of anything else, I allow Natalie to decide that she has exhausted the signs in her mother, rather than deciding for her by not asking the question.

Guy: And what are you most pleased to remember about how you did this with your Mum yesterday? What stands out the most for you about what you did?

This question invites Natalie to make a type of summarising statement, of her highlight of this moment. This is a useful way to bring the examination of a sparkling moment to a close.

Natalie: Erm ... I think ... the fact that I wasn't angry, that I was calm about it, and I didn't, I wasn't rude or anything, I was just like, I just said what was on my mind, erm ... yeah.

Guy: And was that difficult at all, to stay calm, while you were saying things that were on your mind? Was that a difficult thing to do, or did it come easily?

Natalie: I don't know. It just came out yesterday. It just, yeah ... I don't know where it came from. It just, I guess it was the time for it, because, like I said, I'd been feeling so frustrated for the past few weeks, so I guess yesterday was just the time when it just felt as if it had to come out.

The last question is a win-win, in that if it were difficult, this amplifies the achievement that Natalie made, and if Natalie recalls it now as easy, then this can underline progress in becoming calmer – it is getting easier – and give Natalie the message that she will be able to be like this again.

Reflections

- A focus on 'what the client is doing that is working' was at the heart of the development of solution-focused practice. This focus was initially channelled through a search for exceptions, with the emphasis later shifting to instances. What is the difference between exceptions and instances?
- What effect would it have on your practice if you thought in terms of one rather than the other?
- Think of a recent achievement of your own. What questions might a solution-focused practitioner ask you in connection with your achievement? How might they help you to talk about it in detail?
- What might be the purpose of asking someone to talk about instances of the preferred future that are already in place and about what they are doing that is working for them?
- One of the most useful ways of eliciting and following up instances is by using scaling questions, which we will be examining in detail in the next chapter. What do you already know about the solution-focused use of a 0 to 10 scale?

6

Bridging the Preferred Future and Its Instances: Scaling Questions

In the second half of the 20th century, psychology ... was ... learning how to bring people up from negative eight to zero but not as good at understanding how people rise from zero to positive eight.

Shelly Gable and Jonathan Haidt (2005)

Introduction

Scaling questions are the most versatile and adaptable tools available to the solution-focused practitioner. They tend to be used in most structured sessions, both initial ones and follow-up, and can also be useful in a wide range of other conversational contexts, for example in supervision, meetings, sports coaching, one-minute conversations in school corridors, in any situation in fact where talking might help progress to occur. Indeed, the whole solution-focused approach resides within its simple 0–10 scale, which provides a bridge between the preferred future and the instances of this already in place; so coming to grasp how solution-focused scaling works is a sure route to understanding the whole approach. And the structure provided by the scale makes it readily accessible to beginning solution-focused practitioners, who frequently find scaling questions the most straightforward way in to using the approach.

As well as being a tool that practitioners find readily useable, scales also tend to be easily understood by clients. Many people will be familiar with the use of 0–10 scales, though mainly as an assessment tool. For example, if you have chronic pain, a health professional is likely to ask you to rate the intensity of your pain between 0 and 10. However, solution-focused practitioners use scales in a quite distinctive manner, to facilitate change-focused talk rather than to assess, and it is important to be clear about the difference. This chapter will provide a detailed explanation of how to use the general progress scale defined by the overall hoped-for outcome for a piece of solution-focused work. It will also look at some of the many other scales that can supplement the general progress scale and at some alternatives to 0–10 numerical scales for younger children. First though, a brief sketch of the development of the use of scaling in solution-focused practice will help to put it into an historical context.

The development of scaling questions

As with so much of the approach, scaling questions had their origins in ideas that clients brought to their sessions with the Milwaukee team. Steve de Shazer regularly explained their beginnings with stories such as this:

> Early in the 1970s, a client claimed to be feeling better. I asked, how much better. She said 'on a scale from 1 to 10, I've gone from 1 to 7'. This happened spontaneously quite a few times before I started initiating their use.[1]

At other times, de Shazer gave the credit, as he came to do increasingly for the approach overall, to his partner Insoo Kim Berg: 'the first scales were used and spontaneously developed by Insoo and her clients' (Norman et al., 1996).

It took some time for scaling to take its place at the heart of solution-focused practice. At first, scaling questions were found to be useful where there was a degree of vagueness, for example involving feeling states such as 'depression' or abstract topics such as 'communication' (de Shazer, 1994, p. 93), where the numbers were seen to make the conversations more concrete or to help clients to 'describe the indescribable' (Berg and de Shazer, 1993, p. 19). Scales are used in this way in one case example in the seminal 1986 paper (de Shazer et al., 1986, p. 213) as a means of measuring progress and also within a homework task. However, scaling did not figure more generally as part of the session format set out in that paper. By the time Eve Lipchik was delineating a number of ways to facilitate solution-focused interviews in 1988, it was more to the fore, scaling sequences taking their place as a 'variation' alongside the more established exception and miracle question sequences (Lipchik, 1988a, p. 113). A year later, associates of the Milwaukee team, Kate Kowalski and Ron Kral, provided perhaps the earliest systematic treatment of the technique (Kowalski and Kral, 1989).

Whichever of the two had first heard a client spontaneously use a scale, de Shazer appears to be justified in saying, 'the whole development of the range of uses of scaling questions comes from watching (Insoo) work' (Norman et al., 1996; see also West, Bubenzer, Smith and Hamm, 1998). Scaling is placed at the heart of the approach for the first time in Insoo Kim Berg's earliest accounts of doing solution-focused therapy with different client populations (Berg, 1991, 1994; Berg and Miller, 1992), by which time the wider potential for scaling had clearly been recognised. Scales were now being used to elicit, define and assess pre-session change, progress towards goals, confidence in change happening, willingness to work to bring change about, motivation and so on.

Scales became so central to the approach, with scaling used as the predominant means of eliciting exceptions or instances, that de Shazer would later say that solution-focused practice was 'just the miracle question and scaling...' (de Shazer and Berg, 1997), while the BRIEF team in London were using 'scales, scales and more scales' (George et al., 1999, p. 31). This proliferation is reflected later in this chapter when we look at some of the variety of scales that can be used, but it also carries its own dangers of complicating matters and moving away from the simplicity that is such a virtue in solution-focused practice. The final development to trace here is one back to simplicity, reflected in Harry Korman's focus on the 'miracle scale' in the multi-authored *More than Miracles* (de Shazer et al., 2007), referred to by de Shazer himself as the 'progress scale' (1997, 1999). It is important to stay focused on what the client wants, and this endeavour is aided by sticking mainly to the scale defined by 10 being the client's hoped-for outcome, and it is to this *general progress scale* and how to use it that I now turn.

The general progress scale: An overview

Whenever you are working with a client towards a hoped-for outcome, it will be possible to set up and use a scale to help them in moving towards this outcome. It is important to remember that by using a scale you are not assessing the client's progress, and that any assessment taking place is being done by the client themselves. What the scale does is to provide the practitioner with the opportunity to ask a series of questions that can enable the client to develop their descriptions of instances and future progress. There are several important stages in using the scale, which I will first summarise before examining each one in more detail.

The starting point is to define the endpoints of the scale so that it makes sense to the client, and this is typically done by saying that 10 represents the realisation of the client's hoped-for outcome, with 0 usually being either the furthest away from 10 the client has been or the furthest away they can imagine being. In short, 0 is some variation of the worst point. The client is then asked at what point on the scale they see themselves now, and any answer above 0 opens the way for a whole range of useful questions related to that point. It is the difference between this number and 0 that the worker is interested in. If the number given is, say, 3 (a not uncommon answer in a first meeting as it happens), then the questions used to focus on this difference will fall into two main groups:

- What tells you that you're at 3 and not 0?
- What have you done that has got you from 0 to 3?

It will be tempting, especially for the solution-focused beginner, to move quickly on, for example, by asking the client what they could do to make progress further up the scale. However, especially where the preferred future has been described in some detail already, it is important to invite the client to describe the progress that has already been made as fully as possible. It is through an increasing awareness of the ways in which they have been able to make progress so far that the client will be able to build on this to make further progress. That said, having elicited a description of progress already made, the worker will then use the scale to reorient the client to the future, and there are two points further up the scale worth asking about.

The outcome represented by 10 might seem to the client like an unattainable ideal or far-off aspiration, and the sense that the hoped-for outcome of the work is achievable can be increased by the establishment of a 'good enough' point:

- While you aspire to a 10, where might be a good enough point to get to, on the way there?

Once this point has been established, future progress can be made to seem even more achievable by focusing on just one point up the scale:

- What would tell you that you'd moved one point further up the scale?

That sets out in general terms how to use a 0–10 scale in a solution-focused fashion. As with the rest of the approach, it is simple but not easy. I shall, therefore, now set out the steps involved in using the scale in greater detail.

The general progress scale: The details

Creating the scale

The scale is most typically defined as being between 0 and 10, but these endpoints are not set in stone, and, in theory at least, any parameters set some way apart can be used. The parameters do not need to be set by numbers either, as we shall see when considering alternatives for children. Some solution-focused practitioners use a 1–10 scale, but my preference is to start from zero, otherwise the client does not have the opportunity to communicate that *nothing* is ok and that they are at their worst point. In the earlier days of the approach, de Shazer experimented with 10 as the worst, or starting point, and 0 as the desired point, reasoning that going downhill was easier than going up (Molnar and de Shazer, 1987). However, having 0 as the worst point is a better fit with how scales are used in an everyday way, and as solution-focused practitioners should always aspire to fit with how people commonly see things, my preference is to move from 0 towards the desired 10.

As practitioners, we also want to use the specific verbal expressions of our individual clients to make our constructions more meaningful to them. A client who wanted more confidence was trying to clarify what the worker meant by asking what he might do the next day if he had it: 'You mean if I had 100 per cent confidence?' His scale was, therefore, later defined as one between 0 per cent and 100 per cent.

Defining the endpoints

The scale has not been fully created until its endpoints have been defined, since asking only 'Where are you now, on a scale from 0 to 10?' is insufficiently clear. It is the defining of 10 and 0 that makes the scale make sense.

Defining 10

This is the endpoint that needs to be defined most comprehensively and clearly, as 0 can then be defined in relation to it. In short, 10 should represent the realisation of whatever the client has said they want from the work – that their 'best hopes', or 'preferred future', have been achieved. This is not an either/or, but is of course saying the same thing, as the preferred future is simply a detailed account of what the realisation of the client's hoped-for outcome would look like. This is how I set up the scale with Sonia (see Chapters 3 and 4):

> Think of a scale from 0 to 10, where 10 is that things are just like you've described, if you woke up tomorrow, able to be happy, anxiety not a problem, so you were full of energy, confident, and you had all that stuff happening for you, that's 10, and 0 is the other end, the furthest you could get away from that...

Defining 0

There are three main ways of defining 0. The two most commonly used are: the worst the problems have been, or the worst they could become. An advantage of the first way is that any answer above 0 opens up the question: 'How have you moved from 0 to that point?' A second advantage is that an answer of 0 does not imply that the problems could not be worse still, which allows for the question: 'How have you stopped things from becoming even worse?' On the other hand, defining 0 as the worst that things could become has the advantage of deterring a client from saying 0 and helping them to see themselves as doing something constructive in their situation:... 'and 0 is that things have so got so bad that you've given up – you don't even get out of bed in the mornings'. It should be noted that however a worker defines the scale and its endpoints, there will always be some occasions when a client defines themselves at 0. This type of situation will be dealt with in the next chapter.

The third way of defining 0 is to relate it to a time when a decision was made to seek help, for example, '0 is when you decided to do something about this', or 'when you made the appointment...'. This was the 0 usually favoured by de Shazer and his colleagues, and it is a good option to consider in contexts where the work is set in motion by the client proactively calling to make an appointment. To have made such a decision and have taken such a step is likely in itself to provide a boost for the client, which might have led to other beneficial actions being taken, one of the possible explanations for the 'pre-session change' referred to in the previous chapter.

Establishing where now

Having clearly defined the scale, the worker next asks the client to say where on the scale they see themselves at present. This is typically straight-forward, though a client may ask what is meant by 'at present':

> *Client 1*: Do you mean today? I've had such a bad morning, so that would be one thing, whereas it's not been quite that bad for the past couple of days.
>
> *Client 2*: I don't know, it's up and down all the time at the moment.

There are no hard-and-fast rules in this situation, and at one level it does not really matter. The purpose of the rating is not to pinpoint with precision where the client is, but to establish some *difference* from the worst point, so that questions can be asked about that difference. This difference should also be current, or at least recent. There seems little point, for example, in a jaded 40-year-old scaling how they were as a hopeful 20-year-old. Any progress needs to be relevant to where the client is now. The above answers clearly indicate recent differences, so responses could be framed in these ways:

> *Worker 1*: So what point would you've said on either of the past couple of days?
>
> *Worker 2*: What point are you when it's up at the moment?

When working with more than one client, the worker will usually ask each person in turn to say where they are on the scale, before asking each in turn to describe some of the differences between their respective points and 0.

Client's self-rating

As stated earlier, the scale is not being used to assess the client but to help them make progress towards their desired outcome. Any assessment is being done by the client who will be rating their own progress entirely subjectively. The number only has meaning for the client and should be accepted by the worker 'fully and literally' (de Shazer, 1997). In his brief paper on 'radical acceptance', de Shazer recounts a story where a client rated herself at 3 to the surprise of the observing team who, having heard how much things had improved, had thought the client must be considerably higher. It turned out that the client believed 4 was the highest point she could reach, and so she was almost there. It can also be tempting when confronted with a client self-rating of 0 to try to argue the client higher up: 'But you managed to get here today, so you must be slightly above 0'. This should be avoided at all costs, as we shall see in the next chapter.

Scales can be used by workers whose role includes assessment, in which case the worker's own rating does become relevant. The adaptation of solution-focused scales within the Signs of Safety approach to child protection work is an example of this (Turnell and Edwards, 1999). A worker might also have to switch roles *within* a piece of solution-focused work, departing from the solution-focused process and instigating an assessment one, for example, when a client appears at risk of self-harm. Scales are likely to be useful here, though the worker will now be rating the client's safety as well as eliciting the client's own views. In such situations, the worker cannot be said to be using a strictly solution-focused approach, as this does not include an assessment component.

The impact on a client of having their own rating accepted should not be underrated. A support worker newly trained in solution-focused practice[2] introduced a scale to a resident in a shared housing scheme, who then said he did not like scaling because workers would challenge his rating of his situation. The worker tried to reassure the resident, who was not convinced until he heard how the worker responded to his rating. When he said that he was at a 3 or 4, his worker responded by asking 'How come? How come you're at 3 or 4 and not 0?' The resident went on to talk about the differences, but not before saying, with a note of satisfaction, 'Oh, you've not told me I'm at a 1'.

Follow-up questions

Any given point on the scale above 0 opens the door to a whole range of potentially useful questions. The questions tend to emerge quite naturally once you are clear that the difference we are interested in is that between the client's point and 0.

Activity: Asking about 3 again

Imagine that your client tells you that they are at 3 on the scale. What questions occur to you that you could ask in response? You have already considered what to ask at this moment, in Chapter 2, so now you need to come up with at least ten questions before you even consider moving up the scale!

As noted in the overview above, questions about the differences between 3 and 0 can be divided into two groups, the first group – 'What tells you that you're at 3 and not 0?' – inviting a description of those differences. It is important to ensure that a comparison with 0 is made within the questions asked. A client who was asked 'What tells you that it's a 2?' proceeded to list all the difficulties he was experiencing. It took the worker a few moments to realise that the client had also heard an unspoken 'and not higher?' and so was answering a different question to the one intended. It is better to spell out exactly what is meant:

* What tells you that you're at that point and not at 0?
* What are you noticing about yourself (or what have you noticed about yourself) now that you're there and not at 0?

A word best avoided is *why*. The question 'Why do you put yourself there and not at 0?' is superficially similar to the two above but can sound quite different. Remember the importance of accepting the client's answer, and note the challenge implicit in the why question, which could convey the message that the worker sees the client at a different point.

A message that the worker does want to convey is that there will be multiple differences, and this can be signalled by using a plural within the question:

* What are the differences between that point and 0?

After the client's first answer, the worker will have a number of options available for the next question. The simplest way to elicit more description is to ask: 'What else is different now that you're at 3?' Repeating this question will help to elicit a list of differences (see Chapter 5). At times though, follow-up questions will be constructed to draw out the detail of a particular difference, before the next 'what else?'

> *Client*: I've been feeling a little more confident recently.
>
> *Worker*: Yeah? In what ways have you been noticing that?

The worker can ask the client to describe a recent, specific time – a sparkling moment – when they felt more confident; use other-person-perspective questions and so on, and in such ways encourage the richest description of each difference articulated. Another means of eliciting more details of progress made is provided by the question: 'What difference has that made?' as any difference mentioned will inevitably have led to others. In Chapter 2, we saw that Michelle had placed herself at 3 on the scale in her first session, where 10 was that she was moving on in her life exactly as she wished to, and 0 the most stuck she had been.

> *Guy*: 3? Ok, so what are the differences that are making it 3 compared to 0?
>
> *Michelle*: Erm, because of the fact that I've come here, the fact that I've moved to Brighton, and that's it.

By ending her answer with '...and that's it', Michelle was ruling 'What else?' somewhat out of bounds. However, I was confident that there would be a lot packed into Michelle's answer, the second part in particular, knowing that this move had been six months previously. Notice the reinforcing at the beginning of my next response – Michelle nodded and said 'yeah' herself after each of the first three checking questions:

> *Guy*: Moving to Brighton, which was about six months ago, yeah? So that's a good step in terms of moving up the scale, yeah? And coming here? Ok. So what effect has it had moving to Brighton? What differences have you noticed that you're pleased to notice since you've moved to Brighton?

Michelle went on to talk in detail about becoming independent of her family and feeling free to make her own decisions, for example, concerning her children's schools.

The other major group of questions to be used about progress up the scale already being made concerns *how* the progress was made, and in particular the client's part in achieving this progress. As we saw in Chapter 5, narrative practitioners call the questions below 'landscape of action' and 'landscape of identity' questions, respectively. Within solution-focused practice, they have been labelled *strategy* and *identity* questions (Iveson et al., 2012, p. 19):

- What have you done that has helped get you up to 3?
- What does that say about you, that you've gone from 0 to 3?

These questions, and their infinite variations, can be asked about the general movement to the point currently reached, as above, or can be attached to a client's specific answers:

Worker: What tells you it's 4 and not 0?

Client: I've been going out more this week.

Worker: Really? How have you managed to do that?

After further exploration of what the client has done to go out more, and of the differences this has made, the worker can go back to the scale, ask 'What else puts you up at 4?', and then once again find questions to build on that answer. And back again. In this way, the scale remains always present in the background for the worker to return to as needed, unobtrusively focusing the conversation and continuing to build the client's 'progressive narrative' (de Shazer, 1991, pp. 92–93).

Example: Staying with 1

Jake, aged 12, and his father met me on the recommendation of Jake's head of year at school. The hoped-for outcome was about Jake becoming able to keep his cool, and Jake and his Dad have both described detailed preferred futures. I have decided to move to a scale, which I ask Jake first. Although Jake's rating is low, and there is little time left in the session, I will resist the temptation to move up the scale. As Jake is not at 0, there is progress to be elicited.

> *Guy*: So, if 10 is you've achieved what you want for yourself from this, and 0 is the worst it's been, where is it now?
>
> *Jake*: It's not really good actually.
>
> *Guy*: Ok, so between 0 and 10? What number would you put it?

Things may not be 'really good', but any number above 0 will give me confidence there is progress to be elicited, however small.

> *Jake*: 1.
>
> *Guy*: 1, ok.
>
> *Jake*: Because I'm not in school at the moment.

Here Jake was saying why he is at 1 and not higher, so I invite him to think on the other side of his number.

> *Guy*: Um-hum? So how come 1 and not 0? What's different to be at 1 and not 0?

Jake: Erm, maybe because zero is a bit too low, because in general, at home I'm trying, because I'm still keeping myself occupied at home.

Guy: Um-hum?

Jake: And I help around the house a bit.

Guy: Um-hum?

Jake: And I still, like, do work, like, I read 50 pages of a book that's above my reading level.

The *um-hums* have been acting as minimal 'What elses'.

Guy: Yeah? Which book?

Jake: And I wrote a review about it.

Guy: Yeah, which book was that?

Jake: *Little Soldier.*

Guy: Wow, you wrote a review?

Jake: A review of the first 50, 40 pages.

Guy: Ok, so you've done that, that sounds really good. Ok, what else? What else have you done to make it 1 and not 0?

There are follow-up questions that I could have asked before my next 'What else?', but time was short and I decided that the best use of it would be to elicit as many discrete aspects of progress as possible. Each detail added strengthened the platform to build from.

Jake: I've been helping my step-mum in the house, like with my younger brother, because, when my step-mum's busy on the phone, he keeps on running to her, crying, wanting something, and instead of her having to say, 'Alright, I'll call back in a second', I'll go and help instead.

Guy: Ok, and earlier you mentioned the washing-up last night...

Jake: Yeah.

Guy: ...so you're helping your step-mum out, you've been doing that, yeah. Ok, what else? What else makes it 1 and not 0?

Jake: Erm... (*pause*) the way I've been, the way I didn't have, I never had to, this morning when I woke up I never had to ask my Mum if she'd make me some breakfast. I got it for myself.

Guy: Right, and what difference did that make?

Jake: Because I'm getting older now and I need to start taking some responsibility for myself and do things for myself sometimes.

This had the flavour of being something that adults would want for a 12-year-old, so next I check if it is something Jake wants too. Jake's answers to this are fairly minimal, but I have at least shown I am interested in Jake's perspective.

Guy: So is that better for you?

Jake: Yes.

Guy: Ok, how's that better for you?

Jake: Erm, it gives me a bit of responsibility in a way, around the house.

Guy: Ok, so that's a few of the things that make it 1, and not 0 ...

Moving up the scale: A good enough point?

My favourite answer to this question came from a woman who was the single mother of three boys, aged 10, 12 and 14. She was at 2 on her scale, where 10 was defined as the day after the miracle, the miracle question having been used to facilitate a preferred future description. Having plugged away at the differences between 2 and 0, I asked: 'So, given that you probably don't expect miracles to happen in real life, where would you settle for on the scale?' The woman pondered: 'Where would I settle for? Well, if I could just get to 5, and hold it there until they were all 16 and cleared off,[3] then that would do!' Her answer – which was said with a twinkle in her eye – conveyed her feet-on-the-ground quality, which I find is actually quite common when people are trusted to consider what they want from seeing a helping professional. A frequently asked question is whether people express unrealistic hopes when asked what they want, and while this has to be allowed as a possibility, the opposite usually seems to be the case. The vast majority of people place their good enough point around the 7–8 mark. The occasional higher answer can be responded to in an encouraging way, as I tried to with Sonia:

Guy: Where would you settle for on the scale?

Sonia: I want to get to 10.

Guy: You want to go all the way to 10, that's fantastic! Is there a point that would feel was a good place to get to, as you were still aiming at 10, a good point to have arrived at?

Sonia: I suppose 9 wouldn't be too bad!

So far, the examples have all concerned people being at, or aiming at, fixed points on the scale, yet it is not uncommon for people to talk about a range: 'I've been moving between 3 and 5 this week'. If a client spontaneously talks in this way, then it makes sense to cooperate and ask about ranges in return.

When asked what point he was at on the scale in his third session, Dean had said he had been caught on a good day, so it was 'about a 6 or 7 – obviously it's dependent on what the day's been like'. I took this into account when I asked about 'good enough':

> *Guy*: So, let's think about this. Taking your point, Dean, things fluctuate and you have good days and not so good days, so what would be a reasonable range? Between what two numbers would be a good enough place to be?
>
> *Dean*: I'd say at its worst at the moment, it would go to a 5 and I'd still consider that acceptable, and 7 would be really good.
>
> *Guy*: 7 would be good – would you expect to get higher than 7, or would 7 be...?
>
> *Dean*: No, I'd be more than happy with between 5 and 7.

One point up the scale

Establishing a 'good enough' point says in effect, 'Let's not worry about getting all the way to 10', and the sense that change is possible can be increased by breaking it down further: 'Let's not worry about getting all the way to the good enough point at the moment, let's look at one point up the scale'.

Activity: Asking about one point up the scale

Imagine you have elicited a rich description from your client of what 3 is like in comparison to 0, and of what they have done to get there. How might you start to ask about 4?

The most natural question for many would be along the lines of 'What do you need to do to get there?' This is understandable, as it certainly seems as if something needs to be done and that the client is there to see the worker to work out what this might be. However, this type of question has a number of difficulties attached to it. Imagine for a moment how a person who has gone to the extent of seeking help from a professional person might respond if asked 'What could you do to move to a 4?' On reflection, the most reasonable answer is 'I don't know', and a little more reflection suggests that this might quickly be followed up with 'You tell me!' Therefore, this question can all too easily accentuate any feelings of stuckness the client has arrived with and place the worker in an advice-giving role, which in turn can lead to feelings of stuckness on the part of the worker. Asking such questions creates a lot of pressure on that particular conversation to sort out whatever needs doing 'there and then'. However, solution-focused practice involves enabling various possibilities to emerge, rather than following an action planning process that presupposes that it can be known for sure what to do in advance and so looks to lay down a number of fixed steps. The risks inherent in action planning are beautifully articulated in a frequently quoted passage by Joseph Campbell (you saw the italicised sentence already in Chapter 4):

> If you see your path laid out in front of you – Step one, Step two, Step three – you only know one thing ... it is not your path. *Your path is created in the moment of action.* If you can see it laid out in front of you, you can be sure it is someone else's path. That is why you see it so clearly. (quoted in Nelson, 2010, p. 278)

A second issue arising from asking the client what they need to do is that it places the worker in an instrumental position. The suggestion being made to the client is that they need to do something, and really it is no business of the worker whether the client does something or not. An argument for a non-instrumental position was put forward in Chapter 4.

So, the solution-focused practitioner asks the same types of question about one point up the scale as about any other aspect of the preferred future. The focus is on what it would, or might, be like rather than on the process of getting there. And once again, the questions are conditional, *if* being used rather than *when*. The worker does not know what will happen in the future and so does not try to subtly influence the client's beliefs by asking what they *will* notice *when* they have moved a point higher.

- And if you were to move a point higher, what might you notice?
- What might you be doing/thinking/feeling differently?
- Who else would notice, do you think?

* What would be the first small sign that would tell them you were a point higher?

There is nothing set in stone about asking about *one* point higher. The idea is to help the client to think of the smallest signs they might notice; and the lower down the scale, the smaller the difference that might be used. For instance, asking Jake in the above example about a point higher would be to ask him about a point, 2, twice as high as he is at present. Secondly, it is always worthwhile trying to match the client's way of answering. As the resident mentioned above was at '3 or 4' on the scale, the worker went on to ask what '4 or 5' might look like. Another option would have been to ask: 'How would you know you were at a definite 4?'

Returning to the scale in follow-up

Having set up and used the general progress scale in a first session, the worker can return to it in all subsequent sessions, in this way helping to mark further progress and to create a thread that connects the sessions together. The guidance offered above will also be useful when using the scale in follow-up, though there are other issues to consider relating to the place of the scale in the typical first and follow-up session structures. These will be covered in Chapter 8, when we look at 'putting it all together'.

Scale variations

The general progress scale probably accounts for more than 90 per cent of the scaling that we do. In this section, I will describe some useful variations, though this list is anything but exhaustive. Once you are clear about the basic solution-focused structure, the only limit to the different scales you can construct will be your imagination (and your client's).

Specific sub-scales

The word *general* is being used to describe the progress scale to convey the notion of moving towards the whole of what the client wants from the work. There are also occasions when it is useful to focus on specific aspects within the whole. Ian wanted to get his life back on track after years of mental health difficulties and drug use and was describing how he had managed to get himself to 3 on his general progress scale. He suddenly announced that a particular concern was his relationship with his son, Hugh, and both to avoid a shift into problem talk and recognising the importance of this issue, I immediately introduced another scale:

> If we were to have a scale just for that, Ian, where 10 is that you've got the relationship with Hugh that you'd like to have, and 0 is the opposite, where are you now on that scale?

Ian was lower on that scale, between 1 and 2, but simply being enabled to voice this was sufficient for Ian to feel that his concern had been acknowledged, and he was able to list several improvements between him and Hugh 'because it was at a 0, you know, or lower!'.

At times, one or two specific sub-scales will be triggered by a client's comment such as Ian's above, whereas at other times the work will be organised around a series of separate scales more or less from the outset. A typical trigger for such 'multi-scaling' (George et al., 1999, pp. 33–34; Iveson et al., 2012, pp. 95–96) is when a client feels overwhelmed by an assortment of difficulties, feels that each of them needs facing, but is too weighed down to know how or where to begin. Debbie was falling out with her partner, troubled about her ability to control her feelings of rage, worried about her parenting and had difficulties in her relationships with her parents and step-parents. Having elicited an overall hope of 'moving on, in a balanced way', I created four sub-scales, by asking Debbie for a word or phrase to denote 10 in each of the problem areas listed, and calling 0 the opposite of that on each one. I asked about existing progress on each scale and then for signs of a point higher on each. This untangling helped Debbie to turn to a general 'moving on in a balanced way' scale and have a sense of her movement overall. The work was a long way from being done but the multi-scaling had provided a means of lifting Debbie (and me) out of the morass of problems, thereby getting the work underway.

Confidence scales

These should not be confused with a general progress scale used with a client whose best hopes are to become more confident. The confidence referred to here is confidence in desired change taking place or being maintained. One of the earliest scales mentioned in the literature was a confidence scale (de Shazer, 1986), and there are many other examples to be found (Berg and de Shazer, 1993; Berg, 1994; de Shazer, 1994). In part they have been used to gather information about the client in order to inform decisions about tasks to give the client (de Shazer and Berg, 1992). This means that in our more-or-less task-free version of solution-focused practice, we use confidence scales less often, but they are still useful in at least three ways. First, they open the way to identity-related questions. The worker can ask a client at 6 on a confidence scale, where '10 is you know for sure that you'll get to your good enough point, and 0 is you know for sure that you won't':

> 6, ok, good. What is it that you know about yourself that puts you up at a 6, and not lower?

These 'self-knowledge' questions can be supplemented by similar questions eliciting the perspectives of significant others. Modesty often means that people find it easier to list what close friends or family members would say about their qualities. The question

> Of all the people who know you, who would have the most confidence in your ability to make these changes?

can be followed up by:

> What is it they know about you, what qualities do they know you have that gives them that amount of confidence in you?

Secondly, the confidence scale can be a useful check on the achievability of a particular contract. A low rating might prompt the questions 'Are we working towards the right thing? Is it achievable?' A positive answer enables similar questions to the above: 'How do you know you can get there?' A negative one suggests a need to re-contract: 'What else might tell you that our work has been useful?' This might turn out to be coping with the situation rather than resolving it (Ratner et al., 2012, p. 119).

Thirdly, when a good enough point has been reached, usually in a follow-up session, this does not necessarily mean that the work is done, as the client might not be sufficiently confident that they can maintain the progress. In this case, the work simply shifts from the general progress scale to a confidence scale. The work is then done when the client is at a good enough point on the confidence scale.

The 'progress through the work' scale

This is a minor variation of the general progress scale that can be very useful in later follow-up sessions, especially if the work appears to be stuck or drifting (Turnell and Hopwood, 1994, pp. 68–73).[4] The progress is related directly to the work, so that 10 is defined as 'the work here is done and we can say goodbye to each other' and 0 is 'how things were when we first met'. The shift to this scale, through redefining the endpoints in this way and then continuing to use it as the main scale from that point onwards, helps to keep both client and worker focused on the end of the work. It also confirms an expectation that there will be progress during the work, while at the same time allowing for the possibility that the work might be seen to be done even though the client has not met all their original hopes from it. For some people, there is a growing realisation that talking to a solution-focused worker (or any helping professional) will only go so far in helping desired changes to happen, and 'progress' might include an accommodation to this. In this way, the client's sights are lowered to what for them is a more realistic 10.

Coping scales

Another similar shift that can take place is one that was referred to in the discussion of confidence scales above, when sights are reset to coping with a situation rather than resolving it. New scales can be created accordingly, as we shall see in Chapter 7, where we will come across coping scales.

Scaling with children

Children and young people typically like using scales, often finding their concreteness refreshing in comparison with the sometimes abstract and adult nature of words. In my experience, children aged 8 or 9 upwards are usually able to understand and use the simple 0–10 numerical scale quite happily, but for younger children, alternative means of representing progress can be helpful. Fortunately, there are plenty of alternatives. Many of these can be drawn onto a piece of paper, flipchart or white board, and having the child do the drawing is a useful way of gaining and maintaining their interest. The mantra of 'keep things simple' prompts the drawing of mountains and ladders on which the child can draw themselves at the point they have reached on their 'climb' towards their desired point at the top. On the other hand, elaborate pictures of stepping stones across a river or trains arriving at a series of railway stations might better suit the keen artist. Utilising the child's interests to form the scale allows the worker to give rein to their creativity. Remembering that the 8-year-old girl he was working with was a keen swimmer, one creative worker[5] drew a picture of a sea between two islands, Unhappyland and Happyland, and asked the girl to draw herself, showing how far she had swum from the first island to the second. They then wrote a list, next to the swimming girl, of all the things that had been helping her to swim that far.

Using movement is another alternative. One corner of a room to the opposite corner is simple to use, and a child can walk along it or place their chair at the point they have reached. Objects can be useful, such as cut-out footprints to lay on the floor, or a range of faces from the most smiley to the most gloomy. Objects found in a room can also be utilised, as happened in my work with two warring children, Chantelle and Jack, and their mother. Having used a 0–10 scale with Chantelle, aged 9, and suspecting this might not be understood by her 5-year-old brother, I asked Chantelle if she had any ideas about how I could ask Jack the same thing in a way he would understand. Fortunately, we were in a room in a health centre, in which there was a children's height measure attached to the wall. Chantelle suggested using that, and Jack moved the measure up – not very high – to show how much better he felt about things. Chantelle then moved it herself to demonstrate her scale again. In our next meeting, as the children's mother was trying to explain how things had become better between the two, Chantelle, pointing at the measure, asked: 'Can I use that please?' She walked to the measure and pointed, 'It's been that good', and asked her mother what she thought. Her mother thought it was a little higher, prompting Chantelle to say it had 'sometimes been a 9'. Jack then used the measure to show his rating of progress since we had last met.

Scales can also provide an ongoing and easy term of reference, enabling ultra-brief but still useful interchanges. A teacher (Everett, 2005) had used a scale in a conversation with a secondary school pupil, following which they had a number of 'follow-up sessions' which took place as they passed each other in the corridor. '6 today, sir' – 'Excellent, keep it up!' was a typical example!

A warning

People, children and adults, do tend to like scales, but here is a story for anyone who is liable to become too attached to good ideas. A rather feisty woman from a tough part of town arrived for her third session and, before I had uttered a word, said: 'I've had a **** awful week, and if you start asking me any of those **** questions about numbers, I'll throttle you!' If we listen hard enough (and sometimes we do not have to listen that hard) to our clients, we will hear when they let us know not to use certain solution-focused techniques and want us to do something different!

Reflections

- What do you like about scaling questions?
- How and where might you use scaling in your work?
- Think back over your contact with your clients (service users, patients) over the past week or so. Where might the use of a scale have been helpful?
- What would you do if someone said they were at 0? It is difficult to ask 'What tells you that you are at X and not 0?', when X is 0. If you are thinking that this was not addressed in this chapter, then you are right. Answers to this question will be the main concern of Chapter 7.
- If 10 is that you have acquired the knowledge and understanding about the solution-focused approach that you would want to from reading a general textbook about it, and 0 is where you were before you started reading this, where are you now?
- What are you noticing that is different about yourself, now that you are there, compared to when you started reading? What else?
- What might let you know that you were climbing higher up the scale, as you are reading the next chapter or two?

7

Acknowledgement and Possibility: Coping Questions and More

In the middle of winter, I at last discovered that there was in me an invincible summer.

Albert Camus (1952)

Introduction

So what might you do if your client tells you that they are at 0 on the scale? In her account of sequences of solution-focused questions, Lipchik (1988a, p. 117) says that 'the construction of solutions…is greatly facilitated when the clients feel their complaints are accepted as stated and that they are being understood' and that, therefore, 'there are times when focusing on exceptions and potential solutions could prevent the necessary fit from being established and maintained', where by 'fit' she is referring to the collaborative process between client and worker. Different sequences are required, which according to Lipchik were beyond the scope of her chapter. The aim of this chapter is to fill this gap by suggesting ways of responding and continuing solution-focused conversations when clients tell you that they are at 0 or find other means of indicating they are in 'the middle of winter', to use Camus's expressive phrase. The ideas generated will also be useful for those times when clients are feeling stuck, immobilised perhaps by the weight of their problems; when strong negative emotions are being expressed; and in those follow-up meetings when the client responds to 'What's better?' by reporting that nothing is better, the situation is the same, or worse.

Activity: 0 on the scale

Imagine you have created a 0–10 scale with your client, who proceeds to tell you they are at 0 and perhaps goes on to explain at some length why they are at 0. How might you respond? How might your responses continue to establish and maintain a collaborative solution-focused process between you and your client, to use Eve Lipchik's words?

The scope of this chapter

I am using the example of 0 on the scale as a way in to discussions about how to respond in these most difficult situations, though remember the point made in the previous chapter, the whole solution-focused process is contained within the scale. The ideas in this chapter can be generalised and transferred into any context when someone is feeling at their worst, stuck or overwhelmed by their problems. I will begin with the most essential part of any response, which is to *listen*. However, listening by the worker only becomes a useful activity when the client becomes aware that he or she has been listened to, which requires that the worker *acknowledge* the client's difficulties, so that the client feels heard. In solution-focused practice, the worker, always mindful of the focus on movement in the client's desired direction, will try to acknowledge in such a way that leaves open and suggests possibilities for change, and we will examine ways of maintaining this *both/and* position. One way is to draw upon a powerful set of questions collectively known as *coping questions*, and I will focus on their use, alongside other questions which can be asked about clients' constructive actions in the present. Then once it is realised that the client is saying, at least implicitly, that they are at 0 'at the moment', questions about the *past*, when they were higher up the scale for example, and the *future*, in which they are moving up the scale, come into play. Brief examples will be given throughout the chapter, with one case being presented in more detail, to illustrate these ideas. A couple of useful ways of using scales in situations of great difficulty will bring the chapter towards its close.

Listening (revisited)

When a client says they are at 0, we do not invite a description of this point, notwithstanding the practice of eliciting description set out in the previous chapter. The essential aspect there was the description of the difference between the client's point and 0. When the client is at 0, there is no difference, and to ask for a description would be to invite problem talk, which the solution-focused worker has no wish to do. Sometimes, of course, a client will proceed to explain their answer of 0 of their own accord, and then, and at any time that a client is talking about their difficulties, it is, first and foremost, incumbent on the worker to listen.

In Chapter 2, we introduced the idea of 'listening with a constructive ear' (Lipchik, 1988b), and it is all the more important to listen in this way when the client is talking about their problems. We listen for exceptions to the problems; for how the client is getting through them, in terms of both what they are doing and the strengths they are drawing upon; for what they want instead; and for how they would start to notice they were coming out the other side. What we hear with our constructive ears we can then ask about.

Acknowledgement...

Before the worker starts to ask questions, the client needs to know that the worker has heard and appreciated the extent of the difficulties they are going through. Therefore, the worker needs to find a fitting way to acknowledge, both verbally and non-verbally, what the client is communicating. The non-verbal aspect of acknowledgement will be in the worker's tone, pacing and physical expression, and it is not possible to prescribe how these should be, as they will have to fit how the client is at any given time.

So things are incredibly tough for you at the moment...

The verbal content will tend to involve generalised words, such as *tough*, as echoing the specific problem words of the client can have an undesirable reinforcing effect. For example, by responding with 'So you're feeling really insecure at the moment, you're not able to go out, or even to make contact with anyone', the worker might only be digging the holes of insecurity and isolation deeper with the client. At the same time, the worker must show full acceptance of where the client is and not be tempted to suggest that things are any different than the client is saying. It can be tempting to say, in a misguided attempt to help the client see that things are not quite as bad as they first thought, that they must be at least 1 on the scale because, for example, 'you got here today'. Such practice has been deemed 'solution-forced' rather than solution-focused (Nylund and Corsiglia, 1994) and seriously risks damaging the relationship with the client, who is likely to form the impression that the worker does not wish, or is not able, to hear how bad things are.

... and possibility

Yet the art of the approach involves drawing upon a 'both/and' position (Lipchik, 1993) to convey the hearing and acceptance of how bad things are, while simultaneously keeping open the possibility of change. 'Acknowledgement and possibility' has been described as the cornerstone of the approach (Butler and Powers, 1996, p. 229), the idea originating with the American therapist Bill O'Hanlon (1993; O'Hanlon and Beadle, 1996) who encourages us to have one foot in acknowledgement and the other in possibility at all times (personal communication).

Activity: Acknowledgement and possibility

Consider again the acknowledgement 'So things are incredibly tough for you at the moment...' and note how it also allows for possibility, and the words that are doing this work.

Adding the words 'at the moment' is not the same as telling the client that things will improve – 'cheer up, things can only get better' – which would be both crass and belittling of the client's predicament. It accepts how it is here and now and also conveys, quietly and respectfully, that it is unlikely to have always been like this, or that it always will be in the future, which simply reflects the reality of the situation. The sense of possibility will be increased when the worker starts to add questions to the acknowledgements. Questions will flow from what the worker's constructive ear hears, as well as from the implications of 'at the moment' stated above, and I will look at questions focused on the present, past and future in turn. It remains important for the worker not to force matters or to push the client towards possibility. Pacing is key, and the worker will also need to offer continuing acknowledgement amidst the questions, for just as long as the client needs this.

Coping questions

Whether or not the worker has heard the client say anything explicitly about surviving or coping with their difficulties, this will be implicit at the very least. Narrative therapists talk about 'double listening', which is similar to listening with a constructive ear, except that it includes listening for what is not being said, the 'absent but implicit' (White, 2000). While this risks moving beneath the surface of the client's words and looking for hidden meanings there, it is probably unarguable, including by the client, that the client is 'keeping going' in some way, even if they had not been thinking of themselves as doing this until this moment. So, a solution-focused acknowledgement will rarely have a full stop after it, but almost always a comma, after which will typically follow a coping question:

Things sound so tough at the moment, how are you keeping going?

Coping questions were first mentioned in the solution-focused literature in Berg's early accounts of using the approach with particular client groups, people with alcohol problems (Berg and Miller, 1992) and families at risk of breakdown (Berg, 1991, 1994). Ways of responding in situations of extreme difficulty had not figured much in published work prior to this, and a possible explanation may lie in the approach moving beyond the therapy room into contexts where crises and serious difficulties were more common and required appropriate responses. There are many ways of asking coping questions, often following an acknowledgement:

- That situation sounds pretty overwhelming – how are you getting by?
- What is it that you do that helps you to get through?
- What are you doing to look after yourself in this difficult situation?
- That sounds really tough – how are you managing to hang on in there?

Ironically, given the generic name of 'coping questions', my own experience is that using the word *coping* can sometimes cause difficulties:

Client: What do you mean, how am I coping? I'm not coping! Haven't you heard what I'm telling you?!

My own preference is, therefore, to use alternative wordings than 'How are you coping?' or 'How do you cope?'. Even then, there will still be some wordings that do not work for a particular client, so you need to be prepared to reword questions until they fit. The onus is on the solution-focused practitioner to cooperate with the client's way of talking and not vice versa. It is worth gently pushing away with this type of question, beyond some commonly heard answers:

Worker: How are you managing to keep going?

Client: I'm not sure I am. It feels like I'm grinding to a halt.

Worker: So how are you getting by? How have you managed not to come to an absolute standstill?

Client: I really don't know.

Worker: How do you think?

Client: You just have to, don't you?

Worker: Well, some people don't manage to, so how are you doing it?

Client: I suppose I'm taking each day as it comes.

Worker: Ok. What are you doing to get through each day? What did you do that was helpful yesterday?

My experience matches that of Berg and Miller (1992, p. 89), who found that 'coping questions are often successful in gently challenging the client's belief system and her feelings of hopelessness while, at the same time, orienting her toward a sense of a small measure of success'. It is important to note the words 'gently' and 'small' in this quote. There is a need to be cautious, which leads to my next point.

Pacing

The worker is always looking for the balance between acknowledgement and possibility that fits for the client. It is a question of finding the right *pace* to go at. It is important to pay attention to the continuous feedback coming from the client about this (Lipchik, 1994). A couple were attending their first meeting with me, having been referred by their family doctor. When I asked them what their best hopes were, they started to explain how they had been forced to leave their home town due to the violence they had been subjected to and further threatened with. It was a horrendous story, which I responded to with a mixture of acknowledgement, sympathy and coping questions, before returning to what they wanted from coming. They did not respond to the latter question, but continued to detail what had happened, and it became increasingly clear both how awful their experience had been and the corresponding extent of their resources which had enabled them to survive it. This pattern continued for the first part of the meeting, during which I offered further invitations to the couple to consider their hoped-for outcome from the work, which they declined each time, continuing with their account instead. Eventually, I decided not to ask any more about their hopes and concentrated for the rest of the meeting on how they had survived their experience with their family intact. As we finished, the couple thanked me for listening to their story, as this had been the first time they had had the chance to tell it in full. A week later, the couple were able to relate their hopes, which concerned their teenage son's emotional state, and this second meeting followed a typical first session structure. I should stress that this was a most unusual occurrence, as even when a client arrives for a first meeting feeling desperate, causing the movement towards their 'best hopes' to be careful and slow, it is almost always possible to form a contract based around a hoped-for outcome. What was distinctive about this case was that the couple's circumstances had meant they had not been able to tell their story to anyone else up to that point. What happened in the first meeting, therefore, actually fitted with one of the original brief therapy precepts, which was that if something was not working 'do something different' (de Shazer and Berg, 1995). It was a different experience for the couple to relate their problem story, whereas in all likelihood, most clients arriving for their first session have already done so at length elsewhere.

The most straightforward way for the worker to go at the pace of the client is simply to ask the client. Steve wanted to regain his sense of self and, initially finding it hard to imagine this happening, was helped into his desired tomorrow by the miracle question. Describing the differences he would notice in his relationship with his two children, tears suddenly filled his eyes and he paused. Also affected by the poignancy of the moment, I waited for a minute or so, before asking gently: 'Is it ok if I ask you more about this now?' It seemed that the question and its delivery served to acknowledge the emotion evoked in Steve, as well as to assist me in my pacing. Steve nodded and I continued to help him in his description.

Acknowledgement within the question

I said earlier that it is important to acknowledge just how hard it is for the client before launching into asking questions, yet it is possible to acknowledge within the question itself, as the above example shows. Another example came in the second session with Michelle (Chapter 2), when, after she had stressed how scary it had been to go out on her own, I asked: 'How did you get through the scariness, to actually do it?' Coping questions also contain a good amount of acknowledgement on their own, which can be amplified by their wording, together with the worker's tone:

How on earth did you manage to get through all that?

Responding to a problem statement in terms of the client's preferences is another form of acknowledgement that simultaneously invites the client to look forwards:

Client 1: I've lost the ability to think positively at the moment.

Worker 1: And that's something you'd like to regain?

Client 2: I've been down for so long. I'm always miserable and I'm fed up of it.

Worker 2: Sure, you don't want to be like that.

Using coping questions as and when

There is not a particular place where coping questions fit into the solution-focused process, and the worker should be ready to use them at any time and during any question sequence. In this example, I was embarking on the contracting process with a mother of two young children, one of whom had severe intellectual impairment and associated behaviour problems. Though I am joining with the client's humour, the coping questions are there all the same.

Guy: Ok, so what are your best hopes then, from coming here?

Client: That I don't kill him!

Guy: How have you managed to not kill him so far?

Client: erm ...I think Prozac and reserves of patience.

Guy: Reserves of patience?...What, that you...

Client: Yeah...I take a deep breath and take a step back.

Guy: Is that patience that you knew you had or have you found out that you've ... ?

Client: No, I knew I had.

Guy: You knew you had.

Client: Yeah, yeah.

Guy: That's the sort of person you are, is it?

Client: Yeah, I've got a very difficult mother.

Guy: Right, so you've had practice at being patient?

Client: Yeah, I've had practice at being patient, yeah.

Guy: Right, ok.

Client: So I can take a deep breath, and I can take a step back, but it's beginning to wear thin.

Guy: Um-hum, so it's something else that's needed. Well, I guess you do other things as well to cope, and you want something else.

This client had previously described her feelings of quiet desperation and of being a failure as a mother, yet this has now been joined by her patience, which has become a real presence in the room since I took the opportunity offered by the client's jokey 'That I don't kill him!' response.

Preferred ways of coping

A worry is sometimes raised about ways of coping seen to be harmful or potentially harmful, such as drinking, taking drugs or cutting. There is also the possibility that a survivor of abuse, for example, might be coping in more internalised ways that can be harmful, such as dissociating, self-blaming, or keeping the abuse a secret. Follow-up questions can be asked to elicit preferred ways of coping, such as, 'Are you happy with that way of coping?' and 'How would you like to see yourself coping?' (Lethem, 1994, p. 60).

Coping questions focus the client on what they are doing that is helpful to them in the present, as do two other types of question that we will mention before shifting our attention to the past and then the future.

Stopping it from getting worse

If 0 has been defined as the worst that the problem has been or as how it was at the time the client decided to seek help, then by answering 0 the client is not saying that it could not become worse still. In these cases the worker can ask questions of the type 'How are you stopping it from becoming worse?' or 'What are you doing that stops you going to a minus 1?' Some care might be needed though, especially if 0 has been defined as the worst things could be. Becoming worse has been ruled out by this definition, and so the client might feel unheard, or tricked even, if asked how they have not gone below 0. Outside of scaling, however, this is often a useful way to frame questions in the more difficult situations, for example in a follow-up session when a client has reported things becoming worse. In this case it is likely that the client will be too preoccupied with the worsening of the problem to have considered any constructive actions they had taken. The worker can rectify this by asking: 'How come things haven't got worse still?' and 'What did you do to arrest the slide?' By way of acknowledgement, the idea of asking how come a situation is not worse probably originates with Eve Lipchik (1988c), though her sequences which then invite descriptions of the situation at its worst have not found their way into contemporary solution-focused practice.

Working close to the problem: Exception-seeking

In Chapter 5, I described the shift from exceptions to instances, which took place as solution-focused practitioners began to work further away from the problem and became organised more around what the client wanted. However, times remain when the client is so focused on the extent of their difficulties that the solution-focused practitioner needs to revert to work closer to the problem (Iveson et al., 2012, p. 64). Sue's hopes were that she and her 16-year-old daughter, Libby, could live happily together, while Libby, who said this was not possible, would only go as far as hoping for a little less arguing. They both placed themselves at 0 on the scale.

> *Guy*: How come you're still together at the moment?
>
> *Sue*: I don't know, it's on the verge of splitting up I think.
>
> *Guy*: How have you managed to make sure it's not split up, up to now?
>
> *Sue*: Because I'm the one that's trying to... I think if...
>
> *Libby*: The only reason it's not split up at the minute is that I can't find anywhere else to go, because I'm only 16, I haven't got any money to

get a flat, and my sister, she either stays there or she goes in a home, she hasn't much choice. So that's the only reason we're together.

Guy: Some young people end up going into a home, how come that's not happened with you?

Sue: Because I'm determined I want it to work.

After a few further coping questions, which were not engaging Libby in particular, I decided to look for exceptions.

Guy: Libby, for this meeting not to be a waste of your time, you said there needed to be a little less arguing?

Libby: Mmm.

Guy: Ok. At what moments have there been a little less arguing in the past month or two?

Libby: When we're on our own. When we're not all stuck together, that's the only time when there's really not any arguing.

Guy: What about you and your Mum, when there's just you and your Mum? What's it like when there's less arguing between you two?

Libby: There isn't any. We're always arguing and snapping at each other. There's not really any time when we're not arguing.

One of the advantages of working with more than one person is that there is more chance that someone will have noticed some progress, or exceptions in this case (Shennan, 2003a, p. 42). I turned from Libby to Sue.

Guy: Have you noticed any times when there's been less arguing between you?

Sue: Yeah. I don't think we argue all the time. We've been on our own together this morning and we've had a laugh and we've got on ok.

Guy: Ah-hah?

Sue: Well, I thought we did, but obviously not.

Libby: It wasn't so bad this morning.

Guy: What were you having a laugh about?

Sue: It was about cards, and what her boyfriend had done and things like that.

Guy: Um-hum, and before this morning? When did you last notice before this morning when you weren't arguing?

Sue: Last night, Libby's boyfriend was round and we were ok then. I suppose there was someone else there, perhaps that made a difference, I don't know.

Shortly after, Sue rated her confidence of change at 5 and Libby at 3. They had the two further sessions that were available given the agency limits, some modest progress was made, and the family remained together.

Going into the past

So far the suggested questions – about coping, stopping things becoming worse, and exceptions – have all been situated in the present, or at least in the most immediate past. It can also be useful to go a little further back. As has been mentioned, by answering 0, the client is only stating how it is at that moment.

Worker: Can you tell me, when were you last higher up the scale, even a little bit?

Client: Well, it was higher last week, I guess. It was probably a 1 or a 2 before the weekend.

Worker: What was different then?

Client: I was with people I suppose – I went into Connect (*a day centre*).

Worker: What difference did that make to you?

Client: I don't know, took my mind off things I suppose...

Such a sequence of questions can help the client to recall aspects of themselves that have become submerged under layers of difficulty. Clients who are finding it hard to envisage being able to find a way through their current difficulties, or even to survive them, may need to be invited further back still and asked to recall how they overcame other difficult times in their lives. We will see a startling example of the potential effectiveness of this shortly, but before this let us shift forward in time.

Going into the future

If all we know is that the client is at 0 at this moment, then this also does not mean that it will always stay that way. In fact, at these moments we return to our fundamental assumption, that if a person is talking with us, then they must be hoping that something will come from this, which in this case can be translated into the client retaining hope of moving up the scale. But this hope may be hanging on a slender thread, or buried beneath the weight of problem, and just as in the previous chapter I stressed the importance of not moving up the scale too quickly, it is important not to rush hastily to future-focused questions. Being encouraged to dwell on the fact that they are keeping going in some ways, and on how they are doing this, is likely to increase the client's sense that moving up the scale is possible. The worker can also help by being tentative and low-key, and by asking about only a small degree of change. The very fact of the worker asking about future progress conveys possibility, and at the same time, it needs to feel achievable to the client. A useful principle is to ask about smaller differences the lower a client is on the scale. One point up might seem a huge leap to someone at 0. It may be more sensible to ask about a half-point, or to leave numbers out altogether.

> And if things were to be a tiny bit better, what might you notice about yourself?

Usually, the future being described in solution-focused conversations is a very near one, tomorrow, or the next few days and, as the work progresses, perhaps the weeks or months ahead. However, just as going back to a time when people overcame serious difficulties can evoke dormant resources, so leaping forward, perhaps several years, can give someone a rest from their present problems and open up possibility in a different way. A person who cannot see change happening by tomorrow might feel differently about many years ahead. Yvonne Dolan (1991, p. 36) created her 'older, wiser self' approach for empowering survivors of sexual abuse, whereby she would invite a client to imagine that they have 'grown to be a healthy, wise old woman', who could then offer advice to their younger self. This has been adapted by John Henden (2008, pp. 143–144), who asks his suicidal clients his 'Wise Old You' question:

> Just imagine you are much older and wiser than you are now, say 70 or 80 (or if a teenager, 25 or 26!). What advice would you give to you now

about how best to get through this difficult time/sort things out for yourself/get more control over the situation?

Case example: The family who stayed together

This example comes from my time as a social worker, working with families to prevent young people coming into care. John and Linda had four children, Miranda, aged 15; Rachel, 14; Matt, 11; and Joe, 6. They had contacted the department because of the severe difficulties they were having in managing Rachel's behaviour. At the time an experimental service had been set up involving the duty team and the family support team in which I worked, whereby families could be offered appointments quickly, rather than having to wait for a full assessment and possible allocation to an individual social worker, typically a lengthy process. A duty worker and family support team worker experienced in using solution-focused practice saw families jointly for up to three sessions. In their first session, John, Linda and Rachel each stated their 'best hopes' slightly differently though they all revolved around improvements in family relationships, and their scale ratings were at 1, 0, and 0 to 1, respectively. Notwithstanding the low ratings and occasional tension in the room, John and Linda were encouraged that Rachel had come and joined in the session, which had surprised them, and they were keen to arrange a second session. However, a week later, John called to say that something had arisen at work, which meant that he could not attend and so Linda and Rachel could not get to the office either. An appointment was arranged for two weeks later, but on that morning a message was left to say that Rachel would not get in the car, so they were not coming. I later telephoned and spoke to Linda, who told me the situation had deteriorated, she had been signed off work with stress by her doctor, and they were on the verge of asking that Rachel be taken into care. I offered another appointment and saw them again the following week, making it then almost four weeks since the first session. John and Linda arrived alone, as once again Rachel would not come, though they thought this was for the best in any case.

Given the telephone conversation with Linda, I decided to replace the usual first question of a follow-up session, 'What's better?', with the more neutral invitation, 'So, fill us in'. For the first few minutes of the session, John and Linda expressed their frustration with Rachel's behaviour, giving details of what they had been finding so difficult. This included not coming in from school until late in the evening and more lately not going to school at all, staying out late, coming home drunk, smoking, not doing her household chores and constantly arguing. At this stage, all I was doing, along with my duty social worker colleague, was listening, not because we needed to know what the problems were in order to work out what to do about them, but because John and Linda wished to tell us, and as long as they needed to get this off their chests, they needed us to listen.

My first spoken response was to acknowledge what they had been going through, before asking a coping question. Notice how I framed my acknowledgement in a way that left open possibilities for change:

John: So it's very hard at the moment...

Guy: It sounds really hard. I mean, obviously, for the past four weeks, you've, for a fair amount of time, you've been going through a really tough time, and I'm just wondering what's, how you've got through the really tough times in the past four weeks. What's kept you going?

Linda: Prozac!

John (while Linda starts laughing): Tablets for you, isn't it? You've been zonked out of it, haven't you?

Linda: My Prozac and my sleeping tablets.

The possibility lay in my assumption that we were unlikely to have heard the whole story of the past four weeks in that first few minutes of the session, but that John and Linda will have wanted, or needed, to tell us about the most difficult times first. My inclusion of the phrases 'for a fair amount of time' and 'the really tough times' left open the possibility that there had been times that were less tough, which I could ask about later. However, a full acknowledgement of the toughest times was needed first. This was continued by my first coping question, which elicited Linda's use of medication. I might have asked about the difference this was making to Linda, but chose to leave the medication to one side by asking the most simple question I could at this stage:

Guy: Ah-ha, and apart from that, what else has kept you going?

John: We've got jobs to do and we've got the other kids, you know. We both work as well, so...

Linda: We have to keep going, don't we?

John talked a little more about the need to carry on working, to pay the bills and so on, before Linda began to reflect on the difficulty of getting up in the morning. As she had clearly got herself up this morning at least, there was an obvious question to ask. In what follows, notice how I gently pushed away with my coping questions. Even when the answers do not go beyond, 'I don't know', there may still be a positive shift in the client's self-perception.

Linda: You dread getting up every morning…

John: You've still got to go to work, haven't you, at the end of the day.

Linda: Mmm. I look forward to bedtime because she's usually in by then and she's in bed and she's asleep.

Guy: Yep.

Linda: And that's like, 'Oh, thank God', and you go to bed and you go to sleep and you dread it in the morning, and you lie there, sort of thinking, 'Oh God'…

Guy: How do you manage to get yourself out of bed?

Linda :…here we go again…

Guy: How do you manage to get up?

Linda: I don't know, to be quite honest.

John: You struggle some mornings don't you?

Linda: I do.

John: More often than not you're late, aren't you?

Linda: Mmm.

Guy: So how do you do it?

Linda: (*pauses*) Just… (*looks straight at me and pauses again*)…

Guy: Where do you get the strength from to do it?

Linda: I don't know, to be quite honest.

John: Probably your Mum chasing you around: 'Linda, you'll be late'.

Linda: Yeah.

Guy: Who, sorry?

John: Linda's Mum, she's been taking Joe to school of late. She'll just shout upstairs and shout the kids down, or shout 'Hello Linda, have you seen the time?'

Linda: But while I haven't been at work, all I've done really is, is just sort of gone in... I don't know... just (*inaudible*)...

John: Well you haven't, have you, the other kids have been taking themselves to school.

Linda: ... the kids have taken themselves to school. I've got up, sorted out the packed lunches and the breakfasts... like a zombie mode really.

Guy: Um-hum?

Linda: And collapsed back on the settee and gone back to sleep.

Guy: So feeling like a zombie, you're still doing the lunches and the breakfast?

Linda: Mmm.

Guy: Yeah, um, must be hard.

Linda: Mmm.

Acknowledgement is not a one-off event, and here I again acknowledged how hard it must be for Linda, at the same time reinforcing the fact that she was still managing to make the children's breakfasts and lunches. It is important to hold the both/and notion throughout the work and to always be ready to both acknowledge difficulty and to appreciate how someone is coping and what they are still managing to do. Opportunities for further coping questions will also present themselves, and I went on to ask them from another perspective, prompted by Linda's mention of her mother.

Linda: My Mum isn't judgemental. My Dad is – and I love my Dad dearly, but I'd rather tell my Mum, than talk to my Dad. And I tell my Mum absolutely everything.

Guy: So if I were to ask your Mum, 'What are John and Linda doing that's getting them through this really difficult time?', what would she say, do you think?

Linda: I think she'd say the same as me, she doesn't know. Don't you?

John: Probably.

Linda: She quite often says to me, 'I don't know how you keep going. I really don't'.

Guy: So if I pushed her on it and said, 'Come on, so your daughter talks to you all the time and you see a lot of what's going on, and you know Rachel. What the heck are they doing that's keeping them going?'

John: Well, we started out at the onset that we weren't going to let it beat us.

Linda: Because we're ignoring her.

John: We weren't going to let her dictate what's going to happen to the rest of the family. I mean, it does at times, but we're still thinking, 'Ok, you're not going to win'.

Guy: Yeah.

John: 'You're not going to win. No matter how hard you think you're going to hurt us, you're not going to win. And you might not toe the line, you might not come in, but you're not going to win. You're not going to destroy the rest of us, just because you can't do as you're told'. And she just says, 'Well, so what'.

Having asked about their coping in the present, I decided to invite them into the future, to a time when they had come through the other side of their current difficulties. One advantage of working with children and young people is that change can happen fast, as one thing that will certainly happen is that they will become older and grow up. A 19-year-old is typically quite different from a 14-year-old. In this instance, however, my future-focused coping questions resulted in John and Linda moving in the opposite direction, and their strengths and resilience as a couple were brought into stark relief as they described what they had survived in the past.

Guy: How old is Rachel, 14? So just suppose, in about five years' time, Rachel is 19-years-old, and supposing you've got through this really difficult period, just suppose the two of you are reflecting one evening, 'How on earth did we get through that time, with Rachel?' What sorts of things would you be hoping now that you'd be saying to each other then?

Linda: Just going day-by-day.

John: Take each day as it comes, isn't it?

Linda: And ignoring her.

John: The thing is, over the years we've had an awful lot of things thrown at us, and we had my ... We got posted to Catterick when we got married, didn't we? We had four months there, then we were stuck in Cyprus, and ...

Linda: I don't know how we got through the whole lot to be quite honest. We've had obstacles thrown at us all the way through our married life, haven't we?

Guy: Have you?

Linda's voice had suddenly become more animated and, in response, so did mine. My animation also increased because, when Linda stated that they had had obstacles thrown at them all the way through their married lives, what I heard simultaneously was that they had survived these obstacles, as here they were together, now, telling me about them. Therefore, when they began to describe the obstacles in detail and with some relish, I was happy to sit back and listen, for every obstacle mentioned was one more they had overcome, and through this process, John and Linda became increasingly heroic in front of us. Their story included isolation overseas, miscarriages and other losses, difficult births, illness and injury, subsequent discharge from the army and financial hardship. Several minutes later, there was a pause, and I took the opportunity to say something. From this point on, the coin was flipped over, and the focus shifted to how they had got through their difficulties.

Guy: So you couldn't have had it much tougher.

Linda: No.

John: Well, that was then. We nearly split up, didn't we? About seven years ago. I couldn't find work, so I was under her feet all the time, and...

Linda: It was just a nightmare.

John: ...we didn't give each other space, and...

Guy: How did you manage to, you know, not split up, and stay together?

John: We weren't going to let it beat us, were we?

Linda: No, we just talked it through and we decided, you know, got to carry on.

John: Carry on for the sake of the kids and there's the fact that we'd made a commitment to each other, and it doesn't matter how difficult that was going to be...

Linda: We didn't like the life we were leading and we didn't like each other, particularly, at the time. But we decided, that wasn't enough, because the people that we were then wasn't... We weren't the people that had got married at the beginning, so therefore we'd got to...

John: ...get back to how it was, didn't we?

Linda: Neither of us wanted to split up, particularly. We just didn't like each other, how we were now, and we just talked it through and decided that wasn't a good enough reason, because John wasn't John and I wasn't me...

Guy: Right. So when you, so having talked it through, what did you do then? When you talked it through...what did the talking through lead to?

Linda: We started again, didn't we? We threw away the wedding rings, and we started again.

Guy: You threw them away?

John: Well, we bought some new ones.

Guy: Right.

Linda: We bought some new ones and started again.

Guy: Right. And did you find the old John and Linda, or was it a new John and Linda together, or...how did it...?

John and Linda looked at each other.

Linda: It was different...

John: Oh, it was different. We're stronger now for all the things we had thrown at us.

Shortly afterwards I set up a scale, where 10 was that they were coping as well as any parents could hope to in a similar situation with a 14-year-old, and 0 was that Rachel had to come into care immediately. They were at 5 and 6 and I wondered, though did not ask, where they might have said if I had asked that scaling question at the beginning of the session. Before they left, they politely declined further meetings, John saying something that as a solution-focused practitioner I took as a great compliment: 'Despite your best efforts, there's no change with Rachel. It's just that we're coping with her better'. What seemed to have happened was that their focus on overcoming some immense difficulties in the past had reacquainted them with their strengths and coping abilities, including the creativity involved in their symbolic act of buying new wedding rings. Furthermore, the scale of these past challenges perhaps placed in perspective their current difficulties with a teenage daughter. Some time later, when I evaluated this pilot service, I checked what later contacts the families we saw had had with the department. John and Linda had not returned to see a duty worker, so it appears they continued to manage and keep their family together once more.

A both/and, 'enduring and enjoying' scale

The 18th-century English man of letters, Samuel Johnson, once said: 'The only end of writing is to enable the readers better to enjoy life, or better to endure it'. There is, however, a solution-focused both/and alternative to his 'either-or' idea. The scale that I used with John and Linda was a 0–10 coping scale, though any solution-focused practitioner would want to help their clients move beyond just coping to a more positive point. A creative Belgian solution-focused practitioner, Danny Janssen, has devised an ingenious means of doing this, utilising minus numbers and running two scales together.[1] The idea is that we all have limitations or constraints of some kinds in our lives, which we have to cope with somehow, for example illness or disability, financial limitations or the effects of past trauma. At the same time, we have hopes and ambitions for our lives, in spite of, or within, our limitations. So a client can be invited to position themselves on a minus 10 to 0 scale with regard to coping with an ongoing difficulty and to explore how they have moved from minus 10 towards 0. They can also position themselves on a 0–10 scale, where 10 is the achievement of their hopes in spite of their difficulty, and this scale is then used in the normal way. Janssen suggests that 'suffering/coping and surviving/enjoying can go hand in hand', and his concurrent scales idea reflects this beautifully.

Closing thought 1

I would like to finish this chapter with a couple of cautionary notes. First, it can be tempting to assume that a person who has experienced a potentially traumatic event or suffered a significant loss is therefore in need of therapy, and that the scale of their difficulties will be such to trigger the various techniques discussed in this chapter. However, to take one example, bereavement is a normal life event and not an indication in itself that therapy is needed. This can also be the case when bereavement has occurred through horrendous circumstances. I was once requested to provide counselling to the sister and close friends of a teenage boy who had been stabbed to death at a party. Staff at the school they attended were understandably concerned for the young people's well-being, and the counselling was arranged with the agency for which I then worked. I saw the three young people concerned for only one session in each case, as they were all clear that they had adequate supports within their own networks of family, friends and school staff and did not need professionalised counselling in addition. The school was relieved to hear my 'assessment' that this was the case, and this proved a useful lesson in not assuming that being subjected to an awful event or circumstance means that professional intervention is required.

Closing thought 2

Finally, there may be a slight risk in having a separate chapter to discuss ways of responding where people feel at their worst, as this might convey the idea that the sorts of ways discussed – listening, acknowledgement, taking care about pacing and so on – are only important in these situations. However, they are of course important *all the time* and are simply brought into greater relief when people are facing great difficulties. But, when anyone is seeing a helping professional, it is fair to assume that in some way things are not right for them and so they will need this to be acknowledged. At the same time, the person will be wanting change to happen and so the possibility of change will need to be evoked. In other words, the both/and position is especially important to remember when a client is facing their worst moments AND it is always important to remember.

Reflections

- Let me begin with the question I started the chapter with – so what might you do, if your client said they were at 0 on the scale? You should be able to come up with five ideas without thinking now, so come up with at least eight.
- And if your client responded by saying 'Nothing, it's worse', in response to your 'What's better?' in a follow-up meeting? Come up with two more ideas other than ones already contained in your answers to the first reflective question above.
- What if they said 'Nothing, it's the same?' How else might you respond to that?
- Bring to mind someone you are working with where the going is really tough, where things feel stuck and the possibility of change seems slim. Make a list of 10, 15, 25 or more things (the number depending on the time you have available) that you know – about the person, yourself, your relationship, the work done so far – that give you some confidence that change will happen.
- Is there someone you are working with at the moment who you could imagine using Danny Janssen's concurrent scales with? How might that work?
- If you wanted to explain the idea of both/and to someone who had not come across it before, how would you do that? What might you say? What would you say about the value of thinking in this way?
- What do you do yourself when the going gets tough at work (or in life)? What do you do that keeps yourself going? What do you draw upon? What else?

8

Putting It All Together

The whole is greater than the sum of its parts.

Aristotle, Metaphysics

Introduction

In Chapter 2, I presented the overall solution-focused process, and in succeeding chapters, I have broken it down into its component parts. It is now time to put it back together again. In this chapter, I shall be focusing on how to use the whole approach in a structured fashion, session by session. To do this, it is important to be clear about the typical structures of first and follow-up sessions and how the work flows from one to the next. I shall begin with the simplest outlines of these structures, before fleshing these out in more detail, considering each stage of the session in turn. An extended case example will then illustrate 'putting it all together'.

Session structure: Simple versions

The simplest outlines arise naturally from the overall process, which, as we saw in Chapter 2, can be summarised as follows:

- contracting with the client, around what they want from the work;
- helping the client to describe the future realisation of what they want;
- helping the client to describe progress they are making towards what they want.

It is important to note that contracting, as the primary activity, sits over and above the other two areas of enquiry, which can only be followed once a contract and hence a direction for the work has been established. There is an equivalence between these two parts of the process, which therefore might be more accurately presented as in Figure 8.1.

Figure 8.1   Solution-focused process, and typical first session structure – simple version

Even this presentation, while showing future and progress descriptions on the same level, suggests that the future focus takes precedence, given that we read across from left to right. Yet the order of the two is not fixed, and it is by switching the order that we most easily see the difference between first and follow-up sessions. The simplest way to conceptualise their respective structures is to see the first session as beginning with the future focus – what does the client want and how will they know they have got this – and then moving to the progress focus, usually via a scale. In follow-up sessions, the order is simply turned around, with the question 'What's better?' opening the session with a progress focus, before the later return to a future focus, the switch again usually being punctuated by the reintroduction of the general progress scale.

Figure 8.2   Typical follow-up session structure – simple version

The reason for replacing the verb *contracting* with the noun *contract* in the follow-up session map (Figure 8.2) is that the same contract usually flows from one session to the next, with the question 'What's better?' implicitly asking about progress in the direction already established. Therefore, contracting is not ordinarily needed in follow-up sessions, though on occasions when a piece of work loses its direction, or is seen to be heading in the wrong direction, a return to the client's 'best hopes' may be called for. We will see an example of this later, in the case of Anna.

While it is useful to be able to see the shapes of sessions in these minimal ways, in practice more detail is needed. I shall start with the stage-by-stage structure of a first session.

Typical first session structure: Detail

The typical structure progresses stage by stage:

* opening;
* hoped-for outcome – contracting;
* detailed preferred future description;
* instances of preferred future in place – what point on a 0–10 scale?;
* small signs of progress – one point up the scale;
* closing.

The opening and closing stages can be seen as 'bookending' the central part of the session, in which the solution-focused process takes place. As these central stages have been described in detail in the preceding chapters, I will add only a few remarks about how they fit together. Let us take a more detailed look at the bookending stages, beginning with the opening.

Opening stage

The opening stage consists of anything that is done before the worker 'gets down to business' by asking the client what they want. Although this includes activities not specific to solution-focused practice, and may be determined more by the context in which the approach is being used or by the particular style of the worker, adopting a solution-focused approach does influence how a session is started, so it is worth spending a little time on this. The possible activities of the opening stage can be divided into two: first, whatever the worker wants or needs to say to the client; and second, questions the worker might ask of the client.

Introducing and explaining

What the worker might say to the client will be a mix of introductions, information-sharing and explanation. Soon afterwards, the worker will be asking the client what their best hopes *from this* are, which assumes that the client knows what 'this' is and can, therefore, answer the question in an informed way. This may be apparent, for example, when someone has self-referred for counselling, though on other occasions it might be less clear. Once when I was seeing someone in my role as a family support worker, the person told me that her best hopes from this were to obtain a statement of special educational needs for her son. When I said that this was not within my remit and explained what my role was, the person responded politely that she was not looking for that type of help, and after I had informed her how to make contact with the educational psychologist, the meeting ended.

It is worth keeping explanations as simple as possible, first, because simplicity is an aid to clarity and explanations are only worthwhile if they are understandable and, second, because the client is likely to be anxious at this early stage and so unreceptive to lots of information (Doel and Marsh, 1992, pp. 25–26). There are two issues to consider in terms of what might need to be explained: first, the role of the worker and agency; and second, the solution-focused approach itself. Although roles will vary, they must have two features in common, whatever the agency setting, if a context exists in which the solution-focused approach can be used. First, what is on offer will include simply talking; and second, the worker will be able to follow, at least in part, the client's agenda. It can take a little work to create this context, as it did when I introduced solution-focused practice into my work in a statutory children's social work team, and I will share some thoughts on how this can be done in Chapter 10.

These two common features can form the basis of a simple explanation in which the worker's role and the solution-focused approach are linked together. A situation in which I always provide an explanation is when I am seeing a child or young person, who is usually brought by a parent or a professional working with them. I assume that the child might not know what they have been brought to, and so I say something like this:

> In these meetings, we simply talk, because people often find talking helpful. My main job in this talking is to ask questions, to help the talking go a certain way, which I hope will be useful for you. That's why people come and talk here, for it to be useful for them. So, soon, I'll be asking you what you want from this, what you want to be different, and I'll also be asking you about what you're good at, as talking about these things often helps people make changes they want to make.

This can be adapted to fit adult clients, though I might check with them first whether they want any explanation:

> Do you want me to explain a little about the way I work, or should we just launch straight in?

Most clients tend to opt for the latter, in which case I say they can ask any questions about what is happening as the work progresses.

Other information to be shared will include what the worker knows about the client, issues of confidentiality, session length and the number of sessions. There is no need to have any information about someone before starting to do solution-focused work with them, but if a worker does know something from a third party, a referring professional for example, then in the interests of transparency this should be shared with the client. Confidentiality is also not an issue specific to solution-focused practice, though it fits with the principles of the approach for the worker to be as transparent as possible about this and any other agency policies.

Its pragmatism and responsiveness to the individual client create flexibility within solution-focused practice regarding session length. There are no rules such as might govern other approaches, no fixed 50-minute hour for example, though sessions will typically last for less than an hour. Average session length has decreased where solution-focused practitioners have dropped the practice of taking a break and delivering a compliments-based message and task at the end of the session, which I shall discuss shortly. With regard to the number of sessions, where there are no agency constraints regarding this, the client will usually determine when the work will end and there is no way of predicting how long this will take. The average length of treatment is shorter in solution-focused practice than in other approaches (Gingerich and Peterson, 2013), being as low as three to four sessions for the version presented in this book, and it is common for there to be only one or two sessions (Shennan and Iveson, 2011). Therefore, no number is set in advance, and in the opening stage the client can be told that at the end of the session they will be asked if they want to meet again. In other words, every session should be treated as if it might be the last.[1]

Preliminary questions: Starting with strengths

There is an argument that the worker's first question to the client should be the contracting question, for until it is known what the client wants, what mandate does the worker have to ask anything else? (George et al., 2001). And I often do ask my adult clients about their best hopes as soon as I have said all that I need to at the beginning. On the other hand, cast your mind back to the beginning of the first chapter, where Nancy Kline (1999) was quoted as saying that people think better in a meeting if the first thing they do is to say something 'true and positive'. Clients have to think hard during solution-focused sessions, and if Kline is right then it might be doing them a disservice not to invite them to say something positive about themselves at the outset. This view has been supported by research showing that not only is 'resource activation' required for good outcomes in therapy, but that 'successful therapists...focused on their clients' strengths from the very start of a therapy session' (Gassman and Grawe, 2006). A sequence of questions, known as the 'Keys to Cooperation', has proved useful in helping adolescents to do this (O'Leary, 2001, p. 178):

- What do you enjoy doing?
- What are you good at?
- What does it take to be good at that?

If these questions do not seem suited for using with adults, then an alternative way in to ask about their strengths is to start with:

- As I know very little about you, can I start by asking how do you spend your time?

If the client answers in terms of their work, this can be followed up with a question about their interests and vice versa. Within this variety of activities, it is likely that there will be some affirmative answers to the simple checking question 'Are you good at that?', which can lead to a focus on the client's strengths and abilities.

Focusing on strengths can also take place via significant others. Children are likely to have arrived expecting negative things to be said about them. So hearing the worker ask their parents what they are good at can have a powerful effect.[2] A word of caution though – once this question has been asked, the worker has to ensure that the child hears an answer, and both persistence and acknowledgement of the current problems may be required.

> *Worker*: What's he good at?
>
> *Parent*: He's good at staying out late!
>
> *Worker*: Ok! And what's he good at that you're proud of him for?

In a second example, it became clear that the relationship between an angry father and his teenage daughter was, at least temporarily, teetering on the brink.

> *Father*: What's she good at? You're joking, aren't you? I can tell you what she's bad at.

Worker: Well, I can hear that things are pretty awful, for you both I guess, at the moment. What about if I'd met you and asked this before things got as difficult as they are right now?

Father: Oh, I don't know.

Worker: What might you have told me a while back?

Father: Well, one thing that she's doing now is leading her younger sister astray, and she was always helpful with her before…

This type of beginning discussion is sometimes labelled 'problem-free talk' (George et al., 1990, pp. 8–9; Ratner et al., 2012, pp. 49–51), though 'competency talk' might more accurately reflect its purpose (Shennan, 2003a, p. 40). The last piece of dialogue above is an example of talk about the 'pre-problem state', which is a place to go 'when all else fails' (Iveson et al., 2012, p. 72). Solution-focused work is usually done close to the client's present reality, the future being tomorrow or soon after, and the past the time since the last session or since the client decided to get help. Further ahead or back may be less relevant to where the client is now, but if resources are hard to find near to the present, then it is to be hoped that finding them in the client's past can still evoke current possibilities.

The session proper

The central stages of the first session follow the solution-focused process and so make up what we might call 'the session proper'. In terms of their order, the establishment of a contract necessarily comes first, followed usually by the preferred future before progress. Eliciting a detailed preferred future description first both increases the opportunities for the client to come across instances of it in place already and, when it comes to the scaling, ensures that 10 is well-defined. However, there are exceptions to any rule.

Ben,[3] aged 15, was brought for a solution-focused session by his youth justice service worker, and a contract was framed around Ben moving from a life of crime towards a life of work. When the worker invited Ben to imagine waking up the next day having turned his life around in this way, Ben had difficulty coming up with answers about what would be different, mentioning only a couple of things he was doing already: asking his youth justice worker about going to college and spending time only with non-offending young people. It turned out that Ben had come out of prison three weeks earlier and had decided then to go straight. As soon as the worker knew this, it made sense to focus on the last three weeks rather than on the next day, and so a progress focus supplanted the future focus early in the session, early enough in fact for Ben to come up with a list of 50 things he had done to help himself go straight since leaving prison (we encountered Ben earlier when discussing the use of lists in Chapter 5).

In this case, as with Colin who we also met in Chapter 5, a scale was not used. On each occasion, the client started talking about instances and progress spontaneously, making a scale somewhat redundant. What is important is that the worker enables the client to focus on both their preferred future and on progress towards it, and a scale is simply a tool to enable a shift to the latter focus. More commonly though, clients do not talk spontaneously about what is already going well, and it can prove difficult to prompt someone just by asking something like 'What's going well?' – likely replies to this being 'Nothing', 'Not much' or 'I don't know'. There is something about a scale, and a positive number response however small, that enables talk about positive change, as the client has to justify the number given.

It is important for the first session to have both a future and a progress focus for several reasons. First, describing a desired future can give rise to feelings of hope and a sense of possibility, and the more detailed the description, the more real and doable it can seem. Then, when the client becomes aware that they are already making progress, this can increase their expectation that further change will take place, and the worker's focus on the client's successes also promotes worker–client cooperation (de Shazer, 1988, p. 4). A related issue concerns how much time to spend on each part of the session, and there are no hard-and-fast rules concerning this. Every session will be different as every client is different, though typically the future focus takes up the greater share of first sessions while progress has more time in follow-up sessions.

Closing stage

Originally the closing stage consisted of the worker taking a break to consult with the team, or to reflect if working alone, in order to devise an end-of-session message to give to the client, which included compliments and a task. Until the mid-1980s, the Milwaukee team considered that the main active ingredient of change lay in this post-break intervention (Malinen, 2002). However, prompted by their growing realisation that change was already underway before the work had started (Molnar and de Shazer, 1987; Weiner-Davis et al., 1987; Gingerich et al., 1988) and their developing interest in interviewing (Lipchik and de Shazer, 1986; Lipchik, 1988a, 1988b), the team's attention turned increasingly to the pre-break conversation between the therapist and client (Malinen, 2002), which I am terming the session proper. Eventually, de Shazer (1994, p. 272) saw that there was no need to set tasks, or 'fancy tasks' at least, when he realised that 'the therapist doesn't have the magic, the client has the magic' (quoted in Ratner, 2006). The BRIEF solution-focused version has taken this a step further by largely dispensing with the practice of taking a break and streamlining what is said to a client at the end of the session (Shennan and Iveson, 2011).

There is little difference between the closing stages of first and follow-up sessions, except that slightly more might be said at the end of a first session. This is the typical outline:

- summarise;
- decide with the client if and when a follow-up meeting will take place;
- offer a noticing suggestion (optional).

Offering a summary of the session serves at least three purposes. First, an accurate summary, using the words of the client, demonstrates close listening. Second, it gives the client an opportunity to correct anything the worker has misheard or misunderstood. For this reason, and to encourage the client to do this, I usually preface my summarising by saying something like 'Let me just try to summarise what you've said today, to check I've heard you right, and please do let me know if I haven't in any way'. Third, a summary can have a reinforcing effect through the client hearing back what they have said about future possibilities and existing progress.

Prefacing the summary with an acknowledgement of the extent of the client's difficulty can help the worker to continue to get close to the client, a position from which anything else said is more likely to be heard. The worker will then summarise the client's hopes from the work, signs that would suggest their hopes have been realised, progress already made towards this, and what has helped in terms of their actions and their strengths. That it is useful to reinforce the latter in particular is backed up by the research into resource activation mentioned earlier, another finding of which was that successful practitioners 'also made sure they ended sessions by returning to their clients' strengths' (Gassman and Grawe, 2006). Framing how this is done as *summarising* is useful insofar as this privileges the client's ideas and words and keeps the worker close to them, whereas *complimenting* involves the worker in making judgements, which is at odds with the position adopted by the worker at other times during the work. The original purpose of complimenting for the Milwaukee team was to encourage a 'yes set' in the client, so they would be receptive to the assigned task (de Shazer, 1982). In the absence of tasks, then, compliments lose much of their rationale.

After the summary, a decision has to be made about whether another session will take place. The general principle here is to be as client-led as possible, within any agency constraints, as only the client can know when their hopes have been sufficiently realised. If the client does want to meet again, the next decision concerns when this will take place. There is no fixed frequency of sessions, which in a solution-focused piece of work tend to be set further apart than in other approaches, as the focus is on the client making changes in their own ways and in their own time outside the sessions. A typical pattern is for the space between sessions to increase as the client is making progress, but even after a first session if there is significant progress already, there might be a two- to four-week gap before the second.

When the decision about what to do next has been made, that is usually that. On occasions though, the worker might suggest to the client that they notice any signs of progress, however small, before they return for the next session. This sort of 'noticing suggestion' is a leftover from the days of task-setting and is not dissimilar to the Formula First Session Task (Chapter 5). It proves useful when a client has asked directly for advice or has said that they do not know what to do, especially if this happens towards the end of a session. By making a 'noticing suggestion', the worker is responding to this, but in a neutral way, for it is not telling the client to do anything in particular. The problem with giving a task that involves the client doing something is that the idea has come from the worker, and not only might it not fit for the client but it might interfere with the client finding their own way forward.

Typical follow-up session structures: Detail

There is no opening stage as such to a follow-up session, which gets underway as soon as the worker asks:

- What's better (since we met)?

There are good reasons for making this the very first thing asked. Consider this opening exchange of the third session with Michelle (see Chapter 2).

I have just entered the room having switched on the equipment to record the session.

> *Guy*: Can you just pass me that microphone down by your chair? Thanks, I'll just clip that on ... (*Looking up at Michelle, as I start attaching the microphone to my lapel*). So, finally, again ...
>
> *Michelle*: Yeah, how are you doing?
>
> *Guy*: I'm fine, I'm fine. (*Finish attaching the microphone*). And you, so, Michelle, what's better, since we met?

I do not want to respond to Michelle as one might when exchanging social pleasantries upon meeting a friend, but in a purposeful way and also to signal my interest in, and expectation of, progress that Michelle has made since the last meeting. On the face of it, asking 'What's better?' might appear unduly directive, only allowing talk about positive things, and a more neutral first question such as 'How have things been?' might seem more reasonable. And yet one can expect someone who is seeing a helping professional to answer such a question by talking about problems, if only because that is a culturally expected response. In practice, 'What's better?' allows a range of answers, and perhaps a wider range than the seemingly neutral question. Some clients will answer about something being better, while others are not prevented from reporting 'It's the same', or 'Nothing, it's worse'.

Typical structure following a positive response

- Follow-ups to the positive response
  - From the general to the specific, from the abstract to concrete detail
  - How did you do that? What did that take?
  - What difference did that make? What difference is that making?
- What else is better? ...
- Scale – back to the future
- Closing

A simple way to approach this structure is by applying the idea of *widening and detailing* (Tohn and Oshlag, 1997) that we came across in Chapter 4. Having heard a first positive response to the question 'What's better?', the worker will set out to help the client to describe this in detail by utilising the types of follow-up questions listed above. After this 'detailing', the worker will 'widen' by asking 'What else is better?', then detail again, and so on. The particular follow-ups to ask will depend on the nature of the client's answers. It will be useful to bear the following ideas in mind, while remaining flexible about which type of questions to ask and when.

Eliciting specific and concrete detail

A constant movement within a solution-focused conversation is from the general and abstract to the specific and concrete, and this is frequently the case at the beginning of a follow-up session:

> *Edward*: What's better? I guess I'm feeling a bit better, not quite as low as I was.
>
> *Guy*: Ok, and what have you noticed about yourself since you've been feeling a bit better? How have you been able to tell?
>
> *Edward*: I've been going out a bit more, not been stuck in on my own so much.
>
> *Guy*: Yeah? What have you been doing when you've been going out?
>
> *Edward*: I've met up with one or two friends. Been helping a mate move into his own place – helped him move some stuff from his hostel.

How did you do that and what difference has it made?

Having helped Edward to become progressively more concrete, I then had the options of asking about the effects of what he had managed to do – 'What difference has that made to you, helping your mate?' – and of asking about how he had managed to do this. On other occasions, this latter question will be the first follow-up question asked at the start of the session:

> *Worker*: What's better?
>
> *Client*: I've cut down my drinking.
>
> *Worker*: Wow! How have you done that?

As we saw in Chapter 5, it is sometimes worth checking with a client if they are pleased about having done something and whether it had been a hard thing to do, before asking this type of question. Otherwise, by asking 'How did you do that?', the worker may be *telling* the client that he should be pleased and that it was hard.

What else is better?

After each specific aspect of progress has been followed up, and detail about it elicited, including about what others have noticed and the effects on them, the worker can simply ask about another aspect, before 'detailing' again. As with not moving up the scale too quickly (see Chapter 6), it is important not to stint on these 'widening' questions. The eighth or ninth 'What else is better?' becomes easier to ask over time, as solution-focused practitioners learn that there is usually more there. Until then, you must simply trust the client, take a deep breath, and ask!

Scaling in follow-up sessions

At some point, perhaps when there really is no more progress to elicit, there will be a switch to a future focus. Going back to the general progress scale is both a straightforward way to do this and a useful means of consolidating progress made.

> Can we go back to that scale that we used last time, where 10 is you've got what you want from this, and 0 the worst point – where are you now?

On hearing the client's rating, assuming it is higher up the scale, this can be followed with:

> Is there anything else that puts you up at 5, other than what you have already described?

If there is, then more detail can be elicited, though often the client will respond by saying they have covered everything, in which case the scale serves to reinforce the progress made and to punctuate the switch to the future. One point up the scale can be asked about, or the worker may choose to be more indeterminate:

> So, what will tell you that you're moving further up the scale...?

A timescale can be suggested, or once again this can be left vague:

> … over the next few days, or weeks?

Where a client has made progress, the worker may check whether this is a good enough point. If so, this does not necessarily mean that the work is done, as the client might not be sufficiently confident that they can maintain their progress, and the focus of the work can then shift to a confidence scale, as we saw in Chapter 6.

Closing

The closing stage of a follow-up session may include all the same points as in a first session, though will often be briefer. As the worker–client relationship develops, there is less need to acknowledge and summarise formally at the end of a session, and this shortening will tend to happen quite naturally. If the client has encountered setbacks, however, the session will have followed a different path and it might be fitting for the worker to say more at the end. Let us now consider this other follow-up session scenario.

Typical structure following an initially negative response

Tom is a single father with a 12-year-old son, Danny. It is two weeks since his previous session.

> *Worker*: What's better?
>
> *Tom*: What's better? Nothing, it's worse. I've had a terrible time this past week with Danny. I can't do a thing with him, and it's been a real battle to get him off to school each day. This morning, he was playing up so much, I almost lost it with him. To be honest, things have just been piling on top of me and I feel like I'm going downhill again.

Activity: 'It's worse'

Before you read on: How might you respond to Tom's response?

You might have included some of the following, which might be better seen as a list of possible responses rather than a strictly ordered structure.

- Acknowledgement
- Coping questions
- Asking about instances or exceptions
- How have you stopped it getting worse?
- Eliciting difference in the intervening period – better parts
- Option of re-contracting.

Alongside all these options the worker will, as ever, be listening with a constructive ear. In the previous chapter, I introduced the idea of acknowledgement and possibility and the importance of always paying attention to both. Listening constructively does not mean shutting one's ears to problems, and the first thing the worker is likely to do in response to Tom is to acknowledge his difficulties, and they will continue to do this as much as is needed throughout the session. Then there are a number of questions that can be asked, including general coping questions, such as 'How have you been keeping going?', and specific questions, for example about the instance of getting Danny off to school – 'How have you been managing to do that?' – and about the exception of not 'losing it' with his son – 'How did you manage not to lose it with him, what did you do instead?' In the midst of difficulties, there will always be things that the client is still achieving, whether you think of these as instances of what is wanted or exceptions to what is not. They will not always be as immediately apparent as in Tom's first answer, and persistence might be required in eliciting them.

This eliciting will be aided by keeping the idea of difference to the fore, and there are two helpful ways to do this. Imagine Tom later says that he has gone down the scale, from 3 in the last session to 1 now. This suggests that it might have been worse still, as his rating is not at 0, and so the worker can ask 'What have you done to stop it getting worse? How have you made sure it hasn't gone to 0?', with follow-up questions as appropriate, including 'How would you know you're getting back on track again?' A second way of using the scale in these difficult follow-up situations is based on a simple assumption – that no one's experience of any period of time they have lived through is entirely uniform. This idea informs the following question, credited by Harry Korman (2006) to Björn Johansson:

On that scale that we used last time, where 10 is you've achieved what you want from this, and 0 is the opposite, what's the highest point you've been at since we last met, and what is the lowest point?

Coping questions can be asked with regard to the lowest times, before attention turns to the highest point. This is the more useful order to follow, as the client will need to feel that their difficulties have been heard before being able to talk about the better or less difficult times.

On some occasions, where no progress is elicited after the worker has explored these various options, re-contracting may be called for: 'So, what are your best hopes from this meeting?' After all, as the client has returned, it is reasonable to assume they must have some hopes from this. This is what happened in the second session in the work with Anna, which we will follow for the rest of this chapter.

Putting it all together: The example of Anna

Anna was referred for solution-focused work by her general practitioner and had three sessions over an eight-week period before not showing for a planned fourth session. About a year later, when contacted by an independent researcher, she reported that the outcome of the work had been positive. This was despite having answered 'Nothing, it's worse' to the question 'What's better?' at the beginning of each follow-up session. Reviewing the sessions in retrospect, it was possible to see the small ways in which Anna was starting to turn things around during the process of the work.

First session

The contracting was difficult and slow, with Anna saying she had heard that my approach was positive and that she wanted something positive to focus on, but she did not know how 'at the moment'. It is interesting how clients use possibility language themselves, even in their most desperate situations! Anna's desperation became apparent as she talked more about how bad she was feeling and how she had become alienated from others around her. When she said she just needed something positive in her life, I felt this was sufficient to move the work forward.

> *Guy*: Right, so you've decided to come here and give this a go, in the hope that this might help you in bringing something positive into your life, yeah?
>
> *Anna*: Yes.

Guy: Ok. Ok. Suppose it did? Suppose this did do that, and within this incredibly difficult situation you're in, with the way you're feeling, you were to notice this had brought something positive in, even if just in a small way, tonight, tomorrow, what would, what might you notice about yourself?

Anna: I might actually feel the energy to do the housework – my year-old pile of ironing!

Guy: Say you did, say you… what difference would that make to you?

Anna: It would probably mean I'd start getting some order in my life…

Although Anna continued to be distressed, the move into a preferred future had opened up small possibilities. She described doing other jobs in her flat – tidying, finishing unpacking having returned several months ago from temporarily staying elsewhere, beginning decorating, putting pictures up – and walking her dog around the block. The extent of Anna's current isolation became apparent when, having mentioned she would have a more positive demeanour, she said that no one else would notice this other than her dog.

Anna placed herself at 0 on the general progress scale, with 0 as the worse her situation could become. When I asked how she was keeping herself going, she said she just survived each day, by having a bath and making sure she got dressed, having the television on, and that she had managed to walk to the shop for some milk, taking the dog with her. She had also just decided to start taking anti-depressants. I tried two other scales, one where 10 was wanting things to be better and feeling able and willing to work at that, and 0 not caring any more or being bothered about doing anything, on which Anna said she fluctuated between 0 and 10, today being higher than 0 as she had managed to come for this session. For the other scale, I defined 10 as a sense of possibility that at least some of the small signs of future progress described could happen, and 0 knowing that none of it was possible, on which Anna placed herself at between 0 and 1.

Second session

Anna cancelled her next session, following which Christmas and New Year holidays intervened, and the second session ended up taking place in mid-January, six weeks after the first. Anna looked and sounded physically far better, yet said that things were worse and began a lengthy account of a dire family situation that had transpired since our first meeting. In this account, which lasted for half the session, it turned out that Anna had recently been divorced and that the second of her three grown-up children, Chloe, had quite severe learning disabilities and lived in a small residential home. She explained that Chloe spent occasional weekends at home, though since the divorce this had been with her ex-husband and his new partner and not with herself, as she had not been in a position to manage Chloe. However, her husband had announced that he was going away for Christmas, so Anna, thinking that this was unfair on Chloe, had arranged with the care home for Chloe to stay with her. Unfortunately, Anna had found it difficult to manage Chloe, and none of her family knew of the situation until Anna's sister, Maureen, had gone to the care home to see Chloe on Christmas Day and from there went to Anna's. Maureen, angry with Anna, telephoned Anna's ex-husband and they arranged for Chloe to go back into her care home.

This incident had had serious ramifications within the family, with Anna saying that she had been 'disowned' by everyone, including her other two children, even though her intentions had been good and she had apologised for not consulting her ex-husband about Chloe coming to stay with her. While Anna talked in great detail about these events, I could only listen and occasionally ask questions when instance- or exception-like moments arose, for example when Anna mentioned feeling relieved having got certain things off her chest to her sister, who she thought had interfered unnecessarily. However, my question 'What difference did that make, feeling relieved having done that?' only elicited the reply 'Not much', and Anna continued with her story. This pattern was repeated each time I heard a possible opening. After about 30 minutes, it struck me that this detailed problem account had blotted out the solution-focused process instigated in the first session, which therefore needed re-igniting.

> *Guy*: So, Anna, you've had such a difficult time, in terms of your family situation. You did feel some relief having got those things off your chest with your sister. I'm wondering now, what are your best hopes from today's session?
>
> *Anna*: I don't know, don't know. I just … I really don't know. All I know is that I should be here, because I can't do it on my own. And it was a struggle – to get here. But I knew I had to do it.
>
> *Guy*: So how did you get yourself to do it, to get here?

Anna: Knowing that I can't carry on feeling like this, because it will just cripple me completely. And, erm, I don't know. I just don't know how ... I want to move forward, but I just feel very hurt at the moment. And I miss my children. And I hate the fact that they've such a low opinion of me. And my son said that I depress him. Broke my heart. And I've been talking to my best friend, Sylvia, and she keeps telling me 'We've got to forget about what's been happening and just look to today and the future'. And, I was alright Saturday, and I wasn't too bad yesterday in the morning, and in the afternoon, but it just, I just started feeling a bit down again yesterday. Last night I couldn't sleep properly, and I've had nightmares the past couple of nights.

Activity: Next question

What might you ask Anna now?

Anna's statement that she wanted to move forward had re-established a direction for the work, and then her friend, Sylvia, who she had not previously mentioned, appeared almost as a back-up for me! Not only was there a direction, but possible progress too. I asked next: 'What happened on Saturday?', which led to Anna talking about having started volunteering at a local charity shop. How she had managed to do this and the benefits she was experiencing from it took up most of the rest of the session.

Third session

The third session took place two weeks later, and once again, Anna began by saying things were worse, 'certainly on the financial side of things'. She had had the flu the whole of the previous week and had not been able to leave her flat. Therefore she had needed to have her heating on continuously and had missed out on the lunches provided to volunteers in the charity shop.

Anna: It was only Friday I started to feel a bit better. Saturday, another improvement, and then yesterday I was feeling back to normal again.

But, the increase in heating costs and buying food have crippled me a bit financially.

I picked up on Anna feeling a bit better on Friday and Saturday, leading to this response.

> *Anna*: Saturday, yeah, I went out and did a bit of shopping. But spent basically all of Saturday, apart from – what did I do yesterday? Just popped out and bought some more gas and electric. And that was it. But I've been clearing up the flat, which I suppose is positive. Because I've got bags of things, and shelves of ironing that needs to be done. And I had a big case full of clothes that I've had for, since just before Chloe came to stay, which I used to keep in my spare bedroom, and then I shoved all these clothes inside a case, and left it in my bedroom until this weekend. So I've emptied all that out and put stuff away. And done some ironing. Just stuff that I haven't done for a hell of a long time. So the flat's starting to look a bit tidier. That's about the only positive thing.

I elicited more detail from Anna about these activities, resisting any temptation to cheer and remind Anna that these were the sorts of things she said in the first session she would be doing if she were making progress. It was probably good that I did resist because Anna later downplayed this, saying that what was really important was to secure herself financially and for that she needed to find paid employment, which she felt very anxious about as she had not worked regularly since the early years of her marriage. Anna spoke at length about these worries, and the same danger of drift arose as halfway through the second session.

I reminded Anna that she had said in the last session she wanted to move forward and asked her about how else she had been doing this: 'What were you doing that was helping you to move forward before you became poorly last week?' Anna talked about having had time to think, then returned to her reflections about needing a job and about part-time jobs she might be able to get. Another intervention was needed to help bring direction back to the work and to elicit concrete detail about movement in this direction.

> *Guy*: Ok. If I can ask a question that might help see where coming here fits into that? In terms of the future of coming here? So, if you think of

a scale from 0 to 10, where 10 is that you've achieved what you needed to achieve from coming here, and 0 is … say 0 is the point at which you first decided to get some help? Ok? What point on that scale are you at now?

Anna: Probably about … just trying to think … probably about 4 or 5 … yeah, I don't think I'm quite halfway there yet. But it's making, you know, I am starting to think, about the future. I don't have an answer yet. And that's, I don't know who can give me an answer, or how I'm going to find the right answer but I need to …

This appeared to represent significant progress since the first session. Hearing Anna mention the future it occurred to me that, given the truncated preferred future description owing to Anna's distress in the first session and the re-contracting in the second session, the endpoint of the work might need fleshing out in more detail.

Guy: Ok, so, in terms of coming here, and moving forward, overcoming the things that you want to overcome and using here in the way that you want to use it, and you're at a 4 or 5 on that scale … Can I go right to the endpoint of 10? How will you know you've achieved what you wanted from coming here?

Four discrete areas where Anna wanted to see progress emerged: work, her flat, her contact with Chloe, and her relationship with her other two children. To continue to focus the work from this point, I set up some multi-scaling to consider each area in turn. Anna's ratings on the sub-scales ranged from 2 to 5, and she was confident of moving to a good enough point on each one. These scales provided the framework for the rest of the session.

They might well have provided the framework for the fourth session too, except that Anna did not show for it. I wrote to both Anna and to her doctor who had referred her to say that further sessions were available if Anna wished to return, but never saw her again. When I later learned that she had told an independent researcher that things were now 'better', I had no way of knowing if this was as a result of our solution-focused work, as this outcome might have happened in any case. All I could know for sure was that the work had not got in Anna's way.

- 'Solution-focused practice is simple...' Sum up the typical structures for first and follow-up solution-focused sessions in no more than 50 words – altogether!
- '...but it ain't easy!' What is it about following the solution-focused process that might not be easy in practice?
- How might staying with the solution-focused process be worth it for you and your clients?
- I described the opening and closing stages of a session as bookending the central part of the session. How might you bookend a solution-focused process within your work?
- How would you explain the practice of *widening and detailing?*
- Look back over the account of my work with Anna. What did I do that helped to maintain a forward-facing direction for the work?

Becoming clear about the typical session structures, and about how the work flows from one session to the next, is important in getting a firm grip on the solution-focused process, which in turn enables one to apply and adapt it across a range of contexts, as we shall see in the next chapter.

9

Applications and Adaptations

The essence of the beautiful is unity in variety.

Moses Mendelssohn, *Briefe über die Empfindungen*

Introduction

Solution-focused practice is used across a range of settings, with diverse groups of people and within varying activities. Having begun in the relatively small world of therapy, it has long since been applied in virtually every other type of human endeavour where people talk together to help change to happen. As well as in health and social care, solution-focused practice is now widely used in educational settings (Durrant, 1994; Rhodes and Ajmal, 1995; Ajmal and Rees, 2001; Måhlberg and Sjöblom, 2004; Kelly, Kim and Franklin, 2008; Young, 2009) and in organisational work (Jackson and McKergow, 2002; McKergow and Clarke, 2007). One of the features that make solution-focused practice flexible and adaptable for use in such a range of situations is the simplicity of its process. In the preceding chapters, I have simplified further, by mainly explaining and illustrating this process in the context of one-to-one help being provided in structured sessions. In this chapter, I hope to give a flavour of the variety of the approach and to provide and provoke some ideas about how it can be applied outside of this most simple context.

A widely-applicable approach

Added to its blossoming beyond therapy into a wide range of other settings, a second aspect of the approach's versatility lies in the diversity of client groups with which it has proved to be helpful. Questions are often asked on training courses about who the approach can and cannot be used with, with trainees wondering if there are any types of problem where it will not be appropriate or relevant. The straightforward answer is that the approach can potentially be used with anyone, in that there are no client groups or problem categories where a solution-focused approach has not proved useful at some point. This is not the same as saying that it will work for everyone. Although it is an effective approach, as we shall see in Chapter 10 when we consider its evidence base, like all approaches solution-focused practice does not work all of the time. It is just not possible to predict in advance when it will not work.

It will be unsurprising that solution-focused work might be helpful, irrespective of the type of problem someone has, when one reflects that it is not organised around whatever problems there might be. Being organised instead around what is wanted, all it takes for a solution-focused process to be set in motion is a person wanting, or agreeing, to talk, because then it can reasonably be assumed they are hoping that something might come from this talking. To be fully inclusive here, the word *communicate* should take the place of *talk*. As long as the person can communicate, it is the worker's job to find and cooperate with their way of communicating. This might involve using hand puppets with younger children (Berg and Steiner, 2003) or a variety of nonverbal techniques such as 'video exceptions', drawing and role-play with people with intellectual disabilities (Roeden, Bannink, Maaskant and Curfs, 2009). Similarly, the solution-focused practitioner will seek out and work with 'the germs of constructive ideas' in otherwise possibly strange-seeming conversations with patients diagnosed with psychosis (Hawkes, 2003), or with the 'remaining abilities' (Kitwood, 1997) of a person with dementia, where a solution-focused approach has proved to be helpful (Macdonald, 2011).

Solution-focused practice has also proved helpful in palliative care, where it has been shown to help people 'live well until they die' (Bray and Groves, 2007). In a study of solution-focused support provided to patients with cancer, published by the UK's National Institute for Health and Care Excellence, 85 per cent of the patients thought it had made 4 or 5 points difference on a 10-point scale, with 92 per cent finding the work 'very useful' (Bray, 2007). Use of the approach has also been noted as an example of good practice for people with an autistic spectrum disorder (Department of Health, 2006), following work done by Vicky Bliss, also the co-author of a book on solution-focused work with people with Asperger syndrome (Bliss and Edmonds, 2008). Jonathan Prosser (1998), a psychiatrist, has also described work with children with autism. The approach has been used successfully with people with eating disorders (McFarland, 1995; Jacob, 2001), with suicidal clients (Sharry, Darmody and Madden, 2002; Callcott, 2003; Fiske, 2008; Henden, 2005, 2008) and with people experiencing problems arising from bereavement and loss (Butler and Powers, 1996; Simon, 2010) or who have experienced serious trauma (Dolan, 1991; Darmody, 2003; Bannink, 2008).

I have provided references regarding these issues as they are all ones where people have assumed that a solution-focused approach will not be useful, or even possible. There might be other areas where people wonder about its applicability, in which case an internet search should be all that is needed to assuage any doubts. At the same time I should stress that not every activity that a helping professional engages in can be done by applying solution-focused practice. For example, I first started to use the approach when I was a social worker, part of whose role concerned safeguarding children, and I regularly asked my solution-focused teachers 'How do I use it in child protection?' I now see this in some respects as a misguided question, as the activity at the heart of child protection work is risk assessment, and the solution-focused process does not include an assessment component. It is a process of helping someone move towards a desired outcome of their own choosing, and it is in this respect that it might help anyone, and to use it you need to be in a context where you can legitimately follow this process. In the next chapter, I shall share ideas about how you might create such a context in your work. In the rest of this chapter, I shall examine some activities which can be done in a solution-focused way, outside of structured one-to-one work with adult clients, namely supervision and consultation, groupwork, team coaching and work with families and children. This is far from an exhaustive list, and I hope that by providing some experiences of mine, this will provoke some ideas of yours about applying solution-focused practice in your roles.

Supervision and consultation

The terms supervision and consultation are sometimes used interchangeably, and they do both clearly relate to a role of helping workers to do their jobs. The terms also point to an important difference – *supervision* suggesting a managerial role, with an emphasis on *ensuring* jobs are done as much as on *helping* the worker to do them, whereas *consultation* is as likely to take place within a non-hierarchical, peer–peer relationship. Most of what follows concerns consultation, which might also be thought of as non-managerial supervision, but it will be useful to consider managerial supervision briefly first.

Solution-focused thinking has proved useful in the context of management in numerous ways stretching from marketing to staff appraisal (Lueger and Korn, 2006). In terms of managerial supervision, the manager/ supervisor has a legitimate agenda of their own, which at times has to take precedence over that of the supervisee, meaning that at those times a full application of the solution-focused approach is not possible. However, a manager might partly apply it by seeking a supervisee's agreement to work towards an outcome initially imposed by themselves:

> We need to see you working more collaboratively with the rest of the team – do you accept that's reasonable? Will you work with me on this?

Positive answers to such questions will create a form of 'contract' and thus open the door to descriptions of a preferred future of collaborative working and of progress towards this. The manager will be able to use solution-focused questions to enable the member of staff's input into these descriptions. However, the process followed will not be solution-focused overall, as it is fundamentally being led by the manager and the department. The manager is the ultimate judge on whether the contract has been met, so always retains an assessment role, and will also need to decide on actions to take if progress is judged insufficient. Having hopefully sown a seed with these comments about partial applications of solution-focused practice in management contexts, from this point onwards I shall be talking only about non-managerial supervision and consultation.

I begin my (non-managerial) supervision sessions by asking what we need to talk about for them to be useful. The purpose of asking first about content rather than outcome is to ascertain the issues the worker has brought and to agree which ones we will try to address given the time available. I then treat the discussion on each issue as a separate solution-focused conversation, beginning each one by asking 'What are your best hopes from discussing this issue?'

A recent example will provide a useful illustration of what often transpires. The worker[1] stated her best hopes from the discussion as 'to find some new ways in' in her work with a young man struggling with his drug use. This is a common type of answer in this context, and only to be expected when a worker has tried lots of ways in and is currently feeling stuck. Another hope often expressed is to gain some ideas from the consultation. Such answers can lead to the consultant feeling under pressure to provide the worker with ways in or ideas, and indeed the worker may be hoping the consultant will come up with something. Remember though that in the solution-focused approach the aim is not to come up with answers or a plan there and then but to enable possibilities to be aired and resources in the person seeking help to be evoked. This remains the case when the person is a worker seeking a consultation.

Turning back to my example, 'having some new ways in' is an outcome and so, to stay simply solution-focused, my options were to focus on the future realisation of that – 'Suppose you were to find some new ways in, what would you notice?' – or on progress towards it. My preference in these situations, where the worker has been involved for some time already, is to start with a progress focus, which validates the work already done. A useful way to do this is with a version of a confidence scale:

> On a scale from 0 to 10, where 10 is you just know, for certain, there will be other, helpful ways in with this guy, and 0 is there is no chance and you may as well stop working with him, where are you now?

The worker's rating was 3–4. The follow-up questions 'What puts you up at that point and not at 0?' and 'What would be different if you were to move a point higher?' provided the framework for the rest of the discussion. Now, if you look again at how the scale was defined, you will see how these questions encouraged the worker to focus on the client and progress in the work noticed so far, and also on herself in terms of her contribution to that progress and also more generally on her experience and abilities in coming up with ideas in such cases. What was important in helping the worker get to a point where she was looking forward to metaphorically rolling her sleeves up and taking a fresh tack in the next session with her client was paying sufficient attention to all the good work that had been done already.

Frank Thomas, who has written comprehensively on solution-focused supervision (see in particular Thomas, 2013), has described it as 'the coaxing of expertise' (Thomas, 1996), which reflects nicely the process that took place in the above example. If I had succumbed to the temptation to come up with ideas myself, focusing on my own expertise in these situations, this might only have got in the worker's way. There are times, however, when I will share ideas during a consultation, for example if a worker asks me directly about what I might do in a particular situation. In these cases, both the timing and the way the sharing is done are important. If asked at the beginning of a consultation, I say that I will share any ideas I might have, but that I would like to ask some questions first that might help both of us to come up with some, and then launch into the solution-focused process. This means that any ideas I do end up sharing can be added to the worker's own, rather than hinder their emergence. Regarding the way it is done, I try to introduce an idea as something that has worked before, giving specific contextual details of whatever it was that I or somebody else did, rather than frame this as advice about what the worker ought to do in their situation. Advice comes from an expert position, and there are at least two things I will not be an expert on here. One, I do not know, at least fully, the worker's way of doing things and my way might not fit for them; and two, I do not know, at least fully, their situation. So I cannot know what they ought to do.

So far I have described solution-focused consultation done in a formal way, yet far more opportunities arise for it to be offered informally. Imagine you are in your office or staff room and a colleague is telling you about a task they have to do later that day which is filling them with anxiety, and you have a slightly sinking feeling that they are hoping you will come up with some useful advice. The solution-focused approach offers you possibilities for constructive responses that have the added advantage of fitting into even small amounts of time available:

> Have you got five minutes? I can ask you some questions that you might find useful, how about it? Ok, well suppose that you're on your way to do this thing, and you notice that you're approaching it at your very best, what's the first thing you'd notice about yourself? ... [2]

Or you could try:

> Ok, tell me about a time when you did something similar, and it went ok. What did you do that helped it go ok? ...

Or:

> Ok, tell me ten things you know about yourself that make it at least a possibility that you'll do this thing well enough.

Or you could put all these opening gambits together and provide them with a 10-minute solution-focused supervision session. Kidge Burns has usefully described such a process used for peer and student supervision by a group of speech and language therapists working within an acute hospital (Burns, 2008).

Then again, maybe you do not even have 10 minutes. It is important not to underestimate the potential usefulness of one or two questions in helping to shift someone's thinking or actions. A friend and training associate answered my telephone call and told me he was on the lunch break of the first day of a training course in which he was struggling. The people on the course had been 'sent' to take part by their managers and a couple of them had quickly taken a position that what my associate was teaching would not be relevant in their jobs. He had to return to the group as lunchtime was nearly over, and I just had time for a couple of questions: 'What's the first thing you'd notice about yourself, that would tell you that you're going to be at your very best this afternoon?' He told me that he would spring into action and say his first words like he meant them (and as I know him well I could just picture him doing this). I then asked him what the people who wondered about the course's relevance would notice about him, and though he did not have time to answer this on the phone, he told me later that the afternoon had gone better and that he had become more relaxed in his interactions with the sent course members. He may well have done this without the telephone call, but his own view was that this had helped him in bringing to mind what he was like when at his best with reluctant trainees.

Working with more than one person

Contexts in which the solution-focused approach is used with more than one person include groupwork, team coaching and working with families, and although these are distinctive activities, they do raise similar questions of group management, such as who to speak to and when. They also provide similar opportunities given the extra resources in the room. It is useful to distinguish between groupwork, on the one hand, and work with work-based teams or families, on the other. In the first of these, the members of the group typically come together solely for the purpose of the groupwork, whereas teams and families are entities independently of the work being done with them. This has a bearing on the contracting part of the process, for in the latter case, outcomes being worked towards might be team- or family-based, whereas in groupwork they remain individualised. On the face of it, this makes groupwork potentially more straightforward, so this is where I shall start.

Groupwork

Solution-focused practice has been used successfully with groups in a variety of contexts (Metcalf, 1998; Sharry, 2007), including parenting (Zimmerman, Jacobsen, MacIntyre and Watson, 1996; Todd, 2000; Sharry, 2003; Shennan, 2011), mental health (Hoskisson, 2003), substance misuse (Pichot, 2009), anger management (Stringer and Mall, 1999; Emanuel, 2008) and anti-bullying (Young, 2001, 2009). I shall convey how groups can be run in a solution-focused way by describing two groupwork activities I was involved in not long before the writing of this book. Both took place in a school setting, one with adults, where the group was called *Let's talk about parenting* (Shennan, 2011), and the other with children, in a group called *Drawing on our strengths*.

Let's talk about parenting

These groups were for parents of children at an inner-city primary school. Most solution-focused parenting groups are integrative in that they add an educational component (Selekman, 1991, 1999; Zimmerman et al., 1996; Todd, 2000; Sharry, 2003), yet the experiences described here show that a group can be run effectively in a purely solution-focused way. Two groups were each attended by three parents, all mothers, four of Bangladeshi origin, one Pakistani and one Somali, who had been recruited by my co-worker, a learning mentor[3] at the school. We had called the group *Let's talk about parenting* to help with recruitment, as this made clear the group's process, talking, and its content – parenting. The first of these was important as parents were familiar with other groups at the school that were activity-based, and the second because this suggested a common general purpose for the group. In individual work, the ideal is to be as open as possible to the client's choice of content and direction. In groupwork, if the members were each to choose unrelated outcomes, there is a danger they would become a collection of individuals who happen to be sitting in the same room, taking turns to talk, rather than members of a group who are connected and can thereby have more of an impact on each other. Another difference from individual work is that we fixed the number of sessions for the groups (deciding upon five), given the complications that would have arisen from asking the members if they wanted to meet again after each session. After the two groups had been completed, I interviewed the parents about their experiences, and I will include a few of their comments below, having first summarised what we did.

One of the main jobs of the solution-focused groupworker is to ensure that each member has a voice in the group, for it is in their answers that the therapeutic ingredient lies. One of the most useful ways of ensuring this is to instigate turn-taking. Announcing in advance 'I'm going to ask each of you this question' helps to prevent people from feeling the need to interrupt, as they realise their turn will come. So, after introductions and explanations, I asked each member in turn 'What would your children say you're good at?' This sometimes amused and sometimes bemused the parents, one of them later reflecting:

> I liked the question about what your children think you're good at. I went back and asked my son and got positive feedback! At the time, I didn't have a clue!

My next round of questions involved contracting, and here I was influenced by the idea of a group theme (Pichot, 2009) created by having one word representing each member's hoped-for outcome. For example, in the first group, by asking follow-up questions such as 'What difference would that make?', we reached a situation where Nina wanted to be more 'patient'; Deepa, 'calm'; and Radhika, 'happy'. This connected the group members so that, although they were working in individually-defined directions, these directions were linked and dialogue with one could always have some relevance for the others.

I then helped the members to describe their individual preferred futures, the dialogue being always between myself as facilitator and the group member, rather than between the members themselves. In this way we followed a treatment group model rather than a support group model (Pichot, 2009). In the first meeting, I switched to a progress focus by asking each person to describe something they had noticed recently that told them they *could* achieve their hopes. Follow-up sessions all began with 'What's better?' and followed a similar structure to individual follow-up sessions. The ending of the work was low-key, sessions more or less coming to an end after the last question had been answered, the final sessions being little different. This allowed the maximum amount of time for the group members' talking during the sessions, which we believed was more important than anything we might say back to them.

The post-group comments were encouraging in terms of outcome, with five of the six reporting significant improvements (the sixth offering the friendly feedback that she would have preferred to receive some advice), and interesting in terms of process, in two areas in particular. First, several group members commented on the use of questions in the group, this being representative:

> Normally, life is the same routine, getting the children ready for school, cooking and so on. Then you ask these questions and it makes a difference... When Guy asked the different questions I got this new knowledge. So many questions he had to ask me!

Second, although the group members were working towards their individual 'best hopes', there was an added value from the work taking place in a group:

> Listening to other people and the way they did things with their kids helped me to do different things with my own kids.

Drawing on our strengths

Sitting around and talking is an adult-oriented activity, and for children, supplementary means of communication are sometimes needed. In this group session, I worked together with the cartoonist Tim Sanders, and we found a number of ways of weaving talking and cartoon drawing together, while sticking to the simple solution-focused process. The group was for six children, aged 10 and 11, who were chosen by staff at their school after we had agreed with the head that the aim of the group would be helping the children who attended 'to get the most out of school'. This meant the contracting was in effect done with the head in advance, though we followed up our explanation of its purpose to the children at the beginning of the group by asking 'Are you up for this?'. Unsurprisingly they said yes, but asking the question involved the children in the contract and helped to create a collaborative frame for the rest of the group.

A member of the school staff[4] also took part in the group, and we had primed her to help us 'start with strengths' by asking each child's class teacher one thing that child was good at and then mentioning this while introducing each child. The competence-based beginning to the group continued with what the children later called the guessing game. Tim showed them how you could draw something recognisable very simply, line by line. He first drew a vertical line and invited the children to guess who it was, and though none of them could, we encouraged them to call out ideas. Tim then drew a shorter line slanting down from the top of the vertical line and asked the children to guess again. Then another line at an angle, guess again, and so on. As he kept drawing small lines at an angle across the paper, one group member suddenly saw who it was – Bart Simpson! (*Activity: Try it yourself*). We then placed the children in pairs, and one had to draw the other doing something they were good at, line by line, while the rest of the group had to guess what it was. The more mistaken guesses the better, because then the child being drawn heard more things the others thought she or he was good at.

After this, Tim demonstrated how to do a simple three-panel cartoon story and each child created their own, showing part of a day in which they were getting the most out of school. I helped them to represent a concrete interactional sequence (see Chapter 4) by asking them to think who might notice they were having a good day and then to draw themselves with that person, showing first what the other person was noticing and then their response. The beauty of a 'good day at school' story is that it can represent either a future or a progress focus, or perhaps neither, but rather an aspirational present moment which is, after all, the moment in which a child is living. The final activity brought the group together, as Tim drew a magic door at the corner of a large piece of paper, and I invited the children to imagine this had the effect that when they walked through it into school the next morning, they would each have their best day at school ever and make their teachers and parents proud of them. The children all then drew themselves doing something on this day. Adding the adult reaction of pride reflected that the contract was with the head and the school as well as with the children. The 'preferred future', therefore, had to fit the preferences of the school as well as of the children.

Whilst giving compliments has become a rarer practice when working with adults, this is not so with children. We ended the group by giving each child a compliment, both verbally and in the form of a cartoon – Tim drawing the child engaged in some constructive behaviour we had noticed during the group. For this activity, it helps to have a professional cartoonist!

Solution-focused work with teams

Solution-focused work with teams can take two main forms. First, the team might simply be the context for individual consultation discussions, where the presence of a team can have two advantages. One, there is likely to be vicarious learning or supervision taking place for the other team members during the discussion with their colleague; and two, they can act as a resource for their colleague, for example as a 'reflecting team'

(Andersen, 1992). The second form sees the team as the focus of the work and is usually called team building or coaching. In this context, a contract might be created before the work with the team starts, in a not dissimilar fashion to the contracting with the head for the cartooning group, often based on improving relationships in the team or the team's overall performance. Whether or not this is the case, it might still be useful to do a round of 'best hopes' first, either from the work to be done or for the team. More team-based activities are then called for than in the individually-based team consultation, and many simple ones involve breaking into smaller groups and brainstorming answers to such questions as 'How will we/our managers/our clients/other teams know that this is the best team it could be a year from now?' and then pooling these answers together.

One exercise I have developed, where the desired outcome concerns improving relationships within a team, uses the physical representation possibilities inherent in scales. I ask the team members to stand around the circumference of a large imaginary circle, then invite each of them to imagine a scale which starts at the circumference and ends at the centre of the circle, where being at the centre represents the optimal relationships for doing the work of the team, and being on the circumference means getting on so badly the team has to be disbanded. I then ask each member to walk towards the centre until they have reached the point on the scale that represents their current assessment of relationships within the team. This is followed by rounds where I invite people to say what puts them at that distance from the circumference, encouraging as much specificity in their answers as possible, ideally concerning actual interactions between named colleagues. I then invite each person to take a step closer to the centre and to say what would be different if they were at this new point on their scale. Of course, as the team members walk from the circumference towards the centre, they become physically closer to each other, which can add to the positive impact of hearing each other's answers about their current ratings of the team's relationships.

Working with families

Solution-focused practice is used extensively with families (Shennan, 2003a; Lowe, 2004; Backhaus, 2011) and couples (Hoyt and Berg, 1998; Ziegler and Hiller, 2001, 2007; Iveson, 2003; Connie, 2012). In the early days of the approach, working with families was not seen as raising any different issues than working with individuals. For example, when summarising the work done in four different cases – one involving a family of four, one a couple, and two with individuals – de Shazer (1988, p. 151) commented that the process was essentially the same in each case, and that the 'number of individuals was not a complicating factor'. He added that the 'primary emphasis' each time was helping the clients to describe what they did differently when there were exceptions to the problem. In my view the increasing importance of the future focus has given the solution-focused practitioner a little extra to think about when seeing more than one person, so I will focus mainly here on contracting and the preferred future.

Contracting with families

As in groupwork, the idea is to contract with each person in turn. As family work is most frequently triggered by a parent wanting help, it makes sense to ask the parents first what they are hoping for from the work, which also respects the family hierarchy (Shennan, 2003a, p. 40), before going round the group asking each family member the same question. I encourage the children, even if reluctant participants, to voice a desired outcome, as I believe this to be the best way of including them meaningfully in the conversations that will follow. If one of the children does not respond, perhaps repeating 'dunno', then one possibility is to ask them if they want the same outcome as their parents. If they say no to this, then the way is open to ask them again: 'So, what are your best hopes from this?'

Alternatively, a closed question can provide an entry point:

Am I right in thinking that you are not as happy as you'd like to be at the moment? No? So, if this meeting helped you to be happier, would that be good for you?

The actual content of this contract, a desired outcome of happiness, is not really the most important thing here. What an answer of 'yes' does is to provide the worker with a mandate to ask the child further questions, about how they and others would know that they were happier, for example.

A concern often expressed about working with a family is that conflicting hopes will be expressed. It is useful to remember the process and outcome distinction here. Imagine a young person saying they want to go into foster care, while the parent does not wish for this to happen. On the face of it, a solution-focused worker then has a problem, as accepting both answers would involve facing two ways. However, this would be to misunderstand what counts as a contract. Going into foster care is an answer about process, and the young person would then be asked about the difference they are hoping this would make. Desired outcomes – 'moving on', 'getting on better', 'feeling happier' – are less likely to conflict than ideas about processes to achieve them, and it is usually possible to arrive at a series of outcome-based contracts which are compatible with each other.

Compatibility between contracts is also promoted by the fact that they have to fit within the worker's remit or agency expectations. When I worked in a family support team whose role was to prevent the need for young people to be taken into care, our involvement with a family would be predicated on care not being available. I would explain this to the family in the opening stage of our first meeting:

> My team's role is to keep children out of care, and I have become involved on the basis that foster care is not on offer … so, having said all that, what are your best hopes from my involvement?

In the same way, a school-based worker's remit might not allow contracts that include a child changing schools or changing teachers, or a team coach's remit in a piece of conflict resolution might not allow two workers to describe preferred futures of working in different teams. In these situations, if clients insist they want something outside of the worker's remit, then this will need to be responded to, but the response will not take place in the context of solution-focused work, as no contract for this will have been formed.

Preferred futures with families

I have found two contrasting approaches useful for facilitating preferred future descriptions during meetings with couples and families. The simpler perhaps of the two involves turn-taking, asking each person to describe separately so that, in effect, each person has a mini-session within the overall session. As well as being simpler, another advantage of this is that it enables each person to hear clearly what the others want. When Sandra heard her 10-year-old daughter, Sarah, say that having 'Mum's cereal' for breakfast would be one sign that they were getting on better, she was able to act on this the next morning and pass her the muesli at the breakfast table. Though Sandra was not sure if this was connected with the significant improvements she described a week later, it is through such small, everyday actions that close listening and good intentions are demonstrated.

In the second approach, in which I was influenced by observing the practice of Insoo Kim Berg (2000), family members are invited to jointly describe a preferred future, leading to more interwoven descriptions (Shennan, 2003a, p. 41). In the following example, I looked from Pat to her 15-year-old son, Mike, as I asked my first question, to indicate that it was directed at both of them.

> *Guy*: Suppose that you wake up tomorrow to find the things that you've come here for have all happened, ok? In the ways you've each said you want. What's the very first thing you might notice that would tell you that?

By the end of the question, I was looking at the space between Pat and Mike, wanting them to decide who would answer first. Pat grabbed the opportunity.

> *Pat*: Mike would be in the kitchen (*laughs*). I wouldn't have to go and... 'Mike, are you getting up, are you getting up?!'.

It is often the case that people talk first about what they would notice different about someone else in the family. By going on to invite Pat to describe what she would notice about Mike in detail, I was creating an opportunity to then cross over to Mike and invite a description the other way.

> *Guy*: Oh, right... So you'd find him up then?
>
> *Pat*: I'd find him up. He'd actually be out of his bed.
>
> *Guy*: Ok, and what might happen next, then, if things were right tomorrow?
>
> *Pat*: He'd be eating!
>
> *Guy*: Yeah, what would he be eating?
>
> *Pat*: Well, toast, or cereal, anything would be nice...
>
> *Guy*: Yeah, ok, so you'd come in, find him eating some breakfast in the kitchen. What else? What else might you notice about him?
>
> *Pat*: He'd be smiling, and ask if I'd had a good night's sleep. He does that when he's in a good mood. That would be lovely, and, er... yeah.

And the next thing I'd notice is when he went upstairs for his shower, he'd be out in ten minutes! And I wouldn't be still saying an hour later, 'Are you getting out of that shower?!'

Mike: I only stay in there for twenty minutes.

Hearing Mike's interruption, with its slight challenge, and having elicited detail from Pat, I decided this would be an opportune moment to switch, to help Mike weave some description into the picture.

Guy: Well, let's just stay in the kitchen a bit longer. Just suppose that happens then, Mike, that your Mum comes down, and you're up and eating your breakfast, and she comes in and you smile, and ask if she's had a good night's sleep... What do you think you might notice about your Mum?

Mike: She'd start talking to me. She wouldn't keep me in the dark about things until the last minute.

Guy: Ok, so in the kitchen then tomorrow morning, what sorts of things might she start saying to you?

Mike: Anything. If she was planning something it would be 'Oh, are you interested in this? We'll organise it together' kind of thing. So I'd know what's happening and when.

Guy: What else? What else would you notice about your Mum?

Mike: Dunno, smiling I guess.

Guy: What effect would that have on you then, if your Mum was talking to you like that, and smiling?

Mike: That would just make me feel a whole lot better, because then I don't feel wound up about being told five minutes before I have to do something...

Guy: And how would your Mum notice that you were feeling a whole lot better about that?

Mike: Erm... I really don't know... Just that I'd talk to her. We don't talk to each other very much any more.

Guy: And how else might she know you were feeling better?

Mike: Well, I'd say, come on, are you having some breakfast too. She doesn't eat either, you know.

Guy: Would she have some?

Mike: Yeah, she'd have some.

Guy: So you'd have a bit of breakfast together...and you'd be talking, and...ok. So what might be the next sign of things going as you'd like between you tomorrow?

Mike: I'd just want to continue as we'd started, and make an effort to actually make it work.

I continued to interweave by going back to Pat, at the same time helping to propel the description forward through the day.

Guy: Ok, and what would you notice Mike doing then, Pat, after breakfast say, that would tell you he was making an effort?

Interweaving does not mean trying to force family members to agree. A family member can always opt out of a joint description, in which case the worker can revert to questions directed just to the individual.

John (father of Tyla):...he'd be letting his sister have a go on his play station...

Tyla: No way, she always messes it up.

Worker: No worries, Tyla, I'll be asking you what you'll notice in a minute. So, John, what else would you notice about Tyla?

It is only natural for differences to exist, and it is the family's task to manage them. In doing this, they may find questions such as these helpful:

- What would you notice if you were handling your differences in a way that was good for you?
- And if you were getting on as you'd like to, what would you notice about your arguments?
- When things are going well, how do you sort out things like that?

Scaling with families

With scaling, I usually revert to turn-taking, asking each person to say where they are on the scale, before asking each in turn to describe some of the differences between their respective points and 0. Where there has been a jointly described preferred future, this can become the scale's 10, otherwise each scale is defined individually. In the first case, it makes sense to ask 'What have you noticed about *your family* that puts you at that point, and not at 0?' as well as 'What have you noticed about yourself?'.

Working with children

In my own practice, I tend to see younger children together with their parents or carers, or perhaps with a professional who is closely involved with them, as these are the people usually asking for help regarding a child. Where individual work with children does frequently take place is within the school setting, and in this respect there is much to learn from teachers and other school-based staff, including from their experiences handling the ever-present constraint of time. Teachers have to find ways of having ultra-brief conversations, and here I will relate two examples that show how contracting, a preferred future and progress focus, first and follow-up sessions, can be incorporated into conversations each lasting five minutes or less.

One teacher in a Pupil Referral Unit[5] had had a difficult morning with a pupil and managed to find a few minutes for a conversation before the start of the afternoon. She contracted in this fashion:

I think this morning was really difficult for both of us. Would you like this afternoon to go better?

As the pupil said yes, the teacher was able to follow up with a few simple questions about signs of a better afternoon, asking the pupil both what would be different about himself and also what he would notice in the teacher if the afternoon were going better. A nicely complementary example[6] concerns a boy diagnosed with attention deficit disorder, who had been causing frequent major disruptions in his class. The class teacher asked the boy to stay behind for five minutes at the end of every day, to talk about what he had done well that day. The teacher deliberately avoided talking about anything else. This continued over a number of weeks and the teacher found that it made a noticeable difference in the boy's behaviour. However, the most significant improvement for the teacher was in his relationship with the boy, so that even though he still had to correct the boy's behaviour at times, he could now do it without souring their relationship or the atmosphere in the class in general.

Whether work with children is taking place individually or in a family or group setting, it will be helpful for the worker to utilise other forms of communication than just talking. We saw an example of cartooning being used in the groupwork described above, and pictorial and physical movement-based alternatives to numerical scaling were suggested in Chapter 6. Another type of expression which many younger children thrive on involves acting out scenarios, *showing* differences rather than verbally describing them. I was working with a mother whose preferred future included a pleasant walk to school in the morning, her five-year-old son walking nicely beside her. As he was in the room, I asked her son if he could do this, and when he said he could, I asked him to show me. He proudly did so, first insisting that his slightly embarrassed mother walk alongside him. Slightly more elaborate role-plays can be set up, in which children can show, for example, how they can ignore someone trying to wind them up, get on well with each other or behave well in class. This provides opportunities for children to demonstrate what they can do as well as to rehearse behaviours that can be taken into real life. It also has the advantage of engaging children's interest, more than talking only might. And it's fun! (Hackett and Shennan, 2007).

Reflections

- How have you already adapted a solution-focused approach to apply it in one or more of your work contexts?
- What (other) ideas are you having about how you might go on to adapt and apply the approach?
- If you were to adapt the approach so that you are able to use it in one of your roles, what would you need to retain so that you could genuinely say you were still using a solution-focused approach? In other words, what is required, at a minimum, for some work to be called solution-focused?
- What aspects of your work could you not use a solution-focused approach for, however much you adapted and modified it?
- Some people find ways to use the approach in their lives outside of work. Does this occur to you as a possibility and something that you would like to do?

10
Becoming a Solution-Focused Practitioner

Ready Steady Go!

UK pop music television programme (1963–1966)

Try again. Fail again. Fail better.

Samuel Beckett (1983)

Introduction

So by now you will have arrived at the starting line – ready to take your marks. The aim of this chapter is to help you to get set, go and then be able to keep going after the first few laps of the track. I will share some ideas about how and where to get started, including creating a context in which you can use the solution-focused approach. After leaving the starting line, the learning really kicks in, through the hard work of practice, practice, practice. Given that despite being simple 'it ain't easy', I will provide a number of tips that have proved useful to practitioners coming up against the sort of hurdles that can appear when managing solution-focused conversations. I hope they will help you to clear the hurdles and continue round the track, but at times you will hit one and go down. At this point I hope the words of Beckett quoted above will encourage you to get up and go again. Finally, I will answer some of the frequently asked questions that people raise on training courses, including about the approach's evidence base, which has been growing rapidly.

Getting started

The best piece of time management advice I ever received has been pinned up next to my desk since I came across it over 20 years ago: 'Start ... anywhere!'[1] The best way to learn how to use solution-focused practice is to use it, and the best way to start using it is to start using it. I like to reassure people on courses that using the approach is easier in the real world than when practising in a training setting. For a start there is less pressure, as it is unlikely that a client will have read the books and so tell you where you are going wrong. More seriously perhaps, one of the strengths of the approach is that where it is ineffective it does not seem to do any harm (Macdonald, 2011, p. 35). You can have a go safe in the knowledge that if you become stuck and unsure how to carry on with the approach, you can revert to what you know with nothing lost. Nevertheless, where and how to start can still require some thought.

Looking for contexts for using the approach

A useful step is to disentangle your roles in working with people and the contexts in which this work takes place, in order to see more clearly the times when you can ask your clients what they want and through talking help them move towards this. This task is often a straightforward one. There is little to disentangle, for example, for counsellors, coaches and therapists, who spend the majority of their time helping people make changes they want to make in their lives by talking with them in structured ways. It should in fact be relatively straightforward for any worker where at least a part of their work takes place in structured conversational contexts. For example, psychiatric nurses working in acute admission units were able to use the solution-focused approach in their one-to-one sessions with patients after an introductory training course (Hosany, Wellman and Lowe, 2007). It made sense to focus first on these sessions, which made up only a part of the nurses' duties, as their controlled nature facilitated the use of a new approach. A planned, private conversation in a quiet space is conducive to concentrating on an unfamiliar process. The point is not to expect to use solution-focused practice everywhere, but to look for the easiest places to develop your skills, which can later be applied in other, perhaps more unstructured contexts, such as conversations that arise spontaneously in a ward dayroom.

Many workers have roles that encompass the provision of advice and practical help as well as the more exploratory talking that typifies a counselling role and might worry that the former will get in the way of the latter. Workers in a housing support agency made the following comments while explaining how they were using the approach:

> I use it if someone says, 'I need to talk', not if someone, for example, has got a disability living allowance problem.[2]

> I had to sort Sarah's money out first, otherwise she wouldn't have responded. After it was sorted, I said to her I had been on some training the previous week, and I wanted to have a quick chat, as I thought it may help her to feel better...[3]

The first example shows the importance of being led by the client and being ready to start using the approach whenever a client indicates the moment might be right ('I need to talk'), while in the second, the worker is proactive, deciding to attend to practical matters first and then suggesting the possibility of a helpful conversation. This example also illustrates a useful way to introduce the approach with a long-term client. Workers may feel inhibited by a fear that a client they are already working with will notice an awkward change of gear. This can be overcome by a simple and transparent explanation about having been trained in a new approach and a request or suggestion to the client that they try this out. This is likely to gain a positive response, not least by attracting the client's curiosity. By framing it as a 'quick chat', the worker also kept the idea low-key and non-threatening, to fit the approach into the relatively informal nature of her support work. As it happened, a skilfully managed conversation ensued, with Sarah initially placing herself at 0 on the scale and later being helped to describe in detail slightly higher points earlier in the week. Another example from the same agency also shows the approach being introduced with a long-term client at an opportune moment, which is when a worker is feeling somewhere between stuck and desperate, as Kay might have been when she decided to try solution-focused work with Catherine, who we encountered in Chapter 5:

> I started using it with Catherine when she had hit rock-bottom and I thought, 'Neither of us had anything to lose', so I asked her, 'what do you want?'

Creating contexts for using the approach

Further complications arise where workers have other agendas to take into account as well as those of their clients. As a social worker working for a local authority, with statutory duties arising from child care legislation, this was the situation I faced on returning to work after first training in solution-focused brief therapy. I will set out a little of how I put the approach into practice, as I believe that these specific experiences have a more general applicability.

I worked in a children's duty and assessment team, whose role was to field and respond to all referrals concerning children made to Social Services in our given geographical area, which covered one half of a medium-sized English city. On my first day back at work, the team manager asked at the morning meeting for someone to visit a family, where one of the parents had made contact with the office saying they were having trouble coping with the behaviour of one of their children. I volunteered with alacrity, as this immediately seemed to be a context where I could begin to do some solution-focused work. The parents had approached the department, so as a social worker representing the department, asking them about their hoped-for outcome from making their approach made sense. More often, our involvement was triggered by an approach being made by someone raising concerns about a child's safety or well-being. In these situations, our focus was on assessing the risk to the child and taking whatever action was needed to manage that risk and increase the child's safety. The starting point in these cases was not to ask the child's parents what their best hopes were from our involvement. It was my realisation that *all* the referrals made to the department could be divided into one of these two groups – (i) a direct request for help from a parent or carer, and (ii) a third-party expression of concern about possible harm to a child – that opened the way for the creation of a context in which we could use the solution-focused approach in the most planned and structured fashion possible.

This realisation enabled us to focus our efforts regarding the use of solution-focused practice in the areas where it could be used, which was within the first group of referrals. However, it was not relevant for a number of referrals in this group, namely requests for information, advice, practical help, or for services such as a family centre place, for which the team had a gate-keeping role. We, therefore, set up a planned response to the 'request for help' group in the following way. The duty social worker would try to deal with the request on first contact, usually a telephone call, or, if this were not possible, would offer an office appointment, where an attempt to deal with the request could be made face to face. This would give the duty workers the opportunity to deal with requests for advice or practical help. If, by the end of the office appointment, the parents were still wanting help from the department and this was not related solely to practical matters, they were offered a family meeting within the weekly solution-focused surgery we had created within the team. We had in effect set up a series of filters, so that by the time a family sat with us in a weekly surgery session, we could follow the solution-focused process as purely as any counsellor or therapist. The fact that this was a team-based service meant that if any practical issues, or concerns about a child, arose which necessitated a response outside of a solution-focused surgery meeting, then these could be followed up by other members of the team. This enabled the workers in the surgery meetings to concentrate their attention on the solution-focused process.

Activity: Creating contexts for solution-focused work

If only a part of your role involves the use of talking to help people make changes in their lives, spend some time reflecting either on your own or with colleagues on how you could create a context that would best enable you to concentrate on this part of your role – and utilise a solution-focused approach within it – without neglecting your other responsibilities.

Involving colleagues

An important aspect of developing the context described above was the involvement of colleagues. If you work in a team environment where you are developing your interest in solution-focused practice alongside others from the outset, it is fair to say that you will be off to a head start. However, this was not so in my case, as after my first training I returned to a team where no one else knew about the approach. It was then that I realised the truth of the adage: 'To teach is to learn twice' (Joubert, 2005). From that first morning duty meeting, when I volunteered to make a home visit to the troubled family who became my first solution-focused clients, my manager and colleagues became interested in the approach I was beginning to use. When asked to explain it, I found that the simplicity of the process enabled me to do so relatively easily and quickly. The more I explained it, the more streamlined my explanations became and the more my understanding of the approach grew. I therefore recommend, even at a very early stage of using the approach, that you try to explain it to interested others.

Activity: Explaining the approach

A busy manager[4] I was meeting to talk to about a solution-focused service I was developing asked if I could explain the approach to him in ten minutes. I said, with a hint of pride, that I could explain it in five minutes or less. How might you explain it in less than five minutes?

By the time I felt ready to set up the solution-focused surgery, other members of the team had become sufficiently interested to want to be involved, and so it became a team-based service. The format we followed involved two workers seeing a family together, with one worker 'leading' and the other in a consultant role. The lead worker talked directly to the family, while the consultant would direct any comments they made to the lead worker. During the session, the consultant would comment in two different ways. First, they could make suggestions about other questions that could be asked. This could be at the lead worker's request – 'I'm wondering what might be most useful to ask at this moment?' – or the consultant might choose to intervene – 'I'm curious about how John might notice that difference in Jane...'. This format was a useful means of live supervision, providing a safety net when the lead worker was less experienced. Secondly, the consultant would help the lead worker in their end-of-session feedback to the family by commenting on what they had noticed in terms of the family's hopes, progress and strengths. This was done either in front of the family, with the two workers talking together as a reflecting team (Andersen, 1992), or by taking a break to talk outside the room. In Chapter 8, I talked about the shift from complimenting to summarising. However, when working in a team, my preference is that the clients hear compliments from any workers in observational and consultative roles, so that they do not leave the session wondering if negative assessments have been made of them.

After the session, the consultant's attention would turn from the clients to the lead worker's practice. Our rule was for the consultant to comment first on what had impressed them and then only to make other reflections at the invitation of the lead worker. Joint working in this way, with the opportunities it provided for live supervision and immediate post-session feedback and discussion, proved invaluable in developing our skills and confidence in using the approach.

Getting started

- Start using it!
- Separate out that part of your role in which you can help people by talking (or otherwise communicating) with them towards something they are wanting, from your other roles.
- Look for the contexts in which you can use it, starting perhaps with those where it will be easiest to do so.
- Listen for times when your clients are wanting to talk.
- Create contexts which will enable you to use the approach.
- Involve your colleagues, by explaining the approach to them, and by working together if possible.

Practice tips

Solution-focused skills are fundamentally about the connected activities of constructing questions and listening to the client. These activities are not easy, and becoming competent requires a great deal of practice. The following suggestions will help you in developing these skills while you are using the approach in real-life situations.

Lists of questions

The solution-focused practitioner's questions typically emerge from the client's answers, which makes close listening so crucial. In constructing the next question around the client's words, the worker is guided by certain ways of asking questions, certain wordings that occur again and again. With practice, these forms of questions become ingrained in the solution-focused practitioner, in the same way that different vocabulary and constructions do when one has become fluent in a foreign language. Before this, there is an awkward period, when asking solution-focused questions feels unfamiliar and clumsy, not least because remembering the constructions is difficult. So referring to lists of questions can be useful – before, during and after using the approach. Consulting a list before embarking on a session can help questions to be fresh in one's mind. This is harder during a session, though in my early days of using the approach I would have the basic questions representing the different session stages, to refer to as necessary, in front of me. Most usefully of all, as soon as possible after each time I had attempted to use the approach,

I would look through the list of questions I carried around with me, and this had two invaluable effects. First, I felt encouraged when I spotted the types of question I had used; and second, even more usefully, I became aware of other questions that I could have asked at certain points. This acted as a form of self-supervision and played a significant role in my growing fluency in constructing solution-focused questions. For this reason, I am including a list of questions in Appendix 1 and I recommend you try the same activity.

The next question

Although looking through a list of questions beforehand may be useful, it will not provide you with an actual question to ask at any moment during the session, as your questions need to be individually tailored to the person in front of you and their answers. The most important thing is to be listening intently to all that this person is saying. It is hard not to start thinking of what to ask next while the client is still talking, but if you do it is inevitable that you will miss something they say. As de Shazer said, 'If I were to be "thinking", i.e., talking to myself about what to do next, then I would be unable to hear what the client was saying. I would be much too busy listening to myself and thus unable to respond in useful ways' (de Shazer et al., 2007, p. 141).

There are things that can help with the difficult task of only beginning to construct the next question after the client has finished talking. First, it is perfectly fine for there to be a pause while you are working out your next question. In fact, a typical solution-focused session is peppered with pauses, while either the worker is considering their next question or the client is thinking of an answer. A slow pace is useful for solution-focused work. Secondly, you can give yourself time to construct your next question by taking hold of the space between you and the client, showing that you are taking your turn to speak but deciding what to say. My way of doing this is to make some utterance, without saying anything as such, while perhaps looking away from the client:

Ok... So... Let me ask you... What do you think...?

Steve de Shazer in particular had his own idiosyncratic ways of doing this, as can be seen in any of the videotapes of his work.[5]

'Keeping it simple' has been a recurring theme throughout the book and is useful once again here. Often, the next question to ask will be the simplest question that could be asked. For example, after an answer such as 'I wouldn't stay in bed all morning', the simplest question in response is, 'What would you do instead?', and at that moment I would be unlikely to think of asking anything else. So considering what the most simple question next might be can provide a useful guide to what to actually ask. A second way in which staying simple helps comes from remembering the simplicity of the process when feeling stuck about what to ask next. Reminding myself that my next question can come from one of only two groups, future-focused and progress-focused questions, has saved me on many occasions.

I will just add a final thought on asking the next question. It is quite possible that any particular question will lead to an answer that takes a conversation off track, away from a description of a preferred future or of progress towards it. This is likely to happen on several occasions during a session and it really does not matter. You always have a chance to ask another question, which can get the conversation back on track again. Miles Davis, the jazz musician, put it beautifully: 'When you hit a wrong note, it's the next note that makes it good or bad'.

Listening to the client

Once you start to become adept at constructing solution-focused questions, it is tempting to rush in with your next one before the client has said all they want to say. However, listening to the client means not interrupting and ensuring they have the space to answer the present question as fully as they wish to. In Chapter 3, we saw the importance of waiting after the answer 'I don't know', as asking a question immediately after this runs the risk of interrupting the client's thinking. Waiting can be hard, and counting to six was suggested as a helpful strategy. Katy, the housing support worker we encountered earlier working with Sarah, devised her own method:

> I sometimes butt in before someone's finished talking, perhaps because I don't like silences. I resisted butting in and let her think. I pretended I was writing something down, and didn't say anything. It's early days really and I'm still getting to grips with the approach, but I think letting people answer without me butting in is a good thing!

I found that simply making the conscious decision to slow down and allow the client the time and space to think helped me to actually do so. I found that my clients did usually have something more to say, and the result of this was an increasing trust in my clients, that they do have answers. In this way a virtuous cycle develops, the trust increasing an ability to wait for answers to come, which then increases the trust, and so on.

Listening to our ideas about the client can interfere with listening to the client. In solution-focused work, we are not assessing or looking for meanings underneath or behind the client's words or otherwise trying to work the client out. Our intention is to stay on the surface and to accept the client's words at face value, which is another aspect of trusting the client. Again, this is not always easy. I once began a group meditation, determined to empty my mind, but worried I would not be able to and was reassured by the teacher's advice: 'Thoughts will come into your head, and that's ok. When that happens, just be kind to them, and let them drift away'. I recommend doing the same whenever you start to think you know what is going on for your client.

Frequently-asked questions

The questions below are among those I am asked most often on training courses, whether introductory or more advanced ones. As they might well also be occurring to readers of this book, I thought it would be useful to include some responses here.

What about the client–worker relationship?

Some people are taken aback by how a solution-focused worker gets straight on with the business of the work and wonder how this can be done without a relationship being built first. I said in Chapter 4 that in solution-focused work there is no separate getting-to-know-you stage, but this does not mean that solution-focused workers do not believe they have a relationship with their clients. However, rather than seeing the relationship as needing to be created in order to do the work, we adopt the converse view: the relationship arises naturally out of the work being done. In fact, the solution-focused worker's view is even more radically different than the traditional counselling position. When asked how he built rapport with his clients, de Shazer once said: 'The therapist's job is not to build rapport with the client. Rapport is there already, at the start of the work. It is the therapist's job not to lose it' (de Shazer, 2002). This rather elusive idea can be pinned down by associating it with the fundamental assumption of the approach – if a person is wanting or agreeing to talk with someone, then they must want something to come from this. The readiness to talk suggests that a relationship already exists in embryonic form, the development of which is then helped when the client experiences the worker's interest in what they want and in their ways of achieving this.

Do clients get irritated by the repetition?

On introductory courses, people are also struck by the number of questions a solution-focused practitioner asks and by an initial impression that the same question is asked over and over. This leads to an understandable concern that this might become irritating to a client and at worst feel like an interrogation. Bearing in mind that being in a position to ask someone questions puts one in an influential position, my first response is to validate this concern. As our questions can have a powerful effect, I believe it is right to be sensitive about what sort of effect this might be. I then invite people to notice how being on the receiving end of the questions feels, which, as it is usually a positive experience, tends to be reassuring.

It is important to develop the ability to ask a question like 'What else?' again...and again. The question 'Is there anything else?' is easier to ask but can close discussion down, possibly prematurely. Thinking is hard and any of us might accept an invitation to take a break from it if offered, which is what a closed question such as 'Is there anything else?' does. It is highly likely to receive the answer 'no', even if there was more there which the client would have come to by thinking further. Asking 'What else?' keeps the client thinking, is likely to elicit more answers, and yet if there is nothing else it does not seem to prevent the client from saying this. So by asking 'What else?' and not the closed 'Anything else?', the practitioner is in effect letting the client decide that they have nothing further to add at any particular moment, rather than deciding this for them.[6]

The way that questions are asked is important. 'What else?' can appear to disqualify what has just been said, as if it were preceded by a shake of the head and an unspoken comment of 'that answer wasn't good enough'. The sense to be conveyed is one of wanting to build on what has been said and add to it, as if it were preceded by a nod and the comment 'Good...and what else?'

How does the solution-focused approach deal with emotions?

Solution-focused practice has been criticised for neglecting the client's emotions (Kiser, Piercy and Lipchik, 1993). It is true that a solution-focused practitioner is unlikely to ask 'How do you feel about that?', as this question would not help to add to descriptions of preferred futures and progress. I do also tend to discourage trainees from asking too many questions of the type 'How would that feel?' although these questions might help add to a picture of a preferred future. However, I think the criticism is largely misplaced. I shall explain why, first by outlining how solution-focused practitioners *do* deal with emotions.

Dealing with emotions in other helping approaches tends to mean dealing with them as they are happening and affecting the client in the room. These approaches have as their focus what is happening during the session, for example in the relationship between the client and worker, and in feelings that are arising for the client there and then. In solution-focused practice, on the other hand, the focus is on aspects of the client's past and future lives outside of the room, and what the client does in the room is to talk about these aspects. These will include the emotions, as well as the thoughts and behaviours, which the client wants to have. Helping the client to talk about these emotions is the main way that emotions are 'dealt with' by the solution-focused approach. As it happens, when asked in general terms about what they would notice in their preferred future, clients frequently talk first about how they would feel. This is why there is a risk of asking too many 'How would that feel?' questions. For a description to be balanced in terms of feelings, thoughts and actions, it is likely that the worker will more often have to nudge the client towards cognitive and behavioural answers to complement the feeling-based ones.

There is another subsidiary way in which the worker has to deal with emotions during the work. As the object is to help the client to talk about their life outside the room, and sometimes emotion can get in the way of talking, we do have to somehow 'deal with' emotions in the room if they are making it hard for the client to talk. By this I mean doing whatever might help the client to be able to talk, even if this is simply to ask a client who has become upset if it is ok to continue asking questions.

What about recording in solution-focused work?

Many questions asked about the approach are not actually specifically about solution-focused practice but refer more to the context in which the work is done. Recording the work is one such question, and the main determinant regarding this will be the worker's role and agency requirements. Nevertheless, using the solution-focused approach can have a strong influence on recording habits. The more a worker can use the approach purely, by which I mean working entirely to the client's agenda, the more minimal the notes taken can be. Just as the worker is not gathering or retaining information about the client during the session, so there is no need to store such information afterwards. In my case, I have reduced the notes I typically keep to basic factual details, the client's 'best hopes' from the work and their scale rating, yet it is arguable that I do not need to keep even these records. I do not usually need to remember what a client said in previous sessions, as I begin each session with 'What's better?' and then base my successive questions on what the client says from this point, not on anything recorded previously. On the other hand, the recording of factual details is useful, insofar as this reduces the number of occasions that I have to ask my client to remind me what job he does or his partner's name, and so on.

Where I do make and retain more notes is when something has been said that causes me concern about a person's safety. In this case I might then have an agenda of my own, to take protective action, which might involve sharing information with another agency. This potential course of action will need me to have written that information down.

How does it work with someone who does not want to change?

This question suggests that the client is not a voluntary participant in the work, for if they were and it transpired that they did not want to change, then the work could simply come to an end. The implication then is that the work is taking place in some form of statutory context where the client's involvement has been externally mandated. The mandate might come from a court, for instance following the making of a probation order, or from statute, with social workers, for example, having a duty to be involved arising from child care legislation. We saw in Chapter 3 how it is still possible to contract with an involuntary participant. The fact that a person did not choose to see the worker, and would rather be doing something else, does not mean that they cannot hope something might come from their involvement, given that it has to happen.

Of course, the worker may have an agenda and a hoped-for outcome themselves, as did the manager needing a supervisee to work more collaboratively with their colleagues, mentioned in the previous chapter. I suggested that, in this case, although some aspects of the solution-focused process could be used, the work overall should not be described as solution-focused. Another example of this arises in child protection work, where the overriding agenda of the professionals involved is always increased safety for the child. Engaging parents in working towards this hoped-for outcome will almost always be the aim, and aspects of solution-focused practice can prove invaluable in this. However, that the process overall cannot be characterised as solution-focused is clear when we see that the central question in child protection cannot be about the best hopes of the parents. The model of child protection practice most closely associated with the solution-focused approach is the Signs of Safety (Turnell and Edwards, 1999; Turnell, 2012), where the central question is also future-focused but will ultimately be answered by the professionals rather than the clients: 'What do we need to see happening to be satisfied the child is safe in their own family?'.

Does it work?

A rapidly growing body of research is providing a solid evidence base for the solution-focused approach, as numerous outcome studies have been carried out and published since the earliest ones at the Brief Family Therapy Center in Milwaukee (de Shazer, 1985, 1991; de Jong and Hopwood, 1996). Alasdair Macdonald, a psychiatrist and one of the earliest UK-based solution-focused practitioners, acted for many years as the research coordinator of the European Brief Therapy Association and continues to perform a useful service for solution-focused practitioners by maintaining and regularly updating a comprehensive list of outcome studies of solution-focused practice on his website, the details of which can be found in Appendix 2. His latest update, in July 2013, shows 128 relevant studies, including 26 randomised controlled trials, all 'showing benefit from solution-focused approaches with thirteen showing benefit over existing methods' (Macdonald, 2013).

Two recent developments have considerably strengthened the solution-focused evidence base. First was the publication in 2011 of a major text reviewing the current state of the research into the approach, *Solution-Focused Brief Therapy: A Handbook of Evidence-Based Practice* (Franklin, Trepper, Gingerich and McCollum, 2011). Notwithstanding the book's title, it provided a wide-ranging overview of many solution-focused applications outside of therapy, including work with court-mandated offenders and in child protection, education, coaching and management contexts.

Secondly, Wally Gingerich, in updating his first systematic review (Gingerich and Eisengart, 2000), has isolated and reviewed 43 controlled studies of solution-focused practice,[7] where the outcomes were indicated by observed changes in the client, that is, they were not only based on client self-report (Gingerich and Peterson, 2013). In their conclusion, the authors state:

> Based upon our review of the studies, we conclude there is strong evidence that SFBT is an effective treatment for a wide variety of behavioral and psychological outcomes and, in addition, it appears to be briefer and less costly than alternative approaches.

A useful feature of the Cynthia Franklin book is its section on how to measure outcomes of solution-focused practice, which makes it potentially helpful to practitioners wishing to carry out their own research. I have done this in a number of solution-focused services I have helped to set up and run (Masters, 1999; Shennan, 2003b) and found it useful in consolidating my knowledge and understanding of the approach. In this respect, evaluating one's work has the useful side effect of helping to keep going with the work, a few more ideas for which will make up the final part of this final chapter.

Keeping going

To return to the metaphor with which I started the chapter, it is a lot easier to keep running in a group than it is being out on one's own, and one of the most important aspects of keeping going involves gaining support from others. If you are working with others who are also using the approach, then there are ways to maximise the benefits of this. In the previous chapter, I outlined simple structures for informal peer-based consultations, and these can also be used with a colleague about to do some solution-focused work. Earlier in this chapter, I described the invaluable post-session feedback and discussion which can take place if you are seeing clients as a team. It is also well worth discussing work you have done on your own as soon as an opportunity arises, with colleagues who have some knowledge of the approach. It is especially useful to talk about any points where you were uncertain how to proceed and ask colleagues what they might have done. Learning accelerates when questions about the approach are linked to specific experiences in this way. In a team that is making a concerted attempt to use the approach, putting it on the agenda of team meetings is useful. Encouraging team members to talk about specific successful uses of the approach is particularly beneficial and mirrors the solution-focused process in its attention on instances. By asking 'How did you do that?' and similar questions, team members can learn both from hearing the detail of how a colleague was able to use the approach and also by their own use of solution-focused questions in the meeting itself.

If you do not already have others around you who are also using solution-focused practice, then you have an added incentive in talking about it to others. As well as deepening your own understanding by explaining it, you might well engage others' interest in the approach. Here I would sound a note of caution. Following the lead of his mentor the brief therapist John Weakland, Steve de Shazer used to advocate going into 'deep cover' if doing solution-focused brief therapy in an agency setting.[8] I think the idea was that if you were discovered engaged in radical practices, then obstacles would be put in your way, so it was better to remain undetected. I took an entirely opposite view when I began to use the approach. I thought that as I had come across a way of working that was useful and usable, then I should shout about it from the rooftops. From this later vantage point, I can see the pros and cons of each position. Being enthusiastic about an approach might attract some but put others off – 'His keenness was more damping than her scepticism' (Greene, 1943) – while keeping quiet about it might enable undisturbed practice but hold back its development. I now see it as a continuum, on which the most useful point to position oneself will depend on both personal preferences and the characteristics of the context in which one is working.

Activity: Going into deep cover or shouting from the rooftops

Where would be most useful for you to position yourself currently, on the *deep cover – shout from the rooftops* scale, and what would make that point useful?

Seeking other solution-focused practitioners further afield from your workplace will also be useful, all the more so if you are using the approach in isolation. A number of national professional associations have been formed in recent years, and information on them is available in Appendix 2. The UK association holds an annual conference, sponsors regional groups and networks, and operates an email discussion list. Joining a peer-run supervision group is likely to considerably accelerate your learning and support you in maintaining your use of the approach. If there is no local group available, your national association will be keen to assist you in forming one yourself. Internet discussion lists are an excellent resource which are regularly drawn upon by solution-focused practitioners of all levels of experience as a means of consultation and supervision in using the approach. The SFT-L, created and run by Harry Korman, is aimed at people using solution-focused practice as a therapeutic approach, while the focus of SOLUTIONS-L is on its use with organisations. Details of how to subscribe to these lists are also to be found in Appendix 2.

The last word

It was the end of my fourth and final session with a family, and the parents were rating at 9 on their scales and feeling more than confident enough that they could maintain their progress. They were reflecting on what we had done together, and the father said: 'We were telling a friend that we were seeing someone and how much it was helping. He asked what did you do. We said we didn't know!'

I hope that now, you do. I wish you well in your use of the solution-focused approach.

Appendix 1
A List of Solution-Focused Questions

Opening questions

What do you enjoy?
What are you good at?
What does it take to be good at that?

Contracting questions

What are your best hopes from our work together/talking/coming to see me?
How would you know that this had been useful for you?
What difference are you hoping this will make?
What would you notice different about yourself if this turns out to be helpful?
How would you know this was not a waste of (your) time?

Preferred future questions

If you woke up tomorrow and (your best hopes[1] had been met), what is the first
    thing you would notice about yourself?
Imagine a miracle happens tonight while you are asleep, and (your best hopes are
    met) but you are asleep when this miracle happens, so you do not know it has
    happened. What is the first thing you would notice about yourself, that would
    start to tell you that this miracle had happened?
What else would you notice about yourself?
What is the next thing that you would notice, if...?
And after that?
What is the first small sign that would tell you that...?
How would it start to show?

What would be happening instead?
What would you be doing/thinking/feeling (instead)?
How would you know?
What would you notice about yourself, that would tell you that?
How would that show?
Who else would notice that...?
What is the first thing they would notice about you (that would tell them)?
What else? What is the next thing they would notice?
How would they see that?
What effect might that have on them?
What would you notice different about them?
What difference would that make?

Instances questions

What bits of (your preferred future[2]) have you noticed happening most recently?
How did you manage to do that?
What did you do that helped?
What else?
What did it take?
What does that say about you, that you were able to do that?
What skills or strengths did you draw upon?
How did you think of doing that?
Where did you get that idea from?
What difference has that made?
What difference is that making?
What are you doing/thinking/feeling differently since you...?
Who else has noticed?
What have they noticed?
How have they been able to tell that...?
What pleased you most about being able to do that?

Scaling questions

On a scale from 0 to 10, where 10 is (insert client's hoped-for outcome) and 0 is
   the worst/furthest away you have been from 10, where are you now?
What puts you there and not at 0?
What is different?
What have you noticed/are you noticing that is different, now that you are at
   that point?

What are you doing/thinking/feeling differently?
Who else has noticed differences in you, since you have been at that point? What
   do you think they have noticed?
What difference has that made?
How have you got to this point?
What have you done that has helped?
What has it taken?
How would you know that you were a point higher?
What would you notice different about yourself?
What would you notice yourself doing differently?
Who else would notice and what would they notice?
What else? What else? What else? What else? What else? What else? What else?

Coping questions

How are you keeping going?
How are you getting by at the moment?
What is it that you do that helps you to get through?
Where do you get the strength from to even get up in the morning?
That sounds so tough – how are you managing to hang on in there?

Appendix 2

Resources

Internet discussion lists

There are at least three email-based discussion lists which are invaluable resources for people using the solution-focused approach. They provide opportunities for informal peer consultation and discussion about all aspects of solution-focused practice, for people at all levels, from the beginner to the most experienced.

SFT-L

This list is run by Harry Korman, a child psychiatrist who became one of the leading solution-focused brief therapists and trainers in Sweden. Its main focus is the use of solution-focused practice in therapy, health, social care and educational settings. Details of how to subscribe can be found at http://sikt.nu/enginstrsft.html.

SOLUTIONS-L

This is the equivalent of the SFT-L for people applying solution-focused methods to work in organisations, including leadership, change facilitation and coaching. It is run by Solworld and can be accessed via http://solworld.ning.com/notes/The_SOLUTIONS-L_Email_listserv.

The United Kingdom Association for Solution Focused Practice (UKASFP) mail list

The UKASFP runs an email list for its members to share information, ask for help and discuss solution-focused and UKASFP-related topics.

National associations

UKASFP

The UKASFP was formed in 2003 and supports the use and development of solution-focused practice in the UK. It holds an annual conference, hosts an email discussion list and produces an online publication, *Solution News*, and a regular newsletter. It also supports a network of local and regional groups. Full details can be found on www.ukasfp.co.uk.

Solution Focused Brief Therapy Association (SFBTA)

The SFBTA is the American association and was founded in 2002 and also holds an annual conference. They have an excellent website (www.sfbta.org) which is full of resources, including CDs and DVDs of work by Steve de Shazer and Insoo Kim Berg, and links to papers by Steve and Insoo previously posted on the Brief Family Therapy Center website.

Australasian Association for Solution-Focused Brief Therapy (AASFBT)

The AASFBT was formed in 2013. It hosts an annual conference and publishes an international journal, *The Journal of Solution-Focused Brief Therapy*. Their website is at www.solutionfocused.org.au.

Other associations have been and are being created, including in the Netherlands, Poland and Sweden. If you want to find out whether there is an association in your country, one place to find out could be the website of European Brief Therapy Association (EBTA), which is described under the next heading.

International organisations

EBTA

EBTA was the original solution-focused organisation created with the assistance and encouragement of Steve de Shazer and Insoo Kim Berg in the early nineties. It holds a conference each September in a European city and awards a research grant each year. It has set out to support national associations, and also hosts an online forum. Its website is at ebta.eu.

SOLWorld

SOLWorld is an innovative, open network that supports the use and development of solution-focused practice in and with organisations. It too organises an annual conference and has an excellent, interactive website (www.solworld.org).

Association for the Quality Development of Solution Focused Consulting and Training (SFCT)

SFCT provides a voice to solution-focused practitioners working in organisational settings. It produces a journal, *InterAction*, and provides recognition of its members' solution-focused competence (www.asfct.org).

Journals

As well as the journals mentioned above, solution-focused articles are often published in the *Journal of Systemic Therapies*, published by the Guilford Press, and occasionally in family therapy journals around the world.

The *International Journal of Solution-Focused Practices*, a peer-reviewed journal with a free online subscription inspired by the 'Open Source' movement, first appeared in September 2013. It can be found at www.ijsfp.com.

Information about the evidence base

Information on the research into solution-focused practice can be found on several of the websites listed above.

Another excellent resource in terms of research is provided by Alasdair Macdonald. Alasdair, a psychiatrist in the UK, is the former research coordinator for EBTA and has performed an invaluable service for the solution-focused community by keeping abreast of the fast-growing body of research that has been produced to date. He maintains and updates a list of this research on his website (www.solutionsdoc.co.uk/sft.html).

Notes

1 Introduction

1. This idea has been adapted from one I heard used by Eileen Murphy at the 2011 UK Association for Solution Focused Practice conference.
2. Examples based on actual work have been anonymised by altering both names and also some biographical details, without compromising the veracity of the processes being illustrated.
3. I am grateful to my former colleague, Darius Evans, for alerting me to the possibilities this piece of work presented for teaching purposes.

3 Contracting

1. Thanks to Chris Iveson for this particular analogy.
2. Child and Adolescent Mental Health Services.
3. Credit for this wording goes to Sue Young, a solution-focused educational professional from whom I have learned a lot. See Young (2009) for lots of useful ideas for solution-focused conversations in schools.

4 Description I: The Preferred Future

1. Michael Durrant believes that the recognition of the significance of this opening question has perhaps been 'the most important development in the last few years' (Durrant, forthcoming).
2. There are very few new questions under the sun, and I would not claim to have coined many in particular myself. The major 'technique-y' questions, such as the miracle question and scaling frameworks, can be traced back to Milwaukee. I am sure I owe my frequent use of 'notice' to Chris Iveson of BRIEF. 'How would that show itself?' I know I ask having observed Chris's colleague, Evan George, at work.
3. Though Michael White in turn borrowed the idea from Clifford Geertz (1973), who adopted it in turn from Gilbert Ryle (1971).
4. This exercise is similar to one I did on my first course in 1995. I was interviewed by Mark Allenby, now a social work lecturer, and if I had one epiphanic solution-focused moment, that one is certainly in the frame.
5. I owe the phrase to Evan George (I think! It was not often easy to know for sure at BRIEF from which person a particular idea or way of expressing it originated).

5 Description II: Instances

1. Bruner actually used 'landscape of consciousness' but White substituted 'identity' for 'consciousness' for reasons of clarity.
2. The phrase comes from my former colleague Yasmin Ajmal, who in turn told me that the ABC Peer Support Scheme at Acland Burghley School (Hillel and Smith, 2001) helped to shape the idea.
3. Kay Hughes, who works for Caer Las, a housing charity.
4. Catriona Lane.

6 Bridging the Preferred Future and Its Instances: Scaling Questions

1. On SFT-L, an internet discussion forum, in January 2001. Information on how to subscribe to this forum and thus have access to its archives can be found in Appendix 2.
2. Paul Adams, Caer Las.
3. The expression was actually a little stronger.
4. Turnell and Hopwood used the term 'Progress during therapy'. I have altered it here to 'Progress through the work', given the usefulness of the approach in many more contexts than just therapy.
5. Rob Black.

7 Acknowledgement and Possibility: Coping Questions and More

1. Danny shared this on the email discussion list, SFT-L, in 2008. See Appendix 2 for how to subscribe and gain access to its archives.

8 Putting it All Together

1. There is debate about who first coined this phrase, which I thought had originated with Steve de Shazer. Michael Durrant informs me that Steve attributed it to the American solution-focused therapist Charlie Johnson.
2. By way of acknowledgement, I have heard both Insoo Kim Berg and Harry Korman ask this question.
3. This case example, in which Chris Iveson was the worker, was included in our chapter on research studies at BRIEF (Shennan and Iveson, 2011).

9 Applications and Adaptations

1. Ylva Olsson.
2. This type of future-focused interview was first developed by Chris Iveson.
3. Bettina Dobb.
4. Helen Pope.
5. The teacher had been trained in solution-focused work by Yasmin Ajmal, who related the story to me.
6. This time the teacher had been trained by Sue Young, who told the story on the internet discussion list, SFT-L.

10 Becoming a Solution-Focused Practitioner

1. I heard this on a course run by a Derbyshire educational psychologist John Gallagher. I do not know if it was John's original idea, but I am grateful to him for passing on the tip.
2. At the time of this interview, Tony was a support worker with Caer Las.
3. Katy also works at Caer Las.
4. Tony Booth.
5. Available from www.sfbta.org; see Appendix 2.
6. I am grateful to Yasmin Ajmal for this particular way of seeing the benefits of asking What else?
7. Gingerich also refers to solution-focused *brief therapy* (SFBT), but as with Franklin et al., it is clear from the list of studies in the article's references that the applications are not solely by therapists.
8. Steve made this remark more than once on the SFT-L email discussion list.

References

Ajmal, Y. and Rees, I. (2001). *Solutions in Schools*. London: BT Press.

Andersen, T. (1992). 'Reflections on reflections with families', in S. McNamee and K. Gergen (eds) *Therapy as Social Construction* (pp. 54–68). London: Sage.

Backhaus, K. (2011). 'Solution-focused brief therapy with families', in L. Metcalf (ed.) *Marriage and Family Therapy: A Practice-Oriented Approach* (pp. 287–312). New York: Springer Publishing Co.

Bannink, F. (2008). 'Posttraumatic success: solution-focused brief therapy', *Brief Treatment and Crisis Intervention*, 8, 3, 215–225.

Bateson, G. (1972). 'Form, substance and difference', reprinted in *Steps to an Ecology of Mind* (pp. 454–471). Chicago: University of Chicago Press.

Beckett, S. (1983). *Worstward Ho*. New York, NY: Grove Press.

Berg, I. K. (1991). *Family Preservation: A Brief Therapy Workbook*. London: BT Press.

Berg, I. K. (1994). *Family-Based Services: A Solution-Focused Approach*. New York: Norton.

Berg, I. K. (2000). 'Solution-focused brief therapy', two-day workshop at BRIEF, London, 9–10 March 2000.

Berg, I. K. and Miller, S. (1992). *Working with the Problem Drinker*. New York: Norton.

Berg, I. K. and de Shazer, S. (1993). 'Making numbers talk', in S. Friedman (ed.) *The New Language of Change: Constructive Collaboration in Psychotherapy* (pp. 5–24). New York: The Guilford Press.

Berg, I. K. and Reuss, N. (1997). *Solutions Step by Step: A Substance Abuse Treatment Manual*. New York: Norton.

Berg, I. K. and Kelly, S. (2000). *Building Solutions in Child Protective Services*. New York: Norton.

Berg, I. K. and Steiner, T. (2003). *Children's Solution Work*. New York: Norton.

Berg, I. K. and Szabo, P. (2005). *Brief Coaching for Lasting Solutions*. New York: Norton.

Bliss, E. V. and Edmonds, G. (2008). *A Self-Determined Future with Asperger Syndrome: Solution Focused Approaches*. London: Jessica Kingsley Publishers.

Bray, D. (2007). 'Solution focused approaches: effective psychological support in cancer'. National Institute for Health and Care Excellence: Shared Learning Database. http://www.nice.org.uk/usingguidance/sharedlearningimplementingniceguidance/examplesofimplementation/eximpresults.jsp?o=64. Accessed 13 May 2013.

Bray, D. and Groves, K. (2007). 'A tailor-made psychological approach to palliative care', *European Journal of Palliative Care*, 14, 4, 141–143.

Bruner, J. (1986). *Actual Minds, Possible Worlds*. Cambridge, MA: Harvard University Press.

Burns, K. (2008). 'Ten minute talk – using a solution focused approach in supervision', *Solution News*, **3**, 3, 8–12. Accessed 13 May 2013. www.ukasfp.co.uk/file-store/solutionNews/SolutionNews-3-3.pdf.

Butler, W. and Powers, K. (1996). 'Solution-focused grief therapy', in S. Miller, M. Hubble and B. Duncan (eds) *Handbook of Solution-Focused Brief Therapy* (pp. 228–247). San Francisco: Jossey-Bass.

Cade, B. and O'Hanlon, B. (1993). *A Brief Guide to Brief Therapy*. New York: Norton.

Callcott, A. (2003). 'Solution focused assessment and interventions with suicidal and self harming patients', *The Journal of Primary Care Mental Health*, **7**, 3, 75–77.

Camus, A. (1952). 'Return to Tipasa', collected in *The Myth of Sisyphus and Other Essays* (1975 edition). Harmondsworth: Penguin.

Connie, E. (2012). *Solution Building in Couples Therapy*. New York: Springer Publishing Co.

Cooper, M. (2008). *Essential Research Findings in Counselling and Psychotherapy: The Facts Are Friendly*. London: Sage.

Corden, J. and Preston-Shoot, M. (1987). *Contracts in Social Work*. Aldershot: Gower.

Darmody, M. (2003). 'A solution-focused approach to sexual trauma', in B. O'Connell and S. Palmer (eds) *Handbook of Solution-Focused Therapy* (pp. 129–137). London: Sage.

Davis, R. H. (2003). *Jung, Freud, and Hillman: Three Depth Psychologies in Context*. Westport, CT: Praeger.

De Jong, P. and Berg, I. K. (2008). *Interviewing for Solutions* (third edition). Belmont, CA: Thomson Brooks/Cole.

De Jong, P. and Hopwood, L. (1996). 'Outcome research on treatment conducted at the Brief Family Therapy Center, 1992–1993', in S. Miller, M. Hubble and B. Duncan (eds) *Handbook of Solution-Focused Brief Therapy* (pp. 272–298). San Francisco: Jossey-Bass.

de Shazer, S. (1982). *Patterns of Brief Family Therapy*. New York: The Guilford Press.

de Shazer, S. (1984). 'The death of resistance', *Family Process*, **23**, 1, 11–17.

de Shazer, S. (1985). *Keys to Solution in Brief Therapy*. New York: Norton.

de Shazer, S. (1986). 'An indirect approach to brief therapy', in S. de Shazer and R. Kral (eds) *Indirect Approaches in Therapy*. Rockville, MD: Aspen.

de Shazer, S. (1988). *Clues: Investigating Solutions in Brief Therapy*. New York: Norton.

de Shazer, S. (1991). *Putting Difference to Work*. New York: Norton.

de Shazer, S. (1994). *Words Were Originally Magic*. New York: Norton.

de Shazer, S. (1997). 'Commentary: radical acceptance', *Families, Systems, & Health*, **15**, 4, 375–378.

de Shazer, S. (1999). 'The miracle question', notes on BFTC website, revised version at http://www.sfbta.org/BFTC/Steve&Insoo_PDFs/steve_miracle.pdf. Accessed 13 May 2013.

de Shazer, S. (2002). 'Masterclass', BRIEF, London, 9–10 September.

de Shazer, S., Berg, I. K., Lipchik, E., Nunnally, E., Molnar, A., Gingerich, W. and Weiner-Davis, M. (1986). 'Brief therapy: focused solution development', *Family Process*, **25**, 2, 207–221.

de Shazer, S. and Berg, I. K. (1992). 'Doing therapy: a post-structural re-vision', *Journal of Marital and Family Therapy*, **18**, 1, 71–81.

de Shazer, S. and Berg, I. K. (1995). 'The brief therapy tradition', in J. Weakland and W. Ray (eds) *Propagations. Thirty Years of Influence from the Mental Research Institute* (pp. 249–252). Binghamton, NY: The Haworth Press.

de Shazer, S. and Berg, I. K. (1997). 'An interview by Dan Short with Steve de Shazer and Insoo Kim Berg', *Milton H Erickson Foundation Newsletter*, **17**, 2.

de Shazer, S. and Molnar, A. (1984). 'Four useful interventions in brief family therapy', *Journal of Marital and Family Therapy*, **10**, 3, 297–304.

de Shazer, S. and Dolan, Y. with Korman, H., Trepper, T., McCollum, E. and Berg, I. K. (2007). *More than Miracles: The State of the Art of Solution-Focused Brief Therapy*. New York: Routledge.

Department of Health (2006). *Better Services for People with an Autistic Spectrum Disorder: A Note Clarifying Current Government Policy and Describing Good Practice*. London: Department of Health. www.btss.org.uk/better_services_for_people_with_autistic_spectrum_disorder_nov_06.pdf. Accessed 13 May 2013.

Doel, M. and Marsh, P. (1992). *Task Centred Social Work*. London: Ashgate.

Dolan, Y. (1991). *Resolving Sexual Abuse: Solution-Focused Therapy and Ericksonian Hypnosis for Adult Survivors*. New York: Norton.

Doran, G. (1981). 'There's a S.M.A.R.T. way to write management's goals and objectives', *Management Review*, **70**, 11, 35–36.

Durrant, M. (1994). *Creative Strategies for School Problems*. New York: Norton.

Durrant, M. (forthcoming). *Strengths and Solutions: Explorations of Strengths, Resilience and Solution-Focused Brief Therapy*.

Emanuel, C. (2008). 'Anger management', *Solution Focused Research Review*, **1**, 1, 3–10.

Erickson, M. and Rossi, E. (1979). *Hypnotherapy – An Exploratory Casebook*. New York: Irvington.

Everett, J. (2005). 'What number are you?', presentation at Solutions in Education Conference, BRIEF, London, 13 May.

Fisher, M. (ed.) (1983). *Speaking of Clients*. Sheffield: University of Sheffield Joint Unit for Social Services Research.

Fiske, H. (2008). *Hope in Action: Solution-Focused Conversations about Suicide*. New York: Routledge.

Franklin, C., Trepper, T., Gingerich, W. and McCollum, E. (eds) (2011). *Solution-Focused Brief Therapy: A Handbook of Evidence-Based Practice*. New York: Oxford University Press.

Franzen, J. (2013). *Farther Away* (paperback edition). London: Fourth Estate.

Freedman, J. and Coombs, G. (1996). *Narrative Therapy: The Social Construction of Preferred Realities*. New York: Norton.

Gable, S. and Haidt, J. (2005). 'What (and why) is positive psychology?', *Review of General Psychology*, **9**, 2, 103–110.

Gassman, D. and Grawe, K. (2006). 'General change mechanisms: the relation between problem activation and resource activation in successful and unsuccessful therapeutic interactions', *Clinical Psychology and Psychotherapy*, **13**, 1, 1–11.

Geertz, C. (1973). 'Thick description: toward an interpretive theory of culture', in *The Interpretation of Cultures: Selected Essays* (pp. 3–30). New York: Basic Books.

George, E., Iveson, C. and Ratner, H. (1990). *Problem to Solution*. London: BT Press.

George, E., Iveson, C. and Ratner, H. (1995). *Solution-Focused Brief Therapy: Training Course Hand-out*. London: BRIEF.

George, E., Iveson, C. and Ratner, H. (1999). *Problem to Solution* (second edition). London: BT Press.

George, E., Iveson, C. and Ratner, H. (2001). 'Sharpening Ockham's Razor', presentation at European Brief Therapy Association Conference, Dublin, September.

Gingerich, W., de Shazer, S. and Weiner-Davis, M. (1988). 'Constructing change: a research view of interviewing', in E. Lipchik (ed.) *Interviewing* (pp. 21–32). Rockville, MD: Aspen.

Gingerich, W. and Eisengart, S. (2000). 'Solution-focused brief therapy: a review of the outcome research', *Family Process*, **39**, 4, 477–498.

Gingerich, W. and Peterson, L. (2013). 'Effectiveness of solution-focused brief therapy: a systematic qualitative review of controlled outcome studies', *Research on Social Work Practice*, **23**, 3, 266–283.

Greene, G. (1943). *The Ministry of Fear*. London: Heinemann.

Hackett, P. and Shennan, G. (2007). 'Solution-focused work with children and young people', in T. Nelson and F. Thomas (eds) *Handbook of Solution-Focused Brief Therapy: Clinical Applications* (pp. 191–212). New York: The Haworth Press.

Hales, J. (1999). 'Person-centred counselling and solution-focused therapy', *Counselling*, **10**, 3, 233–236.

Hanton, P. (2011). *Skills in Solution Focused Brief Counselling and Psychotherapy*. London: Sage.

Hawkes, D. (2003). 'A solution-focused approach to "psychosis"', in B. O'Connell and S. Palmer (eds) *Handbook of Solution-Focused Therapy* (pp. 146–155). London: Sage.

Henden, J. (2005). 'Preventing suicide using a solution focused approach', *The Journal of Primary Care Mental Health*, **8**, 3, 81–88.

Henden, J. (2008). *Preventing Suicide: The Solution Focused Approach*. Chichester: Wiley.

Hillel, V. and Smith, E. (2001). 'Empowering students to empower others', in Y. Ajmal and I. Rees (eds) *Solutions in Schools* (pp. 74–85). London: BT Press.

Hosany, Z., Wellman, N. and Lowe, T. (2007). 'Fostering a culture of engagement: a pilot study of the outcomes of training mental health nurses working in two UK acute admission units in brief solution-focused therapy techniques', *Journal of Psychiatric and Mental Health Nursing*, **14**, 7, 688–695.

Hoskisson, P. (2003). 'Solution-focused groupwork', in B. O'Connell and S. Palmer (eds) *Handbook of Solution-Focused Therapy* (pp. 25–37). London: Sage.

Hoyt, M. and Berg, I. K. (1998). 'Solution focused couples therapy: helping clients construct self-fulfilling realities', in F. M. Dattilio (ed.) *Case Studies in Couple and Family Therapy: Systemic and Cognitive Perspectives* (pp. 203–232). New York: Guilford Press.

Hudson, B. and Macdonald, G. (1986). *Behavioural Social Work: An Introduction*. London: Macmillan.

Iveson, C. (1994). 'Preferred futures, exceptional pasts', presentation to the European Brief Therapy Association Conference, Stockholm.

Iveson, C. (2003). 'Solution-focused couples therapy', in B. O'Connell and S. Palmer (eds) *Handbook of Solution-Focused Therapy* (pp. 61–73). London: Sage.

Iveson, C., George, E. and Ratner, H. (2012). *Brief Coaching: A Solution Focused Approach*. London: Routledge.

Jackson, P. and McKergow, M. (2002). *The Solutions Focus: The SIMPLE Way to Positive Change*. London: Nicholas Brealey.

Jacob, F. (2001). *Solution Focused Recovery from Eating Distress*. London: BT Press.

Joubert, J. (2005). *The Notebooks of Joseph Joubert* (translated by Paul Auster). New York: New York Review of Books.

Kelly, M., Kim, J. and Franklin, C. (2008). *Solution Focused Brief Therapy in Schools: A 360 Degree View of Research and Practice*. New York: Oxford University Press.

Kiser, D. (1995). *Process and Politics of Solution Focused Therapy Theory Development: A Qualitative Analysis*. Purdue University, CDES, unpublished dissertation, cited in Malinen (2002).

Kiser, D., Piercy, F. and Lipchik, E. (1993). 'The integration of emotion in solution-focused therapy', *Journal of Marital and Family Therapy*, 19, 3, 233–242.

Kitwood, T. (1997). *Dementia Reconsidered: The Person Comes First*. Philadelphia, PA: Open University Press.

Kline, N. (1999). *Time to Think: Listening to Ignite the Human Mind*. London: Cassell.

Korman, H. (2004). The Common Project. www.sikt.nu/Articl_and_book/Creating%20a%20common%20project.PDF. Accessed 13 May 2013.

Korman, H. (2006). The Second Session. www.sikt.nu/Articl_and_book/The%20second%20session.pdf. Accessed 13 May 2013.

Kowalski, K. and Kral, R. (1989). 'The geometry of solution: using the scaling technique', *Family Therapy Case Studies*, 4, 1, 59–66.

Lethem, J. (1994). *Moved to Tears, Moved to Action: Solution Focused Brief Therapy with Women and Children*. London: BT Press.

Lipchik, E. (1988a). 'Purposeful sequences for beginning the solution-focused interview', in E. Lipchik (ed.) *Interviewing* (pp. 105–117). Rockville, MD: Aspen.

Lipchik, E. (1988b). 'Interviewing with a constructive ear', *Dulwich Centre Newsletter*, Winter, 3–7.

Lipchik, E. (1988c). 'Treatment of disturbed parent/child relationships', in R. Cox, C. Chilman and E. Nunnally (eds) *Troubled Relationships: Families in Trouble Series* (vol. 3) (pp. 117–140). Newbury Park, CA: Sage.

Lipchik, E. (1993). 'Both/and solutions', in S. Friedman (ed.) *The New Language of Change: Constructive Collaboration in Psychotherapy* (pp. 26–49). New York: The Guilford Press.

Lipchik, E. (1994). 'The rush to be brief', *The Family Therapy Networker*, 18, 34–40.

Lipchik, E. and de Shazer, S. (1986). 'The purposeful interview', *Journal of Strategic and Systemic Therapies*, 5, 1 & 2, 88–99.

Lipchik, E., Derks, J., Lacourt, M. and Nunnally, E. (2011). 'The evolution of solution focused brief therapy', in C. Franklin, T. Trepper, W. Gingerich and E. McCollum (eds) *Solution-Focused Brief Therapy: A Handbook of Evidence-Based Practice* (pp. 3–19). New York: Oxford University Press.

Lowe, R. (2004). *Family Therapy: A Constructive Framework*. London: Sage.

Lueger, G. and Korn, H.-P. (eds) (2006). *Solution-Focused Management*. Vienna: Rainer Haupp Verlag.

Macdonald, A. (2011). *Solution-Focused Therapy: Theory, Research and Practice* (second edition). London: Sage.

Macdonald, A. (2013). *Solution-Focused Brief Therapy Evaluation List*. www.solutionsdoc.co.uk/sft.html. Accessed 30 October 2013.

Måhlberg, K. and Sjöblom, M. (2004). *Solution-Focused Education*. Smedjebacken, Sweden: ScandBook AB.

Malinen, T. (2002). *From Thinktank to New Therapy: The Process of Solution-Focused Theory and Practice Development*, originally published in Finnish in Ratkes, 2 & 3, 2001. http://www.tathata.fi/artik_eng/thinktank.htm. Accessed 13 May 2013.

Masters, S. (1999). 'Taking a step up the ladder', *Professional Social Work*, October 1999, 16–17.

Mayer, J. and Timms, N. (1970). *The Client Speaks: Working Class Impressions of Casework*. London: Routledge and Kegan Paul.

McFarland, B. (1995). *Brief Therapy and Eating Disorders*. San Francisco: Jossey-Bass.

McKergow, M. and Clarke, J. (2007). *Solutions Focus Working: 80 Real Life Lessons for Successful Organisational Change*. Cheltenham: Solutions Books.

Mearns, D. and Thorne, B. (2007). *Person-Centred Counselling in Action*. London: Sage.

Metcalf, L. (1998). *Solution Focused Group Therapy*. New York: The Free Press.

Molnar, A. and de Shazer, S. (1987). 'Solution-focused therapy: toward the identification of therapeutic tasks', *Journal of Marital and Family Therapy*, **13**, 4, 349–358.

Morgan, A. (2000). *What is Narrative Therapy? An Easy-to-Read Introduction*. Adelaide, SA: Dulwich Centre Publications.

Nelson, T. (ed.) (2010). *Doing Something Different: Solution-Focused Brief Therapy Practices*. New York: Routledge.

Norman, H., McKergow, M. and Clarke, J. (1996). 'Paradox is a muddle: an interview with Steve de Shazer', *Rapport*, **34**, 41–49.

Nylund, D. and Corsiglia, V. (1994). 'Being solution-~~focused~~ forced in brief therapy: remembering something important we already knew', *Journal of Systemic Therapies*, **13**, 1, 5–12.

O'Hagan, K. (1986). *Crisis Intervention in Social Services*. London: Macmillan.

O'Hanlon, B. (1987). *Taproots: The Underlying Principles of Milton Erickson's Therapy and Hypnosis*. New York: Norton.

O'Hanlon, B. (1993). 'Take two people and call them in the morning: brief solution-oriented therapy with depression', in S. Friedman (ed.) *The New Language of Change: Constructive Collaboration in Psychotherapy* (pp. 50–84). New York: The Guilford Press.

O'Hanlon, B. (2001). 'New possibilities in therapeutic conversations', presentation at BRIEF, London, 8–9 February 2001.

O'Hanlon, B. and Beadle, S. (1996). *A Field Guide to Possibility Land*. London: BT Press.

O'Hanlon, B. and Weiner-Davis, M. (1989). *In Search of Solutions*. New York: Norton.

O'Leary, A. (2001). 'Bridges to Babylon', in Y. Ajmal and I. Rees (eds) *Solutions in Schools* (pp. 174–187). London: BT Press.

Pichot, T. with Smock, S. (2009). *Solution-Focused Substance Abuse Treatment*. New York: Routledge.

Prosser, J. (1998). 'Solution-focused brief therapy and autism', workshop at EBTA Conference, Salamanca, 3–5 September.

Prosser, J. (2001). 'Solution-focused therapy', presentation at Solutions with Children & Adolescents Conference, BRIEF, London, 11 May.

Ratner, H. (2006). 'The therapist doesn't have the magic, the client has the magic: the legacy of Steve de Shazer', *Context*, April 2006, **84**, 39–41.

Ratner, H., George, E. and Iveson, C. (2012). *Solution Focused Brief Therapy: 100 Key Points and Techniques*. Hove: Routledge.

Reid, W. and Epstein, L. (1972). *Task-Centred Casework*. New York: Columbia University Press.

Rhodes, J. and Ajmal, Y. (1995). *Solution-Focused Thinking in Schools*. London: BT Press.

Roeden, J., Bannink, F., Maaskant, M. and Curfs, L. (2009). 'Solution-focused brief therapy with persons with intellectual disabilities', *Journal of Policy and Practice in Intellectual Disabilities*, **6**, 4, 253–259.

Rogers, C. (1951). *Client-Centred Therapy*. London: Constable.

Ryle, G. (1968). 'Thinking the thoughts: what is "Le Penseur" doing?', University Lectures, The University of Saskatchewan, reprinted in Ryle (1971) *Collected Papers* (vol. 2) (pp. 480–496). London: Hutchinson.

Said, E. (1978). *Orientalism*. New York: Pantheon.

Sainsbury, E. (1975). *Social Work with Families: Perceptions of Social Casework among Clients of a Family Service Unit*. London: Routledge and Kegan Paul.

Scott, M. (1989). *A Cognitive-Behavioural Approach to Clients' Problems*. London: Tavistock/Routledge.

Selekman, M. (1991). 'The solution-oriented parenting group: a treatment alternative that works', *Journal of Strategic and Systemic Therapies*, **10**, 1, 36–49.

Selekman, M. (1999). 'The solution-oriented parenting group revisited', *Journal of Systemic Therapies*, **18**, 1, 5–19.

Selvini, M. P., Boscolo, L., Cecchin, G. and Prata, G. (1980). 'Hypothesizing – circularity – neutrality: three guidelines for the conductor of the session', *Family Process*, **19**, 1, 3–12.

Sharry, J. (2003). 'Solution-focused parent training', in B. O'Connell and S. Palmer (eds) *Handbook of Solution-Focused Therapy* (pp. 48–60). London: Sage.

Sharry, J. (2007). *Solution-Focused Groupwork* (second edition). London: Sage.

Sharry, J., Darmody, M. and Madden, B. (2002). 'A solution-focused approach to working with clients who are suicidal', *British Journal of Guidance and Counselling*, **30**, 4, 383–399.

Shennan, G. (2003a). 'Solution focused practice with families', in B. O'Connell and S. Palmer (eds) *Handbook of Solution-Focused Therapy* (pp. 38–47). London: Sage.

Shennan, G. (2003b). 'The Early Response Project: a voluntary sector contribution to CAMHS', *Child and Adolescent Mental Health in Primary Care*, **1**, 2, 46–50.

Shennan, G. (2008) 'Solution focused practice in a family support team', *Solution Focused Research Review*, **1**, 1, 11–15.

Shennan, G. (2011). 'A different kind of talking', *Context*, December 2001, **118**, 2–4.

Shennan, G. and Iveson, C. (2008). 'What difference would that make?', *Journal of Family Psychotherapy*, **19**, 1, 97–101.

Shennan, G. and Iveson, C. (2011). 'From solution to description: practice and research in tandem', in C. Franklin, T. Trepper, W. Gingerich and E. McCollum (eds) *Solution-Focused Brief Therapy: A Handbook of Evidence-Based Practice* (pp. 281–298). New York: Oxford University Press.

Simon, J. (2010). *Solution Focused Practice in End-of-Life and Grief Counseling*. New York: Springer Publishing Co.

Stringer, B. and Mall, M. (1999). *A Solution Focused Approach to Anger Management with Children*. Birmingham: Questions Publishing Co Ltd.

Thomas, F. (1996). 'Solution-focused supervision: the coaxing of expertise', in S. Miller, M. Hubble and B. Duncan (eds) *Handbook of Solution-Focused Brief Therapy* (pp. 128–151). San Francisco: Jossey-Bass.

Thomas, F. (2013). *Solution-Focused Supervision: A Resource-Oriented Approach to Developing Clinical Expertise*. New York, NY: Springer.

Thomas, F. and Nelson, T. (2007). 'Assumptions and practices within the solution-focused brief therapy tradition', in T. Nelson and F. Thomas (eds) *Handbook of Solution-Focused Brief Therapy: Clinical Applications* (pp. 3–24). New York: The Haworth Press.

Todd, T. (2000). 'Solution focused strategic parenting of challenging teens: a class for parents', *Family Relations*, **49**, 2, 165–168.

Tohn, S. and Oshlag, J. (1997). *Crossing the Bridge: Integrating Solution-Focused Therapy into Clinical Practice*. Sudbury, MA: Solutions Press.

Turnell, A. (2012). *The Signs of Safety Comprehensive Briefing Paper. Version 2.0*. Perth, Australia: Resolutions Consultancy. www.signsofsafety.net/products-page/booklet/signs-of-safety-briefing-paper. Accessed 13 May 2013.

Turnell, A. and Edwards, S. (1999). *Signs of Safety: A Solution and Safety Oriented Approach to Child Protection Casework*. New York: Norton.

Turnell, A. and Hopwood, L. (1994). 'Solution-focused brief therapy: III. Beyond the first few sessions – ideas for "stuck" cases and case closure', *Case Studies in Brief and Family Therapy*, **8**, 2, 65–75.

Watzlawick, P., Weakland, J. and Fisch, R. (1974). *Change: Principles of Problem Formation and Problem Resolution*. New York: Norton.

Watzlawick, P. and Weakland, J. (eds) (1977). *The Interactional View: Studies at the Mental Research Institute, Palo Alto, 1965–74*. New York: Norton.

Weakland, J., Fisch, R., Watzlawick, P. and Bodin, A. (1974). 'Brief therapy: focused problem resolution', *Family Process*, **13**, 2, 141–168.

Weiner-Davis, M., de Shazer, S. and Gingerich, W. (1987). 'Building on pre-treatment change to construct the therapeutic solution: an exploratory study', *Journal of Marital and Family Therapy*, **13**, 4, 359–363.

West, J., Bubenzer, D., Smith, J. and Hamm, T. (1998). 'Insoo Kim Berg and solution-focused therapy', *The Family Journal: Counseling and Therapy for Couples and Families*, **5**, 4, 346–354.

White, M. (1991). 'Deconstruction and therapy', *Dulwich Centre Newsletter*, **3**, 21–40.

White, M. (1995). *Re-Authoring Lives: Interviews and Essays*. Adelaide, SA: Dulwich Centre Publications.

White, M. (1997). *Narratives of Therapists' Lives*. Adelaide, SA: Dulwich Centre Publications.

White, M. (2000). 'Re-engaging with history: the absent but implicit', in M. White (ed.) *Reflections on Narrative Practice: Essays and Interviews* (pp. 35–58). Adelaide, SA: Dulwich Centre Publications.

White, M. (2007). *Maps of Narrative Practice*. New York: Norton.

White, M. and Epston, D. (1990). *Narrative Means to Therapeutic Ends*. New York: Norton.

Young, S. (2001). 'Solution-focused anti-bullying', in Y. Ajmal and I. Rees (eds) *Solutions in Schools* (pp. 86–96). London: BT Press.

Young, S. (2009). *Solution-Focused Schools: Anti-bullying and Beyond.* London: BT Press.

Ziegler, P. and Hiller, T. (2001). *Recreating Partnership: A Solution-Oriented, Collaborative Approach to Couples Therapy.* New York: Norton.

Ziegler, P. and Hiller, T. (2007). 'Solution-focused therapy with couples', in T. Nelson and F. Thomas (eds) *Handbook of Solution-Focused Brief Therapy: Clinical Applications* (pp. 91–115). New York: The Haworth Press.

Zimmerman, T., Jacobsen, R., MacIntyre, M. and Watson, C. (1996). 'Solution-focused parenting groups: an empirical study', *Journal of Systemic Therapies,* **15**, 4, 12–25.

Index

achievements, 90
acknowledgement, 119–21, 124–5,
    132, 134, 139, 149
  and possibility, 121, 123, 132
action–planning approach, different
    from solution-focused, 63, 111
activities
  0 on the scale, 119
  Asking about 3 again, 104
  Asking about one point up the
    scale, 110
  Asking, listening and summarising,
    18
  At your best, 65
  Constructing questions, 60
  Creating contexts for solution–
    focused work, 186
  Explaining the approach, 187
  Going into deep cover or shouting
    from the rooftops, 197
  It's worse, 154
  Listening for instances, 79
  Next question, 159
  Numbers as prompts for questions,
    22
  Pleased to notice, 1
  Questions of Interest, xii
  What the solution-focused worker
    does and does not do, 16
  Worker positions, 64
  Your preferred reading of this
    chapter, 49
adolescents, 146–7, *see also* children;
    young people
agendas, 41
  different, 41, 166, 185, 194–5
Ajmal, Yasmin, xv, 163, 206n2,
    207n5, 207n6
anger management, 170
anti-bullying, 170
applications and adaptations, 163–81

children, 180–1
  consultation, 165–8
  families, 174–9
  groupwork, 169–72
  introduction to, 163
  supervision, 165–8
  team coaching, 173–4
  wide range of, 163–5
Asperger syndrome, 164
assessment, 72
  not part of solution-focused
    approach, 97, 103–4, 165–6
assumptions
  about small change, 62
  fundamental solution-focused
    assumption, 30, 37, 40, 42, 45
  within questions, 8, 10, 80
Australasian Association for Solution-
    Focused Brief Therapy (AASFBT),
    203
autistic spectrum disorder, 164

Bateson, Gregory, 83
'being positive', 6–7, *see also*
    solution–forced
bereavement and loss, 136, 138–9, 165
Berg, Insoo Kim, xiv, xv, 22, 24, 41,
    50, 51, 59, 75, 80, 98, 99, 114,
    122, 123, 124, 164, 174, 177, 203,
    206n2
best hopes, 19, 36, 43, 48, 131, 142,
    166–7, 174, 194, 199
  see also contracting
  different from expectations, 37
  in family work, 131, 175–6
  from the work, 31, 143
  as immediate focus, 24–5, 145
  and pacing, 123–4
  realisation of best hopes, *see*
    preferred future
  relation to miracle question, 51

best hopes – *Continued*
  relation to scale, 101–2
  returning to in follow–up sessions, 142, 158
  in supervision, 166
  with teams, 174
  unrealistic hopes, 45–7
BFTC, *see* Brief Family Therapy Center
Black, Rob, xv, 206n5
Bliss, Vicky, 164
both/and thinking, 27, 70, 119, 121, 134, 138, 139, 140
Bray, Dominic, 164
BRIEF, xiv, xv, 6, 43, 51, 52, 90, 91, 99, 149, 205n2, 205n5, 206n3, *see also* Brief Therapy Practice
Brief Family Therapy Center (BFTC), 76, 77, 89, 195, 203
brief therapy, 5, 50
  see also solution–focused brief therapy
  MRI brief therapy, 5, 50, 76, 124
Brief Therapy Practice, 6
  see also BRIEF
Burns, Kidge, 168

Cade, Brian, 76
Callcott, Andrew 165
cancer patients, 164
case examples, 12–16, 31–6, 36–40, 53–64, 65–9, 69–70, 71–2, 72–3, 79–81, 82–3, 85–8, 92–5, 107–9, 116, 123–4, 125–6, 127–9, 131–8, 156–61, 166–7, 170–2, 172–3, 177–9
chains of difference, 84
change, 3, 4, 7, 21, 62, 163
  change talk, 77, 97, 148
  client–determined, 26–7, 80, 81, 150
  documenting, 90–1
  effects of, 56, 75, 83–4
  expectation of, 148
  focusing on, 91–5
  in contracting questions, 38, 39, 42–3
  in others, 62

leaving open possibility for, 110, 119, 121, 132, 139, 140
  not wanting to change, 194–5
  noticing change, 54, 59
  pre-session, 77, 85–7, 99, 102
  small changes, 59, 62, 112, 130
checking questions, 82–3, 106, 146, 152–3
child protection work, 72, 165, 195
children, 164
  contracting with, 40–1
  focusing on strengths of, 146–7
  groupwork with, 172–173
  safeguarding, 165, 195
  scaling with, 115–16
  statutory social work with, 46–7, 72, 176, 185–6
  working with, 164, 172–3, 180–1
clients
  best hopes of, 43, 45–7, 51, 131, 142, 145, 166–7, 174, 194
  building on client's answers, 55
  children and young people as, 40–1, 172–3, 180–1
  emotions of, 193
  externally mandated, 41–2, 194–5
  focusing on life outside of session, 25–6
  responses of, 36, 44–7
  strengths of, 17, 145–7, 149
  working with multiple, 169–79
client studies, 4
client-worker relationship, 25, 120–1, 191–2
closed questions, 8, 82, 175, 192
common project, 44
competency talk, 147
compliments, complimenting, 17, 68, 80, 148–50, 173, 187
concrete interactional sequences, 65–9, 173
concretising, 54, 57–8, *see also* personalising
confidence scales, 113–14, 129, 167
constructing questions, 24–7, 60, 188–90

consultation, 165–8, 196, 198, 202
  within a team, 173–4
contracting, 19–20, 29–48, 142
  broad starting points, 47
  client responses, 36, 44–7
  in groupwork, 171, 172
  outcome–based, 30–41
  questions, 36, 42–4, 51, 199
  re-contracting, 142, 155–6,
    158–9
  with a team, 174
  with children and young people,
    40–1, 180
  with externally mandated clients,
    41–2
  with families, 175–6
coping questions, xi, 119, 122–6, 128,
    155, 156
  case example, 131–8
  future-focused, 135
  list of, 201
  other-person perspective, 134–5
coping scales, 115, 137, 138
crystal ball technique, 50

dementia, 164
de Shazer, Steve, xiv, xv, 5, 6, 11,
    22, 24, 38, 47, 50, 51, 62, 75, 77,
    98–9, 101–2, 103, 107, 114, 124,
    148, 149, 150, 175, 189, 191–2,
    195, 197, 207n1, 203
detailed descriptions, 23, 54
  eliciting from others' perspectives,
    60
  in follow–up sessions, 151–3
  inviting, 26
  of preferred futures, 20, 53–62,
    64, 79
  of progress, 21, 76, 83–4, 90–1,
    91–5, 96
  via scaling, 100, 104–6, 107–9
difference questions, 25, 42, 46, 61,
    69, 108, 157, 171, 176, 200
disciplined observation, 11
documenting change, 90–1, *see also*
  recording the work
Dolan, Yvonne, 130, 165
double listening, 122

Durrant, Michael, 163, 205n1,
    207n1

eating disorders, 165
either-or thinking, 138
emotions, dealing with, 118, 193
'enduring and enjoying' scale, 138
Erickson, Milton, 50
European Brief Therapy Association
    (EBTA), 195, 203–4
Evans, Darius, xv, 205n3
evidence base, xii, xiii, 164, 195–6,
    204
exceptions, 17, 75, 76–8, 96, 99, 118,
    120, 128, 155, 164, 175
exception-seeking, 127–9
exception sequences, 88–9
explaining the approach
  to clients, 143–5
  to others, 186–7
externally mandated clients, 41–2,
    194–5

families, 169
  at risk of breakdown, 46–7, 122
  case example, 131–8
  contracting with, 175–6
  preferred futures with, 176–9
  scaling with, 179
  working with, 174–9
first sessions, 85–8, 141–2, 143–50,
    156–7, 162
  in a group, 171
first small signs, 53, 58, 112
follow–up sessions, 12–15, 116,
    131–7, 142, 150–6, 157–61,
    162
  in a group, 171
Formula First Session Task, 76–7,
    150
Franklin, Cynthia, 163, 195, 196,
    207n7
frequently asked questions, 109,
    191–6
future-focused questions, 20, 26,
    53–62, 65–8, 69–73, 85, 109–12,
    130–1, 135, 190
  list of, 199–200

general progress scale, 22–3, 99–112, 142, 157
  client's self-rating, 103–4
  creating, 101
  defining endpoints, 101–2
  establishing where now, 103
  follow-up questions, 23, 104–9
  moving up the scale, 109–12
  overview of, 99–101
  returning to, in follow–up, 112, 153
  variations, 112–15
George, Evan, xv, 6, 43, 59, 99, 113, 145, 147, 205n2, 205n5
Gingerich, Wally, 77, 145, 148, 195, 196, 207n7
goals
  in action planning, 73
  in brief therapy, 50
  replaced by preferred futures, 51
  SMART, 20
good enough point, 100, 109–10, 114, 154, 161
groupwork, 1, 169–73
  case example: Drawing on our strengths, 172–3
  case example, Let's talk about parenting, 170–2
  support group model, 171
  treatment group model, 171

Hackett, Paul, xv, 181
Hanton, Paul, 52
Henden, John, 130, 165
historical sketches, 5–6
  of the future focus, 50–2
  of the focus on what's working, 76–8
  of scaling questions, 98–9
  of coping questions, 122

identity questions, 81, 106, 114, 206n1
'I don't know' answers, 20–1, 36–9, 45, 190
indirect compliments, 80, 81
instances, 75–96
  see also progress
  asking directly for, 88–9

documenting change, 90–1
eliciting, 78–9
emerging within a preferred future, 85–9
exceptions and, 78
focusing on change, 91–5
follow–up questions for, 80–5
history of, 76–8
outside planned contexts, 89–90
possible future effects of, 85
questions, 200
scaling and, 97, 99, 148
in typical session structures, 143, 155
interactional questions, 62, 84,
  see also concrete interactional sequences
international organisations, 203–4
Internet discussion lists, 198, 202,
  see also SFT–L, SOLUTIONS–L; UKASFP
involuntary clients, *see* externally mandated clients
Iveson, Chris, xv, 6, 20, 43, 49, 51, 61, 68, 78, 91, 106, 113, 127, 145, 147, 149, 174, 205n1, 205n2, 206n3

Janssen, Danny, 138
Johansson, Björn, 155
journals, 204

Keys to Cooperation, sequence of questions, 146
Kline, Nancy, 1, 2
Korman, Harry, 44, 45, 99, 155, 198, 202, 206n2
Kowalski, Kate, 98–9
Kral, Ron, 98–9

Lipchik, Eve, 17, 27, 51, 70, 76, 81, 88, 89, 98, 118, 119, 120, 121, 123, 127, 149, 193
listening, 7, 16–18, 119–20, 190
  with a constructive ear, 17–18, 78–9, 120, 155
  double listening, 122
lists, 90–1, 148

Macdonald, Alasdair, 164, 183, 195, 204
management, solution–focused thinking in, 165–6
maximising client choice in framing answers, 54, 63, 84
mental health, 12, 88, 89, 112–13, 170, 205n2
Mental Research Institute (MRI), 50, 76
minimalism, 6, 26–7, 52
miracle question, xi, 50–2, 89, 99, 109, 124, 199
miracle scale, 99
multi–scaling, 113
 example, 161
Murphy, Eileen, 205n1

narrative therapy, 81, 90
 documents, 90
 double listening, 122
 questions from, 81, 106
 sparkling moments, 91
 thick description, 64
national associations, 203
non-directiveness, 62–3, 64, 73
non-instrumentality, 63, 64, 73, 111
noticing suggestions, 149, 150
Nunnally, Elam, 51, 77

Ockham's Razor, 6, 52
O'Hanlon, Bill, 50, 62, 63, 76, 81, 121
open questions, 8, 54, 63, 84
opening stage of sessions, 143–5, 150, 162, 176
 questions in, 145–7, 199
other person perspective questions, 59–60, 105
outcome-based contracts, 30–40
outcomes, 36, 44, 47, 48
 distinct from process, 7, 43
 with more than one person, 169, 170, 176

pacing, 120, 121, 123–4
palliative care, 164
parenting, 113, 170–2

past
 coping, 129, 137
 resources, 149
pausing, 39, 45
peer support, 168–9, 196–8, 206n2, *see also* consultation
people with intellectual disabilities, 164
persistence, 39–40, 68, 89, 146, 155
personalising descriptions, 57–8, *see also* concretising
person-centred approach, 25–6, 62
plurals, thinking in, 25
possibilities, evoking, opening up, 46, 47, 56, 60, 61, 63–4, 68, 74, 85, 111, 121, 147, 157
practice tips, 188–91
preferred future, 49–74
 case examples, 53–64, 65–9, 69–70, 71–2, 72–3, 85–8, 157, 171, 173, 177–9
 concrete interactional sequences, 65–9
 concretising, 54, 57–8
 describing, 53–64
 with families, 176–9
 in first session structure, 143, 147–8
 handling difficulties within, 69–70
 history of, 50–2
 instances emerging within, 85–9
 maximising client choice in framing answers, 54, 63
 more than one agenda, 41, 166, 173
 from perspectives of others, 59–62
 practice principles to aid descriptions of, 53–62
 questions, list of, 199–200
 sequential description, 54–5
 tangible and observable, 58–9, 60
 what would be noticed, 55–6
 widening out, 56, 58, 61
 worker positions to aid descriptions of, 62–4
 zooming in, 57–8, 61
pre-problem state, 147
pre-session change, 77, 85–7, 99, 102
problem-focused assumption, 30

problem-focused brief therapy, *see* brief therapy; MRI brief therapy
problem-free talk, 147
problems, 6–7
  acknowledgement of, 124–5, 132, 134, 139
  exceptions to, 76–8
  getting through, 27
  miracle related to, 51
  MRI view of, 50
  stopping from getting worse, 126–7
  working close to, 127–9
problem talk, 44
process and outcome, 7, 33, 43, 44, 46–7, 175–6
progress, 21–3, 24, 25, 27, 142, 148, 151, 153
  with children, 173
  documenting, 91
  with families, 128
  in groupwork, 171
  via scaling questions, 100, 104–9
  summarising, 149, 187
  in supervision, 167
progress scale, 99
  see also general progress scale
'progress through the work' scale, 115
Prosser, Jonathan, 52, 164
psychiatric nurses, use of the approach by, 90, 183
psychosis, 164

questions, 82–3
  acknowledgement within, 124–5
  amending, 26
  best hopes, 43, 45–7, 131, 145, 166–7
  checking, 82–3, 106, 146, 152–3
  circular, 59–60
  client responses to contracting, 36, 44–5
  closed, 8, 82, 175, 192
  constructing, 24–7, 60, 188–90
  contracting, 31–6, 36–40, 42–4, 51, 199
  coping, xi, 119, 122–6, 128, 131–8, 155, 156, 201
  exception-seeking, 127–9

  follow-up, 76, 80–5, 104–9, 151–6
  future-focused, xi, 63–4, 70–3, 83, 130–1, 135, 199–200
  general to specific, 26
  identity, 81, 106, 114, 206n1
  instances, 78–9, 80–5, 88–9, 200
  interactional, 62, 84
  lists of, 188–9, 199–201
  miracle question, 50–2
  the next question, 189–90
  open, 8, 54, 63, 84
  opening stage, 145–7, 199
  other person perspective, 59–60, 105
  problem-related, 27, 129, 130–1
  relationship, 59–60
  scaling, xi, 9, 22–3, 97–117, 153–4, 155, 200–1
  sequences of, 76
  softening, 39
  strategy, 81, 106
  'what else?', 23, 25, 68, 105, 107, 108, 153, 192
  widening, 61–2, 83, 151–2, 153

radical acceptance, 103
rapport, 191–2
Ratner, Harvey, xv, 6, 43, 90, 114, 147, 149
re-contracting, 142, 155–6, 158–9
recording the work, 193–4
reflecting teams, 173–4, 187
relationship questions, 59–60
research, 10, 195–6, 204
  at BRIEF, 206n3
  client studies, 4
  controlled studies, 196
  outcome studies, 195
resource activation, 146, 149
resources, for solution-focused practitioners, 202–4
Rogers, Carl, 62

Sanders, Tim, xv, 172–3
scaling questions, xi, 9, 22–3, 97–117, 155
  with children, 115–16
  client self–rating, 103–4

scaling questions – *Continued*
confidence scales, 113–14, 129, 167
coping scales, 115, 137, 138
defining endpoints, 101–2
development of, 98–9
with families, 179
follow-up questions, 104–9
in follow-up sessions, 153–4
general progress scale, 99–112
good enough point, 100, 109–10
list of, 200–1
multi-scaling, 113, 161
variations, 112–15
schools
anti-bullying, 170
groupwork in, 170–3
lists with staff group, 91
referrals from, 107, 138–9
use of the approach in, 12, 40–1,
97, 116, 176, 180, 205n3, 206n2
sequences of questions, 76
sequential description, 54–5
session structures, 141–62
closing stage, 17, 148–50, 154, 162
first session, 143–50, 156–7
follow-up sessions, 150–6
frequency of sessions, 150
introductions and explanations,
143–5
length of sessions, 145
number of sessions, 28, 145
opening stage, 143–7
preliminary questions, 145–7
'session proper', 147–8
simple versions, 141–2
SFCT, 204
SFT–L, 198, 202, 206n1, 207n6, 207n8
Signs of Safety approach, 104, 195
SIKT, 43–4
simplicity
of explanation of the approach,
144, 186
of the solution-focused approach,
4–5, 6, 99, 163, 189–190
as a starting point, 1
SMART goals, 20
social work practice, using approach in,
7, 46–7, 71–2, 72–3, 131–8, 185–6

solution-focused approach, 2
advantages of, 4–5
applications and adaptations of,
163–81
BRIEF version of, 5–6, 149
with children, 180–1
contexts for using, 183–6
effectiveness of, 195–6
emotions and, 193
essential characteristic of, 7, 19, 29
frequently asked questions about,
191–6
getting started with, 183–8
involving colleagues in, 186–7
keeping going with, 196–8
problems and, 6–7
recording and, 193–4
session structure, 141–62
with teams, 173–4
two ways of using, 7–8
values of, 10
solution-focused assumption, 29, 30,
37, 40, 42, 45, 48, 130, 192
solution-focused brief therapy, 4, 5–6,
9, 50, 185, 195, 197, 207n7, *see
also* brief therapy
Solution Focused Brief Therapy
Association (SFBTA), 203
solution-focused practitioners, 5,
182–98
frequently asked questions by,
191–6
getting started as, 183–8
keeping going as, 196–8
practice tips for, 188–91
role of, 3, 144
role of, in preferred future
descriptions, 64
types of, 3–4
solution-focused process, 11–28,
141–2, 147, 162, 164, 186
and assessment, 72–3, 104, 165, 166
and scaling, 97, 119
and supervision, 168
solution-forced, 81, 121, *see also*
'being positive'
SOLUTIONS–L, 198, 202
SOLWorld, 204

sparkling moments, 91–5, 105
strategy questions, 81, 106
strengths
  in case example, 135–7
  listening for, 17, 120
  starting with, 145–7, 172–3
  summarising, 149, 187
subjunctive mood, working in the,
  63–4
sub-scales, 112–13, 161
substance misuse, 3, 170
  alcohol, 122, 126
  drugs, 126
suicidal clients, 165
summarising, 17, 57, 149–50
supervision
  of others, 165–8
  of your own solution–focused work,
    187, 97–8, *see also* peer support
  self, 189
support group model, *see* group work

tasks, 17, 150, *see also* Formula First
  Session Task; noticing suggestions
team coaching, 169, 173–4
teamwork, 196–7
tentative approach, 38, 130
terminology, 5
Thomas, Frank, 38, 167
transcripts, 12–16, 32, 36–40, 41–2,
  45–6, 54–6, 58, 60–2, 65–9,

69–70, 71–3,80–1, 82–8, 92–5,
  105–10, 125–9, 132–7, 146–7, 151,
  152, 154, 156–61, 177–9
trauma, 138–9, 165
treatment group model, *see* group
  work
trusting the client, 36–40, 45, 191
Turnell, Andrew, 104, 115, 195, 206n4

United Kingdom Association for
  Solution Focused Practice
  (UKASFP), 202, 203
unrealistic hopes, 45–7, 109

values, of solution–focused practice, 10
video exceptions, 164

Weakland, John, 50, 197
Weiner–Davis, Michele, 62, 63, 77,
  89, 148
White, Michael, 43, 64, 81, 90, 122,
  205n3, 206n1
'what else?' questions, 23, 25, 68,
  105, 107, 108, 153, 192
widening questions, 61–2, 83, 151–2,
  153
William of Ockham, 6

Young, Sue, xv, 163, 170, 205n3,
  207n6
young people, *see* children